Quicknotes

bible

GUIDEBOOK

W9-DDQ-434

Quicknotes
bible
GUIDEBOOK

CAROL SMITH

BARBOUR
PUBLISHING

© 2007 by Barbour Publishing, Inc.

ISBN 978-1-59789-689-4

All rights reserved. No part of this publication may be reproduced or transmitted for commercial purposes, except for brief quotations in printed reviews, without written permission of the publisher.

Churches and other noncommercial interests may reproduce portions of this book without the express written permission of Barbour Publishing, provided that the text does not exceed 500 words and that the text is not material quoted from another publisher. When reproducing text from this book, include the following credit line: "From *The QuickNotes Bible Guidebook*, published by Barbour Publishing, Inc. Used by permission."

365-Day Reading Plan © 1996 The Livingstone Corporation. Used by permission. Permission granted to reproduce this list for personal, group, church, school, or other nonprofit use. Permission must be secured to use this list within a for-profit product or for electronic reproduction (including the Web). Permission may be secured at mail@livingstonecorp.com.

Developed and produced by The Livingstone Corporation.

All scripture quotations, unless otherwise indicated, are taken from the HOLY BIBLE, NEW INTERNATIONAL VERSION®. NIV®. Copyright © 1973, 1978, 1984 by International Bible Society. Used by permission of Zondervan. All rights reserved.

Scripture quotations marked NCV are taken from the New Century Version of the Bible, copyright © 1987, 1988, 1991, Word Publishing. Used by permission.

Scripture quotations marked GW are taken from *GOD'S WORD*, a copyrighted work of God's Word to the Nations Bible Society. Quotations are used by permission. Copyright 1995 by God's Word to the Nations Bible Society. All rights reserved.

Scripture quotations marked NKJV are taken from the New King James Version®. Copyright © 1982 by Thomas Nelson, Inc. Used by permission. All rights reserved.

Scripture quotations marked TLB are taken from *The Living Bible* copyright © 1971. Used by permission of Tyndale House Publishers, Inc., Wheaton, Illinois 60189. All rights reserved.

Scripture quotations marked NLT are taken from the *Holy Bible*, New Living Translation, copyright © 1996. Used by permission of Tyndale House Publishers, Inc., Wheaton, Illinois 60189, U.S.A. All rights reserved.

Scripture quotations marked NASB are taken from the New American Standard Bible, © 1960, 1962, 1963, 1968, 1971, 1972, 1973, 1975, 1977, 1995 by The Lockman Foundation. Used by permission.

Scripture quotations marked NRSV are taken from the New Revised Standard Version Bible, copyright 1989, Division of Christian Education of the National Council of the Churches of Christ in the United States of America. Used by permission. All rights reserved.

Scripture quotations marked KJV are taken from the King James Version of the Bible.

Published by Barbour Publishing, Inc., P.O. Box 719, Uhrichsville, Ohio 44683, www.barbourbooks.com

Our mission is to publish and distribute inspirational products offering exceptional value and biblical encouragement to the masses.

Member of the
Evangelical Christian
Publishers Association

Printed in the United States of America.

Dedication

This work and the efforts that went into it are dedicated to my kindergarten Sunday school teacher. I don't remember her name. I just remember that when she told the story of the Good Samaritan (one of the parables Jesus told), she cried. Sitting in that child-sized wooden chair with my child-sized logic, I felt sure in my soul that if a Bible story made my Sunday school teacher cry, then it must matter.

For me, her passion gave credibility to the power of the Bible. Because of that, I read it myself, and it has proved itself over and over again in my life. This work is her legacy born in a five-year-old heart.

Let's know this Book. Let's be touched by its power. It matters.

(Warmest thanks to Christopher Hudson, Craig Williford, and Roddy Smith for the edits and the sojourn.)

contents

1. THE STORY OF THE BIBLE
The Bible is made up of sixty-six different books, but it's really all one story, a master plan.

2. A BIBLE-IN-HISTORY LESSON
Understanding what the Bible means includes understanding the world at the time the Bible was written. Here's a quick history tour.

3. WHERE DID THE BIBLE COME FROM?

Who wrote it? Who compiled it? How did it get to us in the form that it's in?

4. THE BASIC ANATOMY OF THE BIBLE

Here's a road map for your journey.

5. WHAT DOES THE BIBLE SAY?

The best way to know what the Bible says is to read it. The next best way is to look at the book-by-book summaries here.

6. HOW DO I USE THE BIBLE?

The Bible's not just for sitting on a shelf or carrying to church. It's for reading and understanding. It's for changing our hearts, our habits, and our lives. Here are some tips.

introduction

The story of the Bible is the story of God creating the world and then making Himself available to the people of that world. It is a simple straight line from God's heart to ours.

If the Bible sometimes seems difficult to understand, it's because it was written in another culture, at another time, and in another language. Translating it from Greek and Hebrew is no small task. Translating it from ancient culture to our culture can be just as daunting. Both involve understanding the truth as it was significant to that time and culture, then translating that significance to our lives today. In a nutshell, that is one of the great challenges of understanding the Bible and living according to it. Facing that challenge is a large part of what this book is about.

There is another challenge, as well. Because the Bible was written in that different place, time, and language, it can be easy at times to see it as separate from real life and irrelevant to our lives. On one hand we have the Bible, and on the other hand we have everything else. That is far from reality, though. The issues that the Bible writers were addressing are still the fundamental issues of life. Where did we come from? Where are we going? How do we survive on the way? How do we relate to our Creator? Why do wicked people get ahead? Why is life so unfair? What happens after we die? How can we make a difference in the world? What matters in the big scheme of things?

God addressed all those issues through people who were facing them. He spoke through stories, sermons, songs, poems, visions. . . the very experiences of people who were trying to connect with Him and survive life. What God says to us through those writers is totally relevant to life in any place, time, and language. It's about building a relationship with our Creator and facing life within the context of that relationship. It's about understanding that your life fits within a grand scheme, that we are never unheard or unseen, that we are never forgotten. It's understanding God's role within the universe and our place within His heart. It is that very relevance that makes the Bible unique and powerful.

Abbreviations & Definitions

Throughout this book you'll see Bible references, for example, Gen. 1:1.

The first part (Gen.) is an abbreviation for a book of the Bible, in this case, Genesis. The number before the colon is a chapter of that book. The number after the colon is a verse within that chapter. On the next page is a list of the books of the Bible with their abbreviations for you to refer to.

You'll notice that some of the books come in installments. In the Old Testament those books were probably written as one book but fit on two scrolls (like a double video). The second one is the sequel to the first. In the New Testament the numbered books are letters. So 1 John is the first letter from John that is included. 2 John is yet another letter from John that is included. Get it? They aren't sequels. They are just from the same person. When people talk about the numbered books, you'll hear them say, "First Samuel" or "Second John."

Abbreviations of Bible Books

Most lists of Bible books are organized in the order that they appear in the Bible. That's not very helpful if you aren't familiar with that order, so some Bibles include an alphabetical list in the information up front. Here's a list of the books in the order that they appear, along with their typical abbreviations. Check back here if you need some clarification. (Yes, you can turn down the corner of the page. Just don't tell anyone.)

old testament

Gen.	Genesis	Eccles.	Ecclesiastes
Exod.	Exodus	Song of Sg.	Song of Songs
Lev.	Leviticus		
Num.	Numbers	Isa.	Isaiah
Deut.	Deuteronomy	Jer.	Jeremiah
Josh.	Joshua	Lam.	Lamentations
Judg.	Judges	Ezek.	Ezekiel
Ruth	Ruth	Dan.	Daniel
1 Sam.	1 Samuel	Hos.	Hosea
2 Sam.	2 Samuel	Joel	Joel
1 Kings	1 Kings	Amos	Amos
2 Kings	2 Kings	Obad.	Obadiah
1 Chron.	1 Chronicles	Jonah	Jonah
2 Chron.	2 Chronicles	Mic.	Micah
Ezra	Ezra	Nah.	Nahum
Neh.	Nehemiah	Hab.	Habakkuk
Esther	Esther	Zeph.	Zephaniah
Job	Job	Hag.	Haggai
Ps.	Psalms	Zech.	Zechariah
Prov.	Proverbs	Mal.	Malachi

new testament

Matt.	Matthew	1 Tim	1 Timothy
Mark	Mark	2 Tim.	2 Timothy
Luke	Luke	Titus	Titus
John	John	Philem.	Philemon
Acts	Acts	Heb.	Hebrews
Rom.	Romans	James	James
1 Cor.	1 Corinthians	1 Pet.	1 Peter
2 Cor.	2 Corinthians	2 Pet.	2 Peter
Gal.	Galatians	1 John	1 John
Eph.	Ephesians	2 John	2 John
Phil.	Philippians	3 John	3 John
Col.	Colossians	Jude	Jude
1 Thess.	1 Thessalonians	Rev.	Revelation
2 Thess.	2 Thessalonians		

Definitions

The Bible: In this book "the Bible" means the modern English Bible made up of sixty-six books (thirty-nine in the Old Testament and twenty-seven in the New Testament). There are other versions of the Bible (such as the Catholic Bible) that may include other books. Some other traditional terms for the Bible include: scripture, Word of God, and God's Word. (You might also hear it referred to as a "sword" because a famous verse refers to it as the sword in our spiritual armor.)

Gospels: The Gospels are the first four books of the New Testament that tell the story of Christ.

Canon: This is a term you might hear used that means the accepted, agreed-upon, final list of books that make up the Bible.

Hebrews: Much of the Old Testament centers around the evolution of the Jewish nation. These people can be referred to as the Jews, the Israelites, the children of Israel, the Hebrews, and more. In this book they are usually referred to as the Hebrews.

Holy Land: This is a term used for the land where Jesus lived and worked, particularly the area around Jerusalem.

Passages: A Bible passage is a section. If someone is reading John 1:1–14, then that is the passage he is dealing with. There are not set passages or sections within the Bible like there are chapters and verses. The passage is determined by the study or discussion or reading that you are involved in.

Prophets: Today we often think of prophets as people who tell the future. The prophets of the Bible did have visions of the future, but their role in society wasn't so much to tell the future as to tell the truth. Their nation's spiritual well-being was in their care, and as God inspired them, they spoke.

Messiah: This is the Old Testament term for Jesus Christ, the One God promised from the beginning.

Throughout this book you'll find boxes here and there. These boxes contain one of four kinds of information:

IN CONTEXT: How does this piece of the Bible fit in with the whole Bible? What is the context into which it fits?

THINK ABOUT IT THIS WAY

THINK ABOUT IT THIS WAY: These are organizers for your thoughts. Sometimes we need to see the Bible in light of how it fits into our lives today.

SCRIPTURE BITS

SCRIPTURE BITS: Actual samples of scripture

DID YOU KNOW?

DID YOU KNOW? Facts or concepts that might be new to you

1. THE STORY OF THE BIBLE

The Bible is made up of sixty-six different books, but it's really all one story, a master plan.

The short version

First, God created an ideal world and put people in it. He gave them the choice to build a relationship with Him or not. Those first people made a mess of things.

Then humanity sort of started all over again. Noah and his family became the only survivors of a catastrophic flood. Noah's descendants had the same choice, to build a relationship with God or not. Within a few generations, things were in a mess again.

God has remained intent on building a relationship with the people of the world, though. He established a contractlike covenant agreement with a man named Abraham. Abraham promised to cherish and obey God and to teach his family to do the same. God promised to give Abraham many descendants. God also promised that out of those descendants would come the Messiah, a man who would give His own life on behalf of humanity. That man was God in the form of a human. We refer to Him as Jesus Christ.

Jesus lived and died and lived again. When He left our world, He left behind the message that having a relationship with God requires faith, rather than perfection, on our part. He left behind a group of people who were supposed to keep this message going. He left behind a promise that He would come again, that the world wouldn't always be a broken and disappointing place, that one day all the messes would be cleaned up.

We wait for that time, in faith, trying to keep things as tidy as we can.

That's the story of the Bible in short form.

The not-so-short version

STARTING WITH THE OLD TESTAMENT

The Bible opens with the story of the creation of the world. God created the world and everything in it, including two people, Adam and Eve, and a great garden called Eden. He gave one guideline: Don't eat of this one certain tree. The importance of that guideline was not the tree, nor what kind of fruit grew on it (which, by the way, probably wasn't an apple). The importance of that guideline was their choice to either walk with God or walk their own way. From the beginning, God asked people to show their love and devotion through their obedience. Adam and Eve chose to walk their own way. That changed everything.

Adam and Eve had children (remember the Cain and Abel fiasco?), who had children, who had children, and so on. Each generation ignored God more than the generation before. Of Adam and Eve's descendants, one of the most notable was Noah. By the time of Noah, God regretted even making people (Genesis 6:6). Noah was the one guy of the population who had any concern whatsoever for his relationship with God. God gave humanity another opportunity through Noah. A worldwide flood destroyed everything on earth except the animals and people who moved into Noah's big boat. After the waters receded, the world started over, this time with Mr. and Mrs. Noah, their three sons, and the three sons' wives. (The original *My Three Sons*, pre–Fred MacMurray.)

Noah's children had children, who had children, who had children, and so on, but things didn't get a whole lot better. God gave humanity yet another opportunity, but this time by making a promise kind of agreement with a man named Abraham. God promised He would give Abraham many descendants and that one of those descendants would be the Messiah, the one who would make right this thing that Adam and Eve had messed up. Abraham's part of the promise was that neither he nor his descendants would take their relationship with God lightly and that they would all be circumcised as a sign of their commitment. It was from this agreement that the people we call the Jews or Hebrews descended. The Hebrews are Abraham's descendants.

Abraham had a son, who had twin sons. One of those twins (whose name "Jacob" was changed to "Israel") had twelve sons. Those twelve sons were the patriarchs of the twelve tribes of Israel. They all moved their families to Egypt during a famine, and it was there in Egypt that they began to grow out of an "extended family" and into a "great nation."

Most of the Old Testament is made up of the history of the descendants of these twelve sons. Eventually they became a nation of slaves in Egypt. Through a seeming fluke, a Hebrew baby named Moses escaped slavery and was raised in the king's (Pharaoh's) palace. Moses grew up and led a God-sponsored rebellion, helping his people escape from Egypt. The plan was for Moses to lead his people back to the land that Abraham had settled way back when. That land was called Israel (after one of Isaac's twin sons), or you might have heard it called "the Promised Land."

IN CONTEXT

The first half (roughly) of the Old Testament is all about God's following through on that promise agreement that He made with Abraham: first in Abraham's backyard, then in Egypt, then in the desert, then in their new land. The rest of the Old Testament really revolves around Israel's struggle to worship God and only God. The historical books describe Israel's struggle with idolatry, then with keeping their land, then with returning to their homes after being taken away as prisoners to other lands. The books of wisdom are the truths that carried them through all those times. The books of prophecy record sermons and visions regarding Israel's unfaithfulness and the bad things that would happen to them because of it. These books also prophesy of the coming Messiah, who would deliver them from their physical and spiritual slavery.

Forty years later, through miracles, mishaps, and misunderstandings, the Hebrews finally reached that land. You may have guessed already that the land had been resettled by other people. Even today there are conflicts in that area about land ownership. Under the leadership of a man named Joshua, the Hebrews set out to reclaim the land. God warned them, actually, to make *everyone else* leave that land. The Hebrews did reclaim much of the land, but they didn't make absolutely everyone leave. That's important to remember.

The reason the Jewish people were supposed to run *everyone else* out of the land is because *everyone else* worshiped idols of some kind. During their travels God had given the Jewish people the Ten Commandments, which began with "You'll have no other gods before me." You know how human nature is. If they let idol worship stay in their land, eventually they would be influenced by it.

And that's exactly what happened. The Hebrews kept getting their worship mingled in with the idol worship around them. When they did this, they became weaker and weaker as a nation. As they became weaker (politically and spiritually), they became prey for the surrounding nations. The kingdom divided into two kingdoms. The southern kingdom was Judah, and its capital was Jerusalem.

All during this part of Hebrew history, the prophets cried out to their people to turn back to God and let Him protect them from their enemies. But eventually both the northern and the southern kingdoms of Israel were defeated and taken away from their land into exile. The prophets continued to call out to them even while they were in captivity, asking them to become wholehearted about their relationship with God again. And finally, as they started returning and rebuilding, the prophets were there reminding them to keep from making the same mistakes again.

IN CONTEXT

All the way through the Old Testament, from the first time Adam chose his own way to the last time the ancient Jews rebuilt the temple, there was God's promise. The promise always started with an understood "One day. . ." In the Garden of Eden this promise was to the serpent: One day. . ."he will crush your head" (Genesis 3:15). Later this promise was to Abraham: One day. . ."all peoples on earth will be blessed through you" (Genesis 12:3). Later the promise came through the prophets: One day. . ."the Lord himself will give you a sign: The virgin will be with child and will give birth to a son, and will call him Immanuel" (Isaiah 7:14).

TAKE A BREATH AND REVIEW. . .

All the way through the story so far, there was the promise of one coming who would fix what had been broken when people chose their own way rather than God's way. That's what Jesus' life was all about. The Old Testament asked a question: How can we be right with God since we've chosen our own way? The New Testament answered it: through the grace of God given through the life, death, and resurrection of Jesus Christ.

THE NEW TESTAMENT

The New Testament opens with the life of Jesus. He was God, having put humanity on so that He could give Himself up for our wrongdoings. He enraged the religious leaders of His day because (1) He claimed to be God, (2) He confronted their hypocrisy, and (3) He threatened their authority and power within the community. He said to them in so many words, "God is not about your do's and don'ts. God is about how you live your lives, connect with Him, and love other people." If they gave up their do's and don'ts, then they didn't have a way to control.

At the age of thirty-three, Jesus was sentenced to death through a true conspiracy instigated by religious leaders. Jesus died as He was hanging on crossbeams of wood. This kind of death was called a crucifixion. It was a painful and agonizing execution typical of that period of history. It was amazing enough that an innocent man was willing to suffer such a death. More amazing than that, while He surely did die on the cross, He came back to life a few days later. He spent some more time with the people He was closest to, and then He was gone again, no longer living in a physical body. Before He left the last time, He promised to return again one day to set the record straight once and for all. He also commissioned His followers to spread the message of His sacrifice and to love each other along the way.

IN CONTEXT

The first four books of the New Testament record the events of Jesus' life and ministry. The fifth book records the organization of the early church. The next twenty-one are letters explaining faith and encouraging people and churches. The last book is the prophecy of the end of the world as we know it.

THINK ABOUT IT
THIS WAY

It's like a grocery store coupon. . . .

When people talk about God's plan for keeping us in relationship with Him, they talk about God's redeeming us. They sometimes talk about His plan of redemption. That is really what the big, cohesive plan of the Bible is about—God's process of redeeming us.

Think about it this way. You know those coupons that you (be honest, do you clip coupons?) or somebody you know clips out of the paper? You take them to the store and try to buy the things you have coupons for. When you get to the register, you try to remember to show the coupons to the checkout person, then you hope they'll remember to ring them in. If you do remember and they do remember, then what you are doing is *redeeming* those coupons.

In themselves they really aren't worth much. A two-by-three-inch slick piece of paper is really what they are. Dead tree. But put that manufacturer's seal on them and they're worth something. How much? They're worth whatever the manufacturer says they are worth, that's how much.

God has put into place the necessary scenario for our redemption. He manufactured us. He paid the price—His life. He gave us worth. But we have a part in it. That's why it's not called God's redemption; it's called God's plan for our redemption. He did the work. He made the coupons. He paid the price. He wrote a Book to tell us how to get to the right checkout line. He gave no date of expiration. But we have to choose, through faith, to receive the redemption.

It's something to think about next time you're sitting on the floor with sales papers spread out around you and a pair of scissors in your hand.

Those followers became the first missionaries or church-planters. They went to all the surrounding regions spreading the new and exciting message that Jesus had paid the price for our failure to stay in a right relationship with God. They preached grace and faith. They started churches in major cities. Some of them wrote letters back to the churches they had started to help them understand their role in society until Jesus' return.

That's the story of the Bible. It's the story of God's creating us and wooing us into a relationship with Him.

The Old Testament Asked a Question:

How can we be right with God since we've chosen our own way?

The New Testament Answered It:

Through the grace of God given through the life, death, and resurrection of Jesus Christ.

2. A BIBLE-IN-HISTORY LESSON

Understanding what the Bible means includes understanding the world at the time the Bible was written. Here's a quick history tour.

A TimeLine

Sometimes we forget that while the events recorded in the Bible were taking place, all the rest of world history was happening, as well. We need to understand the biblical events in light of everything that was going on around the world. To add some context, here is a timeline. Keep in mind, there are a lot of differing opinions about the dates. In fact, with a lot of these events, we don't know the exact year. For some, we know of a range that could be as short as three hundred years or as long as one thousand years. In the list below we have often rounded to the nearest century. So remember the figures we've included are ballpark figures (no, not ballpark franks, ballpark figures).

Around this time...	In relation to the Bible...	Meanwhile, elsewhere...
The beginning of time	God created the world. Adam and Eve began their family.	
8000 B.C.	God saved Noah and his family from the flood. The earth began to repopulate.	
3800 B.C.		A people called the Sumerians moved to Mesopotamia and established their civilization. They built cities including Ur, Abraham's hometown. The Sumerians established arithmetic based on ten (because of the ten fingers they could count on), and they divided a circle into sixty subsections, setting up the minutes and seconds that we still use today. They also made great gains in the development of writing.
3000 B.C.		The pyramids were built in Egypt.

2500 B.C.		Egyptians discovered papyrus and ink for writing. They built the first libraries.
2250 B.C.		Horses were being domesticated in Egypt and chickens in Babylon.
2000 B.C.	God asked Abraham (who was in Ur) to move to Canaan and promised him that his descendants would have that land. God made Abraham the father of the Jewish nation by giving him Isaac, his son.	Native Americans immigrated to North America from Asia.
1800 B.C.	Joseph, Isaac's grandson, was sold as a slave into Egypt. Eventually his family moved there, too. The descendants of Joseph and his brothers grew into a nation of slaves in Egypt.	The spoked wheel was invented in the Near East. Egyptian papyrus document describes surgical procedures.
1500 B.C.		The Canaanites invented the first alphabet. Sundials were being used in Egypt.
1400 B.C.	God used Moses to lead the Hebrew people out of Egypt and the slavery there. (This was called the exodus.)	
1350 B.C.	After Moses' death, Joshua led the Hebrews in resettling the land God had promised them—Canaan.	
1300 B.C.	After Joshua's death, the Hebrews were ruled by judges, wise men and women who helped settle disagreements and make good choices. Samson and Ruth (of the Bible books by the same names) lived during this time.	Silk fabric was invented in China. The first Chinese dictionary was forthcoming.

1000 B.C.	God gave Israel their first king: King Saul. Up until this point, Israel was led by wise religious leaders who made decisions based on spiritual insight. That meant that, ultimately, Israel was led by God (a theocracy). The neighboring nations, though, all had political leaders. The Hebrews basically came to God and said, "We want what the other kids have." After much asking, they got it. Things went out of control from there.	Peking was built.
950 B.C.	Solomon (third king) built the temple at Jerusalem.	Celts invade Britain. Assyrians invent inflatable skins (life rafts) for soldiers to cross bodies of water.
900 B.C.	King Solomon died. The kingdom divided into Israel (ten northern tribes, later called Samaria) and Judah (the remaining southern tribes).	
850 B.C.	Elijah rose up as a leader and a prophet among the Hebrews. His successor was Elisha.	
800 B.C.	Isaiah, Joel, Micah, Obadiah, and Nahum prophesied to Judah (the south) while Hosea, Amos, and Jonah prophesied to Israel (the north).	Homer wrote the *Iliad* and the *Odyssey*. Ice skating had become a popular sport in northern Europe.
770 B.C.		The first Olympic Games were held, untelevised, of course.
750 B.C.		Rome became a city. False teeth were invented in Italy shortly after.
650 B.C.		The 33rd Olympics had just introduced horse racing as an event.

600 B.C.	The people of Judah were taken captive into Babylon. The prophets during this time were Jeremiah, Ezekiel, and Daniel.	Japan had just been established as a nation.
550 B.C.		Siddhartha Gautama, founder of Buddhism, was born. Aesop had just written his fables. Confucius was born in China. The lock and key and carpenter's square were invented.
500 B.C.	The first Israelite exiles returned to Jerusalem and began to rebuild.	At the same time in Greece, Pythagoras, a mathematician, discovered that the square of the hypotenuse of a right-angled triangle is equal to the sum of the squares of the other two sides. (Remember the Pythagorean Theorem in geometry?) Halloween originated in a Celtic festival. An Indian surgeon performed the first known cataract operation.
450 B.C.	The rebuilding of the temple in Jerusalem was complete. The ruler at this time was Cyrus the Persian. The Jewish leadership was Ezra and Nehemiah. The prophets were Haggai and Zechariah.	Around the same time (within a decade or so), Hippocrates was born. He grew up to be the "Father of Medicine." (Remember the Hippocratic oath?) He wrote the oldest medical books that still exist. He taught the world that sickness comes from physical causes rather than superstitions or evil.
447 B.C.		The Parthenon was built in Athens.
427 B.C.		Plato was born in Greece.
425 B.C.	Queen Esther was crowned in Persia (a Jewish queen of Persia?).	
399 B.C.		Socrates died.

300 B.C.

Alexander the Great established his empire. Aristarchos stated that the earth rotates on an axis and is not the center of the universe.

250 B.C.

The Septuagint was translated. This was a Greek translation of the Old Testament. Greek was the common language of that time, so this was a *big* deal. Jesus and His disciples probably used this translation.

Meanwhile, Erastitratos discovered that the brain, instead of the heart, was the center of nerve activity.

150 B.C.

A dad and five brothers led a revolt (the Maccabean revolt) against an evil Syrian ruler. Judas, the eldest son, led the Jewish nation into a time of prosperity.

Meanwhile, Eratosthenes, a mathematician, correctly calculated the circumference of the earth.

50 B.C.

Julius Caesar was assassinated and Augustus Caesar became the new Roman ruler. (He is the official who ordered the census that caused Joseph and the very pregnant Mary to travel to Bethlehem, where Jesus was born.) Meanwhile, in Greece, the first steam engine was being envisioned. Also, in Rome, Marcus Vitruvius, an architect, wrote a book on city planning including clocks, hydraulics, and military engines. In Phoenicia, glassblowing was invented.

51 B.C.

Cleopatra became ruler.

30 B.C.

Cleopatra and Mark Antony commited suicide. Sumo wrestling was about to rise to the forefront in Japan.

Beginning of A.D. time	Jesus was born around this time, but probably actually around 5 B.C. Some things are not perfect in hindsight.	
A.D. 30	Jesus of Nazareth was crucified (assassinated) and miraculously returned to life. After He returned to heaven, the Holy Spirit arrived at a time that we now call "Pentecost."	
A.D. 60	Paul wrote his early letters to the churches.	Romans began using soap. Meanwhile, Celsus, a medical writer, suggested using antiseptics on wounds.
A.D. 65	Mark's Gospel, then Matthew's Gospel, then Luke's Gospel and Acts were written.	At the same time, Rome was partly burned, which prompted Nero to blame and persecute Christians. Somewhere, artists began painting on canvas.
A.D. 70	Jerusalem was destroyed again.	
A.D. 80		Mt. Vesuvius erupted in Italy, burying Pompeii.
A.D. 85	John's Gospel was written. Paul made his missionary journeys.	Wang Chung, a Chinese philosopher, declared that any theory must be supported by concrete evidence and experimental proof. (This was the birth of the scientific method at the same time that the greatest miracle of all time was being spread through the civilized world.)
A.D. 90	Individual churches started sharing Paul's letters with each other.	
A.D. 100	The four Gospels were circulated together as a collection.	At the same time, Archigenes, a doctor who was reputed to be the first dentist, made the inaugural drill into a human tooth (while still attached to a living human being). Unfortunately, novocaine had not been invented yet. Meanwhile, the Roman Empire was at the height of its power.

A.D. 120	All thirteen of Paul's letters were pulled together as a collection. (We now call these the Pauline Epistles.)
A.D. 140	A man named Marcion put together a Bible that rejected the Old Testament and and rewrote a lot of the New Testament. This motivated the church leaders to make a decision to recognize officially what books made up the New Testament Canon.
A.D. 145	The church stood against Marcion and recognized all the books of the New Testament. This Testament was almost identical to ours.
A.D. 150	Galen, a surgeon to the gladiators in Pergamum, discovered that human arteries carry blood and not air, as was generally assumed.
A.D. 400	An official council acknowledged what had already been proven as people experienced the power of God's Word: The twenty-seven books that we know today as the New Testament are true and inspired by God.

Geography

most of the story of the Bible takes place around the eastern shores of the Mediterranean Sea. If you have a map, find Africa. In the northeasternmost corner, you'll find Egypt. Let your finger follow the shoreline eastward up and around and you'll find Israel. Israel was Abraham's home, called Canaan. Later it was called the Promised Land for the Hebrews who were set free from Egypt. If you continue on up around the shoreline, you'll find Greece. This is the path covered by much of Paul's missionary journeys, even as far as Rome, Italy.

Today we can travel across oceans and continents in the course of a day. It's hard to imagine that so much of the history of the Bible happened in a relatively small space of land. This points out, too, the beauty of God's timing, entering humanity at a time when the hub of the world was small and the good news could disseminate worldwide very quickly and easily.

That's the big picture. Let's get more specific. Here are the places that the people whom you read about in the Bible encountered as they walked through their everyday lives.

HOUSES AND HOMES

During the Old Testament days, most people traveled with their flocks and herds, so the most common homes were tents made of poles, stakes, and skins. Curtains divided the tents into rooms, and rugs covered the ground inside. The sides of the tents could be folded back to create porches and let fresh air circulate. This was community in a way we hardly recognize with our brick homes and "Close the windows! The air's on!"

As cultures became more stable, they began to build small homes inside of courtyards. Compared to our standards, the homes were small and cramped but held entire families. Occasionally they had separate rooms but seldom doors to the rooms. Usually the homes were made of stone, but near the Jordan they were also made with bricks made of river mud and baked in the sun. The roofs were often beams with brush laid across them.

As time went by, the Hebrews built four-room homes. This structure allowed the builders to build a sturdy roof and then to utilize that roof as a porch or sitting area. Either an outside staircase or just a ladder led to the upper level.

In New Testament times, Middle Eastern homes were built of mud bricks, usually on a stone or limestone foundation. Outside, staircases led to flat roofs that provided a sitting area and extra storage space. Small windows allowed airflow but kept out intruders. Most houses had a small raised area for sleeping. Only wealthier people had upper rooms, courtyards, or gardens.

Whether the homes held rich families or poor families, they typically had much less furniture than we use today. Instead of couches, people often sat on mats and cushions. Instead of tables, they had circular pieces of leather. Instead of bed frames, they had mattresses. Instead of candles and electric lamps, they had oil lamps.

SCRIPTURE BITS

HOUSE RULES

"Every new house you build must have a barrier around the edge of its flat rooftop. That way you will not bring the guilt of bloodshed on your household if someone falls from the roof."

Deuteronomy 22:8 NLT

One day Elisha went to the town of Shunem. A wealthy woman lived there, and she invited him to eat some food. From then on, whenever he passed that way, he would stop there to eat. She said to her husband, "I am sure this man who stops in from time to time is a holy man of God. Let's make a little room for him on the roof and furnish it with a bed, a table, a chair, and a lamp. Then he will have a place to stay whenever he comes by."

2 Kings 4:8–10 NLT

TABERNACLES, TEMPLES, AND SYNAGOGUES

Church buildings are not as important in our communities as they once were, yet we see them everywhere. The phrase "a church on every corner" still translates well in a lot of Western civilization. Religious buildings were far more important in ancient time but were not so ever-present.

Before God's people reached the Promised Land, they wandered in the desert for many years. Because of their nomadic lifestyle, they needed a portable place of worship. A tent, also called the tabernacle, served the purpose. It was the only "church building" in the Jewish camp. It was considered the place where God dwelled.

After the Israelites had settled in the Promised Land and enjoyed a time of peace, King Solomon built the grand temple his father, David, had envisioned. It was a permanent place for the people to worship God and offer sacrifices. The temple was based on the plans of the tabernacle. There was an inner room called the Holy of Holies. This place was reserved for God's very presence. The ark of the covenant (a sacred box with some artifacts from the miracles on their journey) was placed there, as well.

Some other worship centers were established for people who lived far away from Jerusalem. They needed places closer to home to offer their sacrifices. The temple at Jerusalem was the preferred location, though. At least once a year most people traveled there. You might remember when Mary and Joseph took Jesus to the temple in Jerusalem to celebrate the Passover and got separated from each other (Luke 2:41–47).

In the New Testament, local synagogues were the mainstay of biblical instruction. Synagogues may have actually begun as early as during the Hebrew exile in Babylon. Because the people could not return to the temple to worship, they may have begun gathering together to study and encourage each other.

The actual structure of the synagogues varied. They often reflected the

DID YOU KNOW?

The order of a synagogue service

During a service at a synagogue, the women sat on one side of the room and the men sat on the other. The services usually began with a creed of confession. Often it was from Deuteronomy 6:4–5:

> Hear, O Israel: The LORD our God, the LORD is one. Love the LORD your God with all your heart and with all your soul and with all your strength.

The service included prayers and scripture readings (from several different sections of scripture) and then an instructional sermon. There was often a time of question and answer after that. In many liturgical church services today, you can still see the elements of the synagogue service.

SCRIPTURE BITS

Since the synagogues were where teaching was happening, they were some of Jesus' hangouts.

Jesus traveled throughout Galilee teaching in the synagogues, preaching everywhere the Good News about the Kingdom. And he healed people who had every kind of sickness and disease.

Matthew 4:23 NLT

Jesus replied, "What I teach is widely known, because I have preached regularly in the synagogues and the Temple. I have been heard by people everywhere, and I teach nothing in private that I have not said in public."

John 18:20 NLT

community that built them in terms of how elaborately they were built and decorated. Each synagogue would have included at least a chest for the scrolls (like the table with the Bible in front of traditional Western churches), a platform for the teacher, musical instruments, and benches for the learners. Sounds a little familiar, doesn't it?

Food

Keep in mind that this was not a world of meat packaged in cellophane and aisle after aisle of canned foods. This was a time when variety was not at a premium. People often grew their own food. When they shopped, it was at open-air markets. There was no refrigeration, so meat was often cured with salt and dried (like jerky). Spices were not the everyday items that we find in our cupboards today, but some common spices were dill, mustard, and mint. Sugar was not even present.

Typically, a Hebrew breakfast was lighter than a Pop-Tart. It was usually a snack eaten during the course of the tasks of the morning—maybe a piece of bread or fruit. Lunch was light, maybe some bread and olives or fruit. The evening meal was the largest. A family with a modest income probably sat together sharing a big bowl of vegetable stew. Instead of spoons, they probably dipped their bread into the pot to eat. In richer homes the meals may have been enjoyed in courses with pastries or fruit for dessert.

For beverages there were no pop-top soda cans or cream soda. The water wasn't even always safe for drinking. (No, there was no bottled water.) They probably had goat milk, fresh juice, or wine with meals.

In short, there was no kid standing in front of the fridge, door wide open, looking for something to microwave. Foods were blander, coarser, and less varied. Meals were more trouble to make and store. And probably people were a lot more grateful for the food they ate than in the middle-class Western world.

POPCORN AND FIGS

On a wider view, grain was the universal food source in Bible times. In fact, grain was so valuable, it was often used as money. While the men planted, tended, and harvested the crops, the women and children worked to prepare the family's meals. For example, grain seeds needed to be sorted to remove any poisonous kernels; then they were either popped on a hot griddle or ground into cornmeal to make flat cakes.

Grapes, olives, and figs were also abundant in Bible times. Grapes were crushed and fermented for drinking. Olives were crushed for their oil, which was used for cooking, cleaning, lighting, and medicinal purposes. Figs added variety to people's diets. Believe it or not, for a snack, Hebrews sometimes ate locusts, crickets, or grasshoppers (not chocolate-covered, either).

Here are some interesting facts about the Hebrew diet:

- Honey was the main sweetener. There was no sugar.
- Butter was hardly used (because of preservation), but cheese and yogurt were very popular.
- Vegetables were often eaten raw.
- The most common kind of bread was in the form of flat cakes rather than loaves (pita-like).

DID YOU KNOW?

A kosher Diet

You've heard of "keeping kosher." The original guidelines for a kosher diet actually came during the Hebrew's exodus out of Egypt. Moses gave them God's guidelines for a healthy diet. The guidelines included things like the following:

- When eating meat, use this rule of thumb: Eat only animals that chew their cud and have divided hooves. (That leaves out pork—no cud-chewing—and camels—no divided hooves.)
- As for animals that live in the sea, eat only fish with fins and scales (so no turtles or clams or octopus or crab or even scallops).
- Whatever you eat, the blood should be drained from the carcass before cooking.
- Don't cook or eat meat and milk dishes together.
- Don't eat fat.

The list of forbidden food included camels, rabbits, badgers, pigs, reptiles, and certain birds, including eagles, vultures, falcons, owls, and bats. These dietary laws protected a huge group of travelers from disease and contamination.

Fashion

NO NAME BRANDS

Today we have different kinds of clothes for different occasions. We have sports clothes, casual clothes, work clothes, dress casual work clothes, dressy clothes, formal clothes, and so on. Men wear ties for some events and T-shirts for others. Women wear high heels for some events and flip-flops for others. We have a lot of variety in the kinds of clothes we wear. It wasn't that way in the time when the Bible was written. The difference between fancy and casual was just a matter of color and decorative accessories. That was also the difference between the clothes of the wealthy and the clothes of the poor.

As you can imagine, a lot of the fashion decisions from 4000 B.C. until A.D. 400 were determined by weather. The climate around the Mediterranean Sea was hot and dry with full sun exposure. We look at pictures of their long robes and think, *How hot! I'd rather wear shorts!* We forget that their clothes served to shade them from a fierce full sun. The color of their clothes repelled the sun, but the weave of the cloth let air pass through. It was the time of the original natural fibers.

One thing about the Hebrew wardrobe was similar to today. You could often tell a person's occupation from the clothes he or she wore. For example, priests wore special gowns and rabbis wore blue-fringed robes.

DON'T LEAVE HOME WITHOUT IT

The most basic item of clothing for both men and women was a tunic. The tunic was covered with a long wool garment called a cloak. Most people owned only one cloak at a time. They were expensive and time-consuming to make. A cloak was a valuable and versatile possession. It was a blanket to sit on, a carryall, bedding on cool nights, and even a pledge for a debt. In Exodus a law was passed down that a person's cloak should always be returned before nightfall. It was an important item—sometimes it meant a person's survival.

A TRIP TO THE MALL

THE MEN'S SHOP

No, there weren't really malls in Bible times. But if Peter or John had gone to a mall to buy a wardrobe, these are the kinds of items they would have seen on the racks.

Loincloths: Not so fitting as even boxers, they still performed the same function.

Inner tunics: These were undershirts made of cotton or linen. They were thigh-length or ankle-length and were generally for cooler weather.

Tunic coats: These were worn more than any other garment. Most tunics fit about as closely as modern-day shirts. They were often long-sleeved, floor-length, and solid-colored. Working men or slaves sometimes wore knee-length tunic coats without sleeves (think of the messenger in a Roman centurion movie). Very important men wore all white.

Girdles: No, not for tummies. They were cloth or leather belts worn over the tunic coat. They were usually two to six inches wide and sometimes studded with iron, silver, or gold. When cloth girdles were tied in the back, they functioned as belly-packs to carry small items like a snack or loose change.

Cloaks, mantles, or robes: These were large, loose-fitting garments that were worn over everything else. For the working man, a cloak was made of wool, goat hair, or camel hair. For an upper-crust guy, a cloak would be made of linen, wool, velvet, or silk and could be elaborately bordered and lined with fur.

Headdresses: There were usually three varieties: the cap (brimless cotton or wool), the turban (thick linen scarf or sash wound around the head, concealing the ends), and the headscarf (square yard of cotton, wool, or silk draped around the head and held in place by several silk twists). No baseball caps and no visors.

Sandals or shoes: Shoes were made of soft leather in a moccasin kind of style. Sandals were made of a rougher, more durable leather.

Accessories: nose rings, rings. (Yes, on guys. Yes, before alternative music.)

BEST-DRESSED WOMEN

If Mary or Martha had stopped by a boutique, these are the items they would have found hanging on the rounders. The pieces had the same function as the men's clothes, but they were made to look feminine with embroidery and needlework.

Tunics: Ladies' tunics were always ankle-length. They often had fringe at the bottom with a sash of silk or wool.

Headdresses: Mary's headdress would have been a lot different from Peter's. Mary's probably would have been a small, stiff cap with a thin veil to cover most of her face.

Undergarments: Yes, they had them, though not in so many styles as today. What kind of fabric a woman wore had a lot to do with her status. The choices were usually cotton, linen, and silk.

Gowns: Ladies' gowns were often floor-length with pointed sleeves (precursors to the Cinderella-type sleeves).

Petticoats: These were small jackets sporting fine needlework. (Are you thinking *I Dream of Jeannie*? She often wore something like this.)

Accessories: One thing is the same. Ladies had a lot more options with accessories than men did. Maybe that's because men turned their attention more to racing their camels. Ladies' accessories included earrings (also called chains or pendants), nose rings, anklets (spangles), bracelets, and elaborately braided hair.

society

GENDER ROLES

This might hurt a bit, ladies, but the Bible reflects a culture in which women didn't really have full rights as people. They were not even considered reliable witnesses in legal matters. Often when you read an account of a crowd in the Bible, you will just be given the number of men in the crowd. (That can make the event even more amazing when you add in women and children. See Matthew 14:19–21, for example.) Basically, in Bible times, men were trained for farming, hunting, and fighting in wars. Women typically tended the children and cared for the needs of the home.

There were exceptions, though. Deborah was a judge (Judges 4:4). Miriam was a worship leader (Exodus 15:20). Anna was a prophetess (Luke 2:36).

When you understand the typical role of women in the ancient world, then you understand how revolutionary Jesus' life and ministry were. He honored women as people (John 4:7–9). He allowed them to minister alongside Him and even support Him in His ministry (Luke 8:1–3). Today, when women still struggle against gender stereotypes, Jesus' style would be refreshing. In the time in which He lived, it was downright radical!

SERVANTS

The ancient world described in the Bible had more than its share of barbarism. You can be sure of that. Prisoners of war were often horribly mistreated, tortured, and killed. If they weren't killed, then they were probably taken into slavery. The kind of treatment they received as slaves was probably dependent upon the ruler of that time. When the Israelites were slaves in Egypt, they were given impossible tasks and were ill-treated (Exodus 1:11–14). But every time slavery is mentioned in the Bible, it does not have the connotations of cruelty and inhumane treatment.

Slavery in ancient days was often a way to pay off debt. In fact, a person could choose to sell himself as a slave to change his financial situation. There was also a system in place for a slave to choose to become a lifelong slave. This often happened because he or she was happy in his or her place in life and chose it almost like we would choose a career today.

The quality of a slave's life depended almost entirely on the nationality and character of his master. Roman law decreed that slaves were the legal property of their master, giving Roman masters complete control and authority over their servants. Jewish law provided slaves with limited rights, although they were still expected to obey their masters. Scripture required Jewish people to grant their Hebrew slaves freedom in the seventh year and a special year of celebration known as the Jubilee Year (Leviticus 25:39–42; Deuteronomy 15:12). Most slaves were forced to do manual labor, but some were nurses, tutors, and even doctors. In fact, some educated people would sell themselves into slavery for a limited period of time to acquire Roman citizenship.

IN CONTEXT

The whole book of Philemon in the New Testament is rooted in a slavery scenario. A slave named Onesimus ran away from his master and then became a Christian. The book of Philemon is actually a letter of commendation that the apostle Paul wrote to accompany Onesimus as he returned to his master, Philemon. While Paul taught over and over again that we are free in Christ, slavery, as a societal role, was an accepted part of that culture.

MARRIAGES AND MISTRESSES

To the modern female mind, the concept of concubines can be quite hard to take.

A concubine was a woman who became a part of a household in much the way a wife would. The husband and head of the house assumed the obligations of a husband to this woman, but she didn't have the rights and privileges of a wife. She was responsible for part of the household. She bore children by her "husband," and her sons had the same right to inheritance as the sons of the wives. She couldn't be sold away or gotten rid of, but she was always a concubine rather than a wife.

In the Bible, polygamy (having more than one wife) and concubines are mentioned as a matter of course. It's important to note, though, that the Bible also lists the negative outcomes of households with multiple wives and concubines. It was not a happy or healthy arrangement.

The story of Sarah and Hagar in Genesis 16 is a powerful example. Sarah gave her Egyptian slave, Hagar, to her husband, Abraham, to bear children for her. In that day, giving substitute wives for childbearing was a common practice, even a requirement. (Having children was the ultimate accomplishment and purpose for a woman in those days. It was a shame for her not to give her husband any kids, particularly sons. It was a greater shame than giving him another woman.) After Hagar served as a surrogate mother and bore Abraham a son, Sarah mistreated and abused her because she was jealous of her ability to conceive. Hagar's son, Ishmael, fathered the Arab nation. Sarah's son, Isaac, fathered the Jewish nation. If you watch the news, you know that conflicts between the two continue even to this day (Genesis 16:1–12).

Some kings in ancient times had so many concubines that they built a separate building for them near the palace called a harem. The harem was filled with young virgins taken from their homes for one reason—to serve the king and fulfill his sexual needs. Some of these women lived in the harem all of their lives, only to be summoned by the king once. In the book of Esther, you'll read the story of a young Jewish girl who became part of the harem of a Persian king named Xerxes (Esther 2:7–17).

King Solomon was famous for his seven hundred wives and three hundred concubines. He often married foreign princesses to build political alliances with surrounding nations. Because of that, they influenced him to worship their foreign gods. This led to the downfall of his kingdom and his faith.

WAR AND PREJUDICE

The accounts in the Old Testament describe a world that is war-filled and barbaric. Sometimes as a reader you can feel like you're reading the stories of Conan the Barbarian or the Klingons in *Star Trek*. The truth is that the ancient world was full of mutual hatred and intense rivalries. The globe that would fit that time had no set boundaries drawn in. Land was always up for grabs. "Conquer or be conquered" was the law of the land.

Longtime enemies of Israel included the Philistines, Assyrians, Ammonites, and Egyptians. As you read through historical accounts, as well as the Psalms and the Prophets, you'll find these enemies listed over and over again. It was not a "love your enemy" kind of time. It was an "eye for an eye" kind of time. Much of the story of the Old Testament has to do with God's preserving that family line through which Jesus would come. Jesus would then inaugurate a new way of living that had the potential to put war and prejudice away completely. To preserve that family line often meant battle lines were drawn. The Bible tells of some amazing and miraculous victories. The Hebrews also suffered severe defeats.

Even in the New Testament, you'll read about the hatred Jewish people had for Samaritans. Major racial tension. Here's the history—when the Assyrians invaded the northern kingdom of Israel in 722 B.C., they deported many foreigners to settle there. Over time, the Jewish people and Assyrians intermarried, creating a mixed race called the Samaritans. "Pure-bred" Jewish people from the southern kingdom refused to associate with Samaritans because they considered them "half-breeds." Understanding this piece of history gives you more of an understanding of the parable of the Good Samaritan (Luke 10:29–37), as well as Jesus' boldness in talking with the Samaritan woman at the well (John 4:7–9).

The Job Market

EMPLOYMENT OPPORTUNITIES

The days described in the Old Testament were mostly agricultural. In New Testament times, both agricultural industries and service industries began to organize. Importing and exporting were a part of the trade. Much like today, cities produced livelier trade and more career options than villages and small towns. Also, cities that were built around ports or trade routes had a greater variety and more accomplished technology. Here's a list of descriptions from the job market in the Middle East during Bible times.

SCRIPTURE BITS

---

career Day

Lamech [Cain's great-great-great-grandson] married two women—Adah and Zillah. Adah gave birth to a baby named Jabal. He became the first of the herdsmen who live in tents. His brother's name was Jubal, the first musician—the inventor of the harp and flute. To Lamech's other wife, Zillah, was born Tubal-cain. He was the first to work with metal, forging instruments of bronze and iron.

Genesis 4:19–22 NLT

FARMERS

As early as the fourth chapter of Genesis, farming was a way of survival. In fact, when God banished Adam and Eve from the Garden, He told them that they would find their food in the ground and that it would be hard work.

And to Adam [God] said, "Because you listened to your wife and ate the fruit I told you not to eat, I have placed a curse on the ground. All your life you will struggle to scratch a living from it. It will grow thorns and thistles for you, though you will eat of its grains. All your life you will sweat to produce food, until your dying day. Then you will return to the ground from which you came. For you were made from dust, and to the dust you will return" (Genesis 3:17–19 NLT).

Through Old Testament history, most peasant families supported themselves through farming. After the fall rains, when the soil was soft, farmers used wooden plows to prepare the dirt for planting. Seeds were hand-scattered, then farmers depended on steady spring rains to bring the crops. They harvested by pulling out whole plants by hand or by using a wooden sickle to cut the grain stalks. The husks were separated from the grain on the threshing floor, a hard, smooth area outside of the house. A large forked tool was used in the winnowing process to toss the grain into the air, allowing the evening wind to blow away the chaff. The quality grain left was measured and prepared for meals in the home or for sale in the village market.

It was in this kind of setting that Ruth met Boaz (Ruth 2:1–3) and that God called Gideon to be a leader of Israel (Judges 6:11).

FISHERMEN

During Old Testament times, the Israelites were often wandering from home to home, like nomads in the desert. They did not depend heavily on fishing. But by the time of the New Testament, the people were settled in their land and there was a flourishing fishing industry around the Sea of Galilee. Fish were so abundant that some fishermen stood on the shores, threw out a circle of netting (weighted around the edges), and pulled in a good catch of fish. Most fisherman, however, used boats to take them farther out into the lake. Often a net with weights on the bottom and corks on the top would be thrown out between two fishing boats and dragged to shore.

Bible stories tell us a lot about the fishing business during this time. Sometimes fishermen worked all night at their job (John 21:3–4). Some of the greatest dangers of fishing were the unpredictable storms on the Sea of Galilee (Matthew 8:23–27). Simon Peter and his brother, Andrew, were career fishermen before becoming disciples of Christ (Matthew 4:18–19).

One day as Jesus was walking along the shores of the Sea of Galilee, he saw Simon and his brother, Andrew, fishing with a net, for they were commercial fishermen. Jesus called out to them, "Come, be my disciples, and I will show you how to fish for people!" And they left their nets at once and went with him (Mark 1:16–18 NLT).

ARTISANS AND CRAFTSMEN

"He will be able to create beautiful workmanship from gold, silver, and bronze; he can cut and set stones like a jeweler, and can do beautiful carving; in fact, he has every needed skill. And God has made him and Oholiab gifted teachers of their skills to others. (Oholiab is the son of Ahisamach, of the tribe of Dan.) God has filled them both with unusual skills as jewelers, carpenters, embroidery designers in blue, purple, and scarlet on linen backgrounds, and as weavers—they excel in all the crafts we will be needing in the work" (Exodus 35:32–35 TLB).

From almost the beginning of the Bible, craftsmen were recognized. A craftsman among the Hebrews was someone who supported his family by producing crafts and artifacts to sell. Today we value things that are "handmade." In those days, that was everything!

Potters were in great demand. Copper containers were often expensive, and leather hide bottles (like those used for wine) couldn't be used for everything. So clay or earthenware pottery was essential. Potters made clay cooking and eating utensils. A Hebrew potter probably kneaded the clay with his feet, then molded it into various shapes of vessels on his potting wheel.

Woe to those who try to hide their plans from God, who try to keep him in the dark concerning what they do! "God can't see us," they say to themselves. "He doesn't know what is going on!" How stupid can they be! Isn't he, the Potter, greater than you, the jars he makes? Will you say to him, "He didn't make us"? Does a machine call its inventor dumb? (Isaiah 29:15–16 TLB).

Carpenters made plows, winnowing forks, and threshing tools for farming, as well as roofs, doors, window frames, and furniture for homes. They used tools such as saws, awls, and hammers. Sometimes carpenters worked with metal and stone as well as wood. Joseph, Jesus' earthly father, was a carpenter, and Jesus was known to His neighbors as a carpenter.

"He's just the carpenter, the son of Mary and brother of James, Joseph, Judas, and Simon. And his sisters live right here among us" (Mark 6:3 NLT).

Tanners fashioned cowhide and goatskin and the hides of other animals into sandals, bags, tents, shields, flooring, and water sacks. Because tanners worked with animals that were considered unclean, the trade was scorned and tanners were often required to work outside of the city. Tanners often used bone tools to scrape the hides. They used lime and bark from certain trees to tan the skins. The Bible mentions that Peter stayed with a tanner named Simon when he was in Joppa.

Masons worked in stone. They molded and shaped limestone rocks to be used in construction. They built walls and foundations. Their tools included a plumb line (an ancient vertical level), a measuring reed, and a variety of hammers and chisels. The prophet Amos, among others, used the mason's plumb line as an example of God's judgment of the faithfulness of Israel.

Other craftsmen included **coppersmiths, goldsmiths, silversmiths,** and **weavers.**

HERDSMEN

Herdsmen were the sharecroppers of livestock. They often did not own the animals that they tended, but their pay was in the form of products from the herd. Herdsmen tended to oxen, sheep, goats, and camels. Theirs was an honorable profession. Probably the most prominent herdsmen in the Bible were the shepherds.

Shepherds were usually responsible for a flock of sheep and goats mixed together. Their tasks included feeding the flock, leading it to green pastures, protecting the animals from wild animals, and keeping track of the flock. Shepherds sometimes had to travel far with their herds to find pastures, especially in the hot summer months.

Both goats and sheep were valuable: goats for milk, meat, and their hair, which was used to make clothing, and sheep for their wool and meat.

In the Bible you will find the role of the shepherd used over and over again as a metaphor for God's care for us. About God, Isaiah wrote,

He tends his flock like a shepherd: He gathers the lambs in his arms and carries them close to his heart; he gently leads those that have young (Isaiah 40:11).

David wrote,

The LORD is my shepherd, I shall not be in want (Psalm 23:1).

Jesus even said,

"I am the good shepherd; I know my sheep and my sheep know me—just as the Father knows me and I know the Father—and I lay down my life for the sheep" (John 10:14–15 NIV).

To the modern world these comparisons are poetic and beautiful. To the ancient world they were familiar and understandable. There was a direct connection to their everyday lives.

PRIESTS

There were two different kinds of workers in the temple. The Levites were responsible for the upkeep of the temple and the operations. Levites were descendants of Levi, one of the twelve sons of Israel (and the tribe that Moses descended from).

Moses' brother, Aaron, was the first high priest. The priests in the temple all descended from his particular bloodline in the Levite tribe. (Talk about needing a census.) The office of priest was established by God to mediate between God and the nation of Israel. Priests were responsible to help the common people maintain a right relationship with God, as well as to oversee the everyday operations of the temple and maintain the system of daily sacrifices.

Though this is a very loose comparison, the closest comparison to the modern Protestant church would be this: The Levites would include all the church staff and particularly those who handle the administration and upkeep of the church and its buildings. The priests would be those of the church staff who handle worship and the spiritual development of the people of the church.

The book of Hebrews compares Jesus' role in our lives to that of a high priest.

Therefore, it was necessary for Jesus to be in every respect like us, his brothers and sisters, so that he could be our merciful and faithful High Priest before God. He then could offer a sacrifice that would take away the sins of the people (Hebrews 2:17 NLT).

That is why we have a great High Priest who has gone to heaven, Jesus the Son of God. Let us cling to him and never stop trusting him. This High Priest of ours understands our weaknesses, for he faced all of the same temptations we do, yet he did not sin (Hebrews 4:14–15 NLT).

JUST A FEW MORE. . .

Here are a few more common occupations listed in the Bible:

- **Bakers:** made bread or baked dough that customers brought in (Genesis 40:1)

- **Barbers:** cut hair, most often worked on the street (Ezekiel 5:1)

- **Counselors or advisors:** advised the king or another official (1 Chronicles 27:32)

- **Diviners:** seemed to have access to secret knowledge, particularly future events (1 Samuel 6:2)

- **Dyers:** extracted color from natural sources and dyed cloth (2 Chronicles 2:7)

- **Elders:** were chief men or magistrates of the cities (Genesis 23:10)

- **Merchants:** imported and made merchandise available for sale to the public (Luke 19:45)

- **Nurses:** acted as tutors, guides, foster parents, or nannies (Genesis 24:59)

- **Perfumers:** dealt with anything fragrant, including apothecary as well as cosmetic items (1 Samuel 8:13)

- **Physicians:** understood and practiced the art of healing (Jeremiah 8:22)

- **Scribes:** handled correspondence, kept accounts, and transcribed documents (Ezra 7:6)

- **Politicians:** held positions as rulers, senators, magistrates, anyone involved in government (1 Chronicles 23:2)

- **Singers:** functioned as trained or professional vocalists
  (1 Chronicles 15:27)

- **Soldiers:** held rank in professional military service (Judges 9:4)

- **Tax collectors:** gathered taxes for the Roman government (Matthew 9:9)

church History 101

The political and social world of the Bible was very different than our modern world. The world of the church was different, as well.

There's a church on every block in many Western cities. There are small churches and big churches and loads of different denominations. As they grow, they often add buildings to their campuses. Sometimes they build gyms or family life centers. They add libraries. They clear off softball fields.

That is nothing like the early church. In fact, the early church had nothing to do with buildings at all. The early church was just the people who believed in Jesus and the miracle of His resurrection. They were identified by the cities they lived in. They united to spread the news and to encourage each other. They didn't meet because it was what they always did. They met because they needed each other. They didn't have buildings. In fact, during times of persecution, a church building would have been the most dangerous place to be.

When you read the books in the New Testament that are letters (called epistles), you realize that most of the churches were called by their city names. The Ephesian church was all the believers in Ephesus. The Philippian church was all the believers in Philippi. They hadn't divided into denominations. They were just the followers of Christ who were willing to admit their faith and join together to continue Jesus' ministry. You've probably heard ministers today encourage the modern church to become more like the New Testament church in this way.

THE MINISTRY

What do you think of when you think of someone who is "in the ministry"? Do you think of clerical collars? Hospital visits? Preaching from pulpits? Church offices?

Today we often think of a pastor who goes to one church for a while, then goes to another church, probably in the same denomination. That church pays him a salary and probably provides some kind of benefits package.

Ministry for the prophets of the Old Testament and the early church leaders of the New Testament was a whole different thing. They were most often "itinerant," which was like being a freelance pastor who traveled around to different congregations. They were often in a dangerous profession. They withstood persecution. Often there were other religions in their area that were as fervent in their beliefs if not more so. There were no salary packages or benefits. The pastors and teachers depended on the people of the congregation to sustain them. Many, such as the apostle Paul, were bivocational, which means they had a day job (like tent-making) that they used to support themselves so they could minister in their off time.

currencies, weights, and measurements

or all of our societal evolution, two things about the marketplace are the same now as they were in the days described in the Bible: (1) Shoppers wanted to get the most for their money, and (2) merchants wanted to get paid well for their products/services.

Because of this, from the beginning of civilization, money and measurements were developing into standard systems.

It is difficult to imagine a world like the early Old Testament world in which standard weights or measurements shifted from one place to another. In one city a shekel or cubit could mean one thing. In another city it meant something else entirely. In one marketplace, barley was measured by the handful. Whose hand? In one place distance was measured by a bow shot or a day's travel. Which archer? Whose legs?

By the time of the New Testament, everything in life was more standardized because more of the world was under one rule. A money system was in place and there were government-established standards for weights and measurements. (Yes, the government was already stepping in with its standards. No FDA yet, though.)

MONEY

As you read the Bible, some terms you will find for money include the terms below. You'll notice that some equal weights rather than currency. That is because scales were used in the marketplace. These weights or coins were put on one side of the scales and the merchandise was put on the other side. That would make for a heavy change purse, wouldn't it?

Bible term		Approximate modern equivalent
Farthing		¼ cent
Quadrans		¼ cent
Mite		⅛ cent
Denarius	a day's wage	1 cent
Drachma		16 cents
Didrachma	½ Jewish shekel	32 cents
Shekel (temple)	½ or ⅓ shekel	0.2 ounce
Shekel (common)		0.4 ounce
Shekel (royal)		0.5 ounce
Mina	50 shekels	1.6 pounds
Talent (light)	3,000 shekels	66 pounds
Talent	125 libra	88 pounds

WEIGHTS AND MEASURES

Liquids, like wine or oil, were measured in rectangular containers shaped a little like a bathtub. They were called baths and came in different sizes. Solids, like cereals and grains, were measured in tublike containers of different sizes. The largest was an ephah and was big enough to hold a small adult. Another way to measure was with scales. Premeasured weights were placed on one side of the scales and the merchandise was placed on the other side and priced according to weight.

Here are some weights and measurements that you might see as you read the Bible. Keep in mind, though, that in the Old Testament they were less standardized.

Bible term		Approximate modern equivalent
Liquid Measures		
Log		0.5 pint
Hin	⅙ bath	6 pints
Bath		38.5 pints
Cor		48.5 gallons
Homer	10 baths	90 gallons
Dry Measures		
Kab		3.5 pints
Omer	⅒ ephah	38.5 pints
Ephah		⅕ bushel
Distances		
Finger span		¾ inch
Palm		3 inches
Span	½ cubit	9 inches
Cubit		17.5 inches
Pace		1 yard
Fathom		6 feet
Reed	6 cubits	8 feet
Furlong		202 yards

3. WHERE DID THE BIBLE COME FROM?

Who wrote it?

Who compiled it?

How did it get to us in the form that it's in?

HOW the BiBLe came to Be

SO HOW WAS THE BIBLE ACTUALLY WRITTEN?

We know the Bible now in rearview. We can look back from our viewpoint through history and see how it all came to be. But in order to really understand the Bible, we have to be able to look from the perspective of the writers, as they were experiencing life.

The people whose writings make up our Bible didn't know that their work would one day be collected into the holy scriptures. They weren't thinking they were going to be on a best-seller list. They were like we are: driven by the problems they were trying to solve and the ideologies they felt passionately about.

- Moses wrote because he didn't want the history of God's provision to be forgotten. He wrote in the style in which he felt comfortable— narrative. He just told the facts as they happened, or as God told him they happened. He is the only person we know of who actually took dictation from God, at least when he wrote down the Ten Commandments.
- David didn't set out to write psalms that could be translated into praise music today. He just wrote about the parts of life that he was processing (even the less-than-shiny ones), and they became a part of Psalms.
- Jeremiah didn't make a plan to write a book that would fall three books after Ecclesiastes in the Bible. Jeremiah's heart was broken because his people continued, over and over, to fall away from God. Jeremiah knew that this would lead to their own destruction. So when God called Jeremiah to be a prophet, Jeremiah pulled out all the stops to convince them to turn back. He used metaphors. He used dramatic language. He forecast the consequences of their behavior. His style of writing poured out of who he was and how he communicated.

Each person who wrote a part of the Bible wrote from his specific place and time in history. What made their writing unique was that God breathed His truth through them. He used them exactly where they were, but guided them to record exactly what He needed. Today we think of this kind of thing as dictation, but that's not how it worked (except the one time with Moses). God didn't speak the words and let the writers take shorthand. It was more miraculous than that. He breathed His words into their lives so that when they wrote from their hearts, God was in it.

SO WHO DECIDED WHAT BOOKS TO INCLUDE IN THE OLD TESTAMENT?

By the time civilization was grown up enough to keep historical records, the Old Testament was already collected into pretty much the same books that we have in our Old Testament today. The books were considered sacred because of their history and because of the power that evidenced itself when they were read. The first five books (called the Books of the Law, the Torah, or the Pentateuch) were the basis of the Hebrew faith. The books of the prophets were studied and quoted in Hebrew worship. Each book had proven itself over and over again. Eventually this collection was called the Old Testament.

Remember that as the Old Testament was being written, the world was rather new and in the process of organizing itself. Languages and nationalities were being born. Technology was being birthed and then advancing. We humans were figuring out how to keep track of ourselves. In the midst of all that, the early theologians (which usually meant wise men who worked in the temple or synagogues) were discussing and rediscussing the power of the Bible, which at that time was called something like "the Law and the Prophets." They were also discussing what their responsibility was in caring for the manuscripts and in passing them down through the generations. Task forces were formed (called councils) specifically to discuss and decide about these kinds of things.

In the final roll call, there were several different organizations of the Old Testament. Some versions kept 1 and 2 Kings as one book. Others made them two books. Some included some books written after 400 B.C. (called the Apocrypha), but others didn't. The thirty-nine books listed on page 14 as the Old Testament were present in all of the versions, though they were organized in a variety of ways.

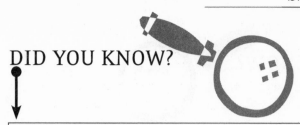

DID YOU KNOW?

One of the big tests for the authority of Old Testament books was the test of the writer. The first five books (Genesis, Exodus, Leviticus, Numbers, Deuteronomy) were believed to be written by Moses. The rest were believed to be written by prophets (people to whom God manifested His truth). Some of the later books that don't appear in our Bible but appear in others were discounted because their authors were closer to historians than prophets.

SO WHO DECIDED WHAT BOOKS TO INCLUDE IN THE NEW TESTAMENT?

By the time the New Testament was "canonized" (officially recognized as a complete collection of books), a very important discovery had been made among church leadership: the committee. While a task force or two had been involved in recognizing the Old Testament canon, the early church had plenty of committee meetings about what books really were inspired by God and were to be included in what we call the New Testament.

By the late fourth century, the same twenty-seven books that you find in your New Testament were considered the finished New Testament. Even though committees or councils met, however, the canon of the New Testament wasn't something that arbitrary groups of people decided. These people merely recognized what books were standing the tests of authorship and authority. The books stood for themselves. It's just that by that time, humanity was organized enough to recognize it in a corporate kind of way.

If you want more details, grab a Bible dictionary or encyclopedia and look up "canonicity." You'll find a lot of information about what scrolls were found where and what historians mentioned what books. You can be sure that there has been no shortage of cross-referencing and cataloguing or research. What we often treat as casual and everyday was taken seriously in the time when the New Testament and Old Testament were being recognized as finished and complete.

DID YOU KNOW?

chapters and verses

Today when you open most Bibles, you will find the books of the Bible divided into chapters and verses. This is not the way the Bible was originally written. Originally the books in the Bible were just writings. They were letters. They were sermons. They were stories. Except for the Psalms, which were numbered as songs, the other books were written in the form of letters, sermons, and stories.

By the fifth century, in some manuscripts the Gospels were divided into chapterlike divisions. Then in the Middle Ages a variety of systems were used to mark off texts that could be used for public worship. It wasn't until the thirteenth century, though, that Stephen Langton (chancellor of the University of Paris) divided the Vulgate (a widely used Latin translation) into chapters. Then around 1551 Robert Estienne (a printer in Paris) divided Langton's chapters into verses. These divisions became standard and have been used ever since.

Can you imagine how much harder it would have been to find John 3:16, or any other verse, without the 3:16?

where'd we get the translations?

making copies of the Bible, before printing presses, was a *huge* deal. Men called scribes dedicated their whole lives to the tedious task of copying the manuscripts l-e-t-t-e-r by l-e-t-t-e-r, line by line. Translating the Bible from its original language into another language was an even *bigger* deal. It meant that mere people were going to make choices about what God was actually saying.

The Old Testament was originally written in Aramaic and Hebrew (two closely related languages). This makes sense when you know that all of its writers were Hebrews. The New Testament was originally written in Greek because that was the common language of that day. (Alexander the Great had conquered the whole area by then and the standard language was Greek.)

The first translation that we know of was when the Hebrew Old Testament was translated into Greek. It was called the Septuagint (sep-TU-a-jint). It was called that because the translation was completed by seventy-two men, six from each of the twelve tribes of Israel. (Remember, "sep" often means seven. A "septuagenarian" is a seventy-year-old.)

Since the Septuagint, there have been many translations. Maybe the most famous is the King James Bible, famous for its Old English thees and thous. Other translations you might have heard of are the New International Version, the Revised Standard Version, and the New American Standard Bible.

People often talk about Bible translations in the same tone of voice in which they talk about politics or religion. In other words, they don't take it lightly. In fact, they can come to blows disagreeing about it. On one hand, it's a good thing that we take seriously the way we treat God's Word. On the other hand, the purpose of the Bible is to teach us to live lives that please God. We honor God's Word the most when we obey it, not when we defend a particular version of it.

There are two main schools of thought about translating.

- **Word-for-word:** Each individual word is translated into its equivalent in the new language. These translations can be a little tougher to read and sometimes a little awkward. Some languages use articles and prepositions differently than others. Sometimes there is not an equivalent word. Sometimes you end up with more technical-sounding words in an effort to be exact, so overall the translation is harder to read.

- **Thought-for-thought:** Rather than translating each word one at a time, the translator looks at the whole phrase or sentence and asks, "How can I translate this thought into a phrase that means the same thing?" Because of this, these versions are often easier to read.

Which method is better? They both have their place. *Word-for-word* translations (like the King James Version or the New American Standard Bible) are great for doing in-depth studies of a single verse or word. But a *thought-for-thought* translation (like the New International Version or the New Living Translation) is great for daily reading and understanding. You might hear word-for-word translations called "study translations" and thought-for-thought translations called "reading translations." It wouldn't be a bad idea to have one of each on your bookshelf.

Here is how the most popular versions of the English Bible fit on the spectrum:

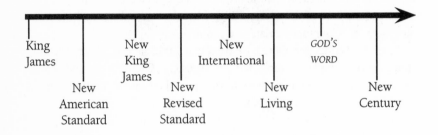

word-for-word   Thought-for-Thought

King James

New King James

New American Standard

New Revised Standard

New International

GOD'S WORD

New Living

New Century

WOULD YOU LIKE STUDY HELPS WITH YOUR BIBLE?

These days you can buy a Bible with as many options as a new car. You can buy a plain Bible, or you can buy a Bible with lots of extra stuff to help you understand and apply the information inside. You can buy a leather-bound Bible to last a lifetime or a paper-bound Bible to hopefully last through middle school camp. You can buy a Bible with colorful maps and a concordance in the back for those times you want to look up a verse or a specific word. You can buy a Bible with lists in the back so you can find verses that will apply to your specific situation. All of these features help you better understand and navigate your Bible.

There are other features you can choose from, too. *Study Bibles* give you background, historical data, and explanations of hard-to-understand verses. *Devotional Bibles* often give you a devotional plan for reading the Bible each day. They give you a daily Bible passage to read and give you a devotional thought (kind of like a short sermon) on the passage.

If you are motivated to read and understand the Bible, you'll want to find a Bible that works for you. If it looks too complicated for your purposes, look around some more. Ask people you know and respect who read the Bible what they like about their translation. Ask the clerks in the store what they know about the translations on their shelves. As long as you are using trustworthy translations, find the Bible that will be most inviting to you to spend time reading it. If you aren't reading it, you won't benefit from its power to change your life.

DID YOU KNOW?

which Translation?

You'll note some initials after most Bible references that are listed in a book. If you don't see any initials, look on the copyright page of the book and you'll probably see that one specific translation is used or that one is used unless otherwise noted. In this book, if there are no initials, the translation is the NIV or New International Version. Here are some typical translation abbreviations you may see.

GW	God's Word
KJV	King James Version
NASB	New American Standard Bible
NCV	New Century Version
NIV	New International Version
NKJV	New King James Version
NLT	New Living Translation
NRSV	New Revised Standard Version
TLB	The Living Bible

4. THE BASIC ANATOMY OF THE BIBLE

Here's a road map for your journey.

The Basic Info

The Bible is the story of God's reaching out to His creation, to people, to us. It opens with the creation of the earth and closes with the end of life as we know it. There are two main sections of the Bible. The first is the Old Testament, written before Christ came to earth. The second is the New Testament, written after Christ's birth, life, death, resurrection, and return to heaven.

OLD TESTAMENT

The Old Testament is made up of thirty-nine different "books." These books were inspired by God (see "How the Bible Came to Be" on page 61) but written by different people in many walks of life and for many different purposes.

Some of the books are just one step beyond oral tradition. They are stories to be passed down to generations to come. Some of the books are almost legal documents; they are the rules and regulations of the day. Some are poetry, songs, hymns, proverbs. Some are sermons and prophecies.

The writers wrote out of their own abilities and context. It wasn't like they were saying to themselves, "I'm going to write a book, and *just maybe* it will be included in the Bible one day." No. They wrote because an issue needed to be addressed or some history needed to be recorded. They responded to that need in the most effective way they could think of. God wrote the Bible through these writers as they responded to life around them.

Even though the Old Testament doesn't speak about Jesus in the same biographical way that the New Testament does, the focus of the Old Testament is on God's solution to humanity's problem: the future coming of Christ. In the Old Testament, Jesus is referred to as the promised one, Messiah, Immanuel, the Redeemer. God's promise to Abraham included a promise that Jesus would come through Abraham's bloodline, the Jewish people. This is why the history of the Jewish people was so important: Jesus was climbing down that family tree. This is the significance of all the sacrifices you read about in the Old Testament: Jesus was promised as the ultimate sacrifice for sin.

NEW TESTAMENT

The second section of the Bible includes twenty-seven different documents or books. All of these books were written in the first hundred years after Jesus lived. Like the Old Testament, they were written by different people in different circumstances and for different reasons, but inspired by God. These documents were all pulled together and recognized as the collection we call the New Testament.

The New Testament is made of books that tell the story of Jesus' life, death, and resurrection; books that tell the story of the church; and letters written to encourage and instruct those churches.

oLd Testament organization

Typically the Old Testament is broken down into these categories:

THE LAW

Written by Moses himself, these books tell about the beginning of the world and the Jewish nation. They tell history through stories. They also give guidelines for life and worship. They are a mixture of narratives and instruction.

These books (also called the Torah or Pentateuch) are the basis for the Hebrew faith.

- Genesis
- Leviticus
- Deuteronomy
- Exodus
- Numbers

HISTORY BOOKS

These books tell true stories of historical events. They span the time from when the Hebrews reentered Israel after leaving Egypt, through the divided kingdom and the exile into Babylon and Assyria, and then until the Hebrews reentered Jerusalem after the exile. (Theirs is a rocky past.)

- Joshua
- Judges
- Ruth
- 1 and 2 Samuel
- 1 and 2 Kings
- 1 and 2 Chronicles
- Ezra
- Nehemiah
- Esther

WISDOM BOOKS

These books are more experiential. Some are stories, but they are not from an informational point of view as much as a grappling-with-life point of view. Jesus would have called these books the Writings. Others have called them "wisdom literature."

- Job
- Psalms
- Proverbs
- Ecclesiastes
- Song of Songs

PROPHETIC BOOKS

The prophets were the philosophers of the day, the street preachers, the Billy Grahams of the ancient Hebrew world. They told it like it was. In the process, through God's guidance, they also sometimes told it the way it would be when Christ came hundreds of years later. Even if they did do a little future-telling, they were not like fortune-tellers or psychics. They talked about the future for the purpose of their people having hope and living clean lives within that hope. The prophetic books are divided into two categories. The first five books are books by the "major" prophets. It's not so much that these prophets were greater than the others, but their writings are longer and we do know more about them.

- Isaiah
- Jeremiah
- Lamentations
- Ezekiel
- Daniel

The rest of the books are by prophets considered "minor" prophets. The lives of the prophets below were more obscure and their writings are shorter.

- Hosea
- Joel
- Amos
- Obadiah

- Jonah
- Micah
- Nahum
- Habakkuk

- Zephaniah
- Haggai
- Zechariah
- Malachi

IN CONTEXT

The prophecies of the Old Testament do not appear in the Bible in the order that the prophets lived or worked. (If anything, they are roughly in order by length from the longest to the shortest.) So when you read through their messages, keep in mind that they are not chronological. But they all preached to Israel or Judah during the time that the Hebrews resettled the land, went into exile in foreign lands, and eventually returned home. These writings were the spiritual guides of that time.

New Testament organization

The New Testament is typically thought of as being divided into these categories:

THE GOSPELS
These are similar to biographies of the life of Jesus Christ, though some writers organized events in different order.

- Matthew
- Mark
- Luke
- John

HISTORY BOOKS

There is only one history book in the New Testament besides the Gospels. It's really a sequel to the Gospel written by Luke. It is the story of the beginning of the New Testament church and the spread of the good news of Christ.

- Acts

THE LETTERS (OR EPISTLES)

We know the first thirteen letters were written by the apostle Paul. The last three of those letters are called his pastoral letters because they were written to pastors rather than whole churches. The letters after the letter to the Hebrews are called general epistles (uh-pis-uhls) because they weren't written to any one specific person or church.

- Romans
- 1 and 2 Corinthians
- Galatians
- Ephesians
- Philippians
- Colossians
- 1 and 2 Thessalonians
- 1 and 2 Timothy

- Titus
- Philemon
- Hebrews
- James
- 1 and 2 Peter
- 1, 2, and 3 John
- Jude

PROPHETIC BOOKS

There is only one book of prophecy in the New Testament. This book is about the "end times" or the "second coming" (meaning, of Jesus). It could also be called apocalyptic (meaning, end of the world).

- Revelation

writing styles

Because the Bible was written by so many different authors facing so many different slices of life, it is written in a lot of different literary styles. We read each book best when we understand the perspective of the author. Here are some categories that might help.

HISTORICAL NARRATIVES

Genesis, Exodus, Judges, and Acts are some prime examples of historical narratives. They teach us about history, but not just the facts of history. They tell us the story of history, the people, the places, the marriages, the family conflicts. Historical narratives were one step above oral tradition. They were the way history was passed down. The author wanted to describe events and to tell about heroes and villains.

WISDOM WRITINGS

Often these books are called poetic, but not the "Roses are red, violets are blue" type of poetry. Hebrew poetry wasn't so concerned with rhyming as with symmetry and profound thoughts. It was called poetry because of its structure and style. Psalms, Proverbs, Ecclesiastes, and Song of Songs are classic poetry books, perhaps even poetic philosophy books that cut a slice of life and place it on a plate with presentation as a primary concern. Wisdom writings are to be experienced, savored, rolled around in your mind, and digested bit by bit. They are life's encounters recorded through one writer's perspective and applied as it was meaningful for him.

PROPHECIES

A bulk of the Old Testament is made up of prophetic passages. Isaiah through Malachi (the last book) are prophetic books. These prophets spoke to their own culture, as well as to the future. When they were writing, the only Bible to speak of was the Book of the Law (the first five books of the Old Testament). Today when we think of hearing God speak or of His revealing Himself, we think of the wealth of His words we have in the Bible. Back then, though, they were still waiting for fresh news from God. They got it through the prophets. The prophets were the guys who simply could not sit still watching their people decay spiritually.

TEACHING PASSAGES

Many passages are specifically meant to teach us. They aren't giving us a story and letting us draw our own conclusions. They aren't poetry or narratives. They are lay-it-on-the-table, this-is-how-it-is-and-will-be truth. They are intended to train us and to teach us, to inform us and to form us. The Gospels are filled with teaching passages from Jesus. Many of the epistles or letters in the New Testament include them as well.

PARABLES

The Gospels include many of Jesus' parables. The importance of these passages was not the facts of the story. The importance was the principles underneath the story line. When we read the story of the woman who continues to knock on someone's door until he answers, it's not important what the woman wanted or whether a woman would have knocked on a door that long. What is important is that when we keep seeking answers from God, we have a better chance of finding them the longer we persevere.

EPISTLES OR LETTERS

Much of the New Testament is written in the form of letters, personal letters to churches and to individuals. They include personal information at the beginning and the end. It's like reading someone else's e-mail. You understand it best when you know what questions the writer was answering. So the more we know about the churches that received the mail, the better we understand the letter.

THINK ABOUT IT
THIS WAY

Cable Station Synopsis
It might be easier to understand the whole writing-in-style thing if you think about cable TV stations. TV is going the way of radio these days in that each station is finding a niche or format and fitting its shows within that format. Except for the traditional networks, the cooking shows are on a channel about cooking. The sports shows are on a channel about sports. If books of the Bible were assigned to cable channels, they might divide up like this:

Television for Women
Esther, Ruth, and Song of Songs: These would definitely fit in with "chick" TV. Women's stories, problems, issues, and interests.

Science Fiction or Psychic Channel
The writings of the prophets of the Old Testament and the book of Revelation would definitely fit into this kind of genre, even though there is nothing fictional or fake about them. No per-minute charges, either, on their hotlines. But amazing visions and a future like you wouldn't (but can) believe.

Real-Life TV
Joshua, Judges, 1 and 2 Samuel, 1 and 2 Kings. Talk about action, suspense, and adventure. If they had a cameraman running behind, we'd be watching them whether they fuzzed out the Philistine faces or not.

Advice TV
Proverbs: everyday wisdom to make decisions by—without the fights, the weird clothes, and the tearful confrontations.

History Channel or the News
Genesis, Exodus, 1 and 2 Chronicles, and Acts: These books would be prime targets for who, what, when, where. They record not only what happened, but often what impact it had on the culture.

Music Station
Music video programming has never seen the likes of the lyrics in the Psalms. Just what kind of spin would you put on Psalm 18? Talk about special effects.

Biography Channel
Ezra, Nehemiah, Job, and the Gospels: All of these books give the story of one man's life.

Christian TV
The epistles or letters of the New Testament could be the meat and potatoes of Christian TV stations. These were letters written specifically to Christians dealing with real issues. Put a host writer in front of a microphone and let him go.

The Whole Bible in one-Liners

The whole next section is dedicated to the content of the Bible, book by book. Before you take on that mass of information, though, here is the whole Bible in one-liners.

Old Testament

Genesis:	God created the world, gave us the choice to love Him, and began His plan to restore us through a good man named Abraham.
Exodus:	In Egypt, Abraham's descendants grew into the Hebrew nation; then they headed back home.
Leviticus:	God gave the Hebrews guidelines for worship and sanitation to survive their journey.
Numbers:	Because of their lack of faith, the Hebrews took a forty-year detour through the desert.

Deuteronomy:	Moses said good-bye, gave a history lesson, and gave some guidelines for loving and worshiping God.
Joshua:	The Hebrews resettled their land after more than four hundred years away by facing down the squatters in every city.
Judges:	The Hebrews organized into a nation back in their homeland and were led by wise judges.
Ruth:	One family's story about God's provision.
1 and 2 Samuel:	Samuel led Israel and then anointed King Saul. After Saul, King David reigned and his family suffered.
1 and 2 Kings:	King Solomon ruled Israel, and then the kingdom divided in two. Finally, the Hebrews were exiled to foreign lands.
1 and 2 Chronicles:	Israel's story from David's reign until the exile into Babylon, but from a spiritual (not political) perspective.
Ezra:	The Hebrews returned from exile in Babylon and rebuilt the temple.
Nehemiah:	More Hebrews returned from Babylon and rebuilt Jerusalem's wall.
Esther:	The Hebrews survived exile in Persia because of a Jewish "royal beauty contest" winner.
Job:	Bad times don't change the nature of God.
Psalms:	Lyric sheets from Old Testament temple worship. Songs about facing life and worshiping God.
Proverbs:	Nuggets of wisdom for dealing with everyday life.
Ecclesiastes:	I had it all, and it didn't mean anything without God. Sincerely, King Solomon.
Song of Songs:	I'm passionately in love, and I can't stop thinking about her! By Solomon.
Isaiah:	Pay attention. God has a master plan in the works, and we need to be a part of it.

Jeremiah:	Prepare to face the consequences of living apart from God. Know that God's plan is still in place.
Lamentations:	What we dreaded has happened. Our sin has destroyed us. My heart is broken.
Ezekiel:	Here are some visions I saw from God's perspective on how we've lived our lives and of heaven.
Daniel:	Here are the stories of Daniel, a Jewish exile in Babylonia, and his visions of the future.
Hosea:	Ephraim, you are as unfaithful to God as a prostitute to her husband. Turn around!
Joel:	Because of our sin, it's going to get worse before it gets better. But it will get better one day.
Amos:	By human standards, you're looking okay, but by God's standards, you're failing.
Obadiah:	Attention, people of Edom: You've bullied Israel, and now you'll answer to God Himself.
Jonah:	Jonah unwillingly prophesied to a wicked place and was disappointed at the good turnout.
Micah:	We are immoral at every level and headed for destruction. Only God can deliver us from ourselves.
Nahum:	No matter how strong evil seems, God will do away with it when He is ready.
Habakkuk:	God, why don't You stop bad things from happening?
Zephaniah:	God will hold us accountable for our actions. All of them.
Haggai:	Don't ignore what matters most—your relationship with your God and Creator!
Zechariah:	Finish the temple and get your relationship with God in working order. The Messiah is coming!
Malachi:	Worshiping God is not about doing the least to get by. Be wholehearted instead.

New Testament

Matthew:	Hebrew friends, Jesus is the Messiah that God promised through the prophets, and here's how I know.
Mark:	Hey, Romans, Jesus was a servant-king. Look what He did!
Luke:	Amazing news! Jesus is God and yet totally human. He understands our journey.
John:	It really is true. Jesus Christ is God Himself.
Acts:	A new church organizes: Jesus' sacrifice makes us right with God. Spread the news!
Romans:	Dear church: The only way we can be right with God is through faith.
1 Corinthians:	Dear church: Don't be like the world around you. Be who God made you to be, pure and effective.
2 Corinthians:	Dear church: Here's who I am. Now let me tell you who you should be.
Galatians:	Dear church: You can't earn God's approval by obeying rules. It takes faith.
Ephesians:	Dear church: Receive God's amazing love for you. Then love each other well.
Philippians:	Dear church: Knowing you brings me joy. Knowing God brings us all joy.
Colossians:	Dear church: Faith in Christ is enough. Don't add anything else to it.
1 Thessalonians:	Dear church: Look forward to Christ's return!
2 Thessalonians:	Dear church: Look forward to Christ's return, but keep living full lives and working hard!
1 Timothy:	Dear Tim: You're doing well. Here are some things to remember about leading a church.
2 Timothy:	Dear Tim: Come soon. I don't know how much longer I'll be here. Keep the faith!

Titus:	Dear Titus: Here are some helpful hints about leading your church.
Philemon:	Dear Philemon: Forgive Onesimus not as a runaway, but as your brother in faith.
Hebrews:	To all Jewish Christians: Now that Christ has come, focus on Him rather than the rituals that pointed you to Him.
James:	Yes, salvation is by faith, but faith without action is useless.
1 and 2 Peter:	These are difficult times. Let your faith help you endure. Don't let go just because troubles come.
1 John:	Ignore false teaching. Live righteously. Love each other. Know that Jesus was God in the flesh.
2 John:	Keep your chin up and your hearts open, but keep a close watch on your faith.
3 John:	Keep up the good work! I'll be there soon to deal with the power struggle.
Jude:	Watch out for people who use God's grace as an excuse for irresponsibility!
Revelation:	Here's the last page of world history—the end of the world as we know it.

5. WHAT DOES THE BIBLE SAY?

The best way to know what the Bible says is to read it. The next best way is to look at the book-by-book summaries here.

what does the Bible say?

That's a big question. The following sections are a medium-sized answer divided into a book-by-book summary. Each book is categorized for you so that you'll know up front what kind of situation the writer was facing and what kind of information he was giving. Each book is a slice of life laid out on a platter. It's a little piece of somebody's life that God spoke through.

SCRIPTURE BITS

Before you read about what the Bible says, read what the Bible says about itself:

For the word of God is full of living power. It is sharper than the sharpest knife, cutting deep into our innermost thoughts and desires. It exposes us for what we really are.
Hebrews 4:12 NLT

All Scripture is inspired by God and is useful to teach us what is true and to make us realize what is wrong in our lives. It straightens us out and teaches us to do what is right. It is God's way of preparing us in every way, fully equipped for every good thing God wants us to do.
2 Timothy 3:16–17 NLT

And remember, it is a message to obey, not just to listen to. If you don't obey, you are only fooling yourself. For if you just listen and don't obey, it is like looking at your face in a mirror but doing nothing to improve your appearance. You see yourself, walk away, and forget what you look like. But if you keep looking steadily into God's perfect law—the law that sets you free—and if you do what it says and don't forget what you heard, then God will bless you for doing it.
James 1:22–25 NLT

Just a little note: You'll find throughout the Old Testament that God taught people a lot through object lessons. The feasts that the Jews instituted and celebrated were reminders of significant events in their history. God asked them to build memorials from time to time. The prophets often used objects or actions to teach. It's a pretty cool thing to realize that God works with people in practical ways. He did the same thing when He embodied Himself in the New Testament. He taught in parables, everyday stories, down-to-earth examples. It makes you wonder, doesn't it, where we ever got the idea that God is a distant deity who doesn't dig into our lives. If the Bible reveals anything, it's that God meets us right where we are and teaches us in every possible way that we'll understand.

old Testament Book summaries

The following pages include a little information about each of the books in the Old Testament. They are marked off in sections (law, history, poetry, prophecy). The books are in the order that they appear in the Bible.

For each book you can read some stats and a one-line overview, or you can dig a little deeper and read the major stories or points of that book.

DID YOU KNOW?

As with anything else in this world, there are a lot of differing opinions about a lot of the details listed here. Sometimes there are different guesses about who the author was or whether he was the only author. For our purposes you'll see the most generally accepted facts listed. For instance, there might have been other writers included in the Psalms, but we've told you the ones we're sure of. In the back of this book is a list of sources that you can use to explore all of the possible scenarios for these details.

THE LAW

The first five books of the Bible are called the Law of Moses or the Books of the Law (also the Torah or Pentateuch). In the New Testament, when Jesus is quoted talking about "the Law and the Prophets," the "law" refers to these first five books. Moses is credited with writing all five of these books.

These first five books lay the groundwork for a lot of life. They were the survival manuals for the Jewish nation, the descendants of Abraham, the recipients of the covenant he established with God. It is in these five books that we learn the stories of the beginning of the world itself, as well as the beginnings of the different cultures and languages of the world. It's in these books that we discover how the Hebrews learned to survive as nomadic people in their desert wanderings (from how to deal with mold to what to do about PMS). It's in these books that the Hebrews built their first church and learned how to maintain it. It's in these books that the priesthood was established, as well as the kosher diet and the first pyramid personnel management system. It's in these books that a people began their journey of knowing God and living in peace with Him.

THINK ABOUT IT THIS WAY

The stories in these books aren't necessarily G-rated even though we teach them in simple form in children's Sunday school. They are set in a primal, violent time in world history. God worked through these people as they were. He didn't pretty them up before He told us about them.

IN CONTEXT

The Law of the Old Testament

- Genesis

- Exodus

- Leviticus

- Numbers

- Deuteronomy

Genesis

IN CONTEXT

Here's the scoop. . .

Written: *around 1450 B.C.*

Written by: *Moses*

Writing style: *historical accounts of true stories*

One-liner: *God created the world, gave us the choice to love him, and began His plan to restore us through a good man named Abraham.*

THE LAY OF THE LAND

The book of Genesis covers a lot of historical ground. The places, the people, and the events that you'll read about through the rest of the Bible all find their roots in Genesis.

It is in this book that God established the world and His relationship with the people of that world, first through Adam and Eve, then Noah, then Abraham and his descendants.

CREATION

Genesis describes the creation of the world in very concrete terms. God spoke us and our surroundings into being. The world was ideal when God made it. The first people were placed in a paradise called the Garden of Eden and asked to tend that garden, to build a friendship with God, and to obey Him. You probably know how that story goes. The dad was Adam, the mom was Eve. . . .

THE FIRST DYSFUNCTIONAL FAMILY

Adam and Eve were the first and only earth-dwellers to experience the world as innocent adults. They woke up for the first time able to walk and run and love and enjoy God's creation. Before long they did the one thing God asked them not to do, and innocent adulthood was gone forever. They left the ideal garden, and the kind of life we know began: sweat, labor, pain, and disappointment. They lost their first two sons to violent, fatal sibling rivalry. It was not a happy time. But Adam and Eve did what we do today. They picked themselves up and dusted themselves off, and with the forgiveness and guidance of almighty God, they started all over again. Their world was changed forever, but their God was still the same.

NOAH

The descendants of the first family disregarded God more and more. The world became a mess. (Perhaps more of a mess than it is now.) It was such a mess that God thought about scrapping the project altogether (Genesis 6:5–8). There was one man, though, who remained faithful. God preserved that man's family: Noah, his wife, and their three married sons.

God preserved Noah by asking for his obedience. God told Noah to build a very big boat. There is a good chance that until this point it hadn't even rained in the world yet, so building a boat was a wild thing for Noah to do. Then came all the animals; then came the floods. Everything on the earth was destroyed except the creatures on that boat.

When it was all over, Noah recommitted himself, his family, and this freshly laundered world to follow the Creator once again. We are all descendants of Noah's family.

ABRAHAM

One of Noah's descendants (more than a few generations down) was Abraham. (At one point he was known as Abram.) God established a special relationship with Abraham. He promised that Abraham would be the father of a great nation. At the time of this promise, Abraham was very old and had never had children! God also asked Abraham to pick up and move to a new place, Canaan. Canaan was the place that we know as Israel today.

Eventually Abraham and his also-old wife, Sarah, did have a child, Isaac, way past their childbearing years. Today Abraham and Sarah would have had top-selling autobiographies as well as incredible tabloid marketability. But in their day and time, they were just two people who (after some laughter and an "Are you sure?") believed God would do what He said.

If you've hung around kids' programs at church much, you may have heard the motion song "Father Abraham Had Many Sons." The song can go on forever. Abraham's descendants did, too. All from two little old people who believed God could do the impossible.

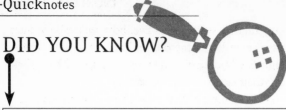

DID YOU KNOW?

You also may have heard of Sodom and Gomorrah, some pretty wicked cities. Abraham's nephew, Lot, lived in one of these cities. Abraham saved Lot from destruction just before God burned the towns to the ground. It was Lot's wife who looked back at her home and died immediately, transformed into salt.

THE ISRAELITES

Genesis is really about a family tree. First it's about the family tree of the whole world. Then it's about Abraham's family tree. This is why you'll find genealogies galore. (As irritating as it may be to women today, most genealogy was defined according to the dads. That's an ironic twist, considering that the test of whether a person is Jewish depends on the nationality of Mom more than Dad.)

Abraham's son Isaac had twin sons, Esau and Jacob. In an amazing turn of events (not to mention deceit and disguise), Jacob, the younger of the twins, got the birthright. Because of that, he became the leader of the family. God changed Jacob's name to Israel. (Names meant a lot more back then than they do now, and there wasn't any paperwork to fill out.) Thus Jacob, or Israel, became the head of the family, and his descendants were called the Israelites (or Israelis or Hebrews or Jews as we know them today). The land they settled in was also called Israel.

Jacob had twelve sons and one daughter. His sons became the patriarchs (or head honchos) of their families, called tribes. (You'll sometimes hear them described as the twelve tribes of Israel.) It was a Middle Eastern *Bonanza* in the making.

JOSEPH

Jacob's favorite sons were his two youngest, Joseph and Benjamin. They were the sons of Jacob's favorite wife, Rachel. (He had two wives, Leah and Rachel, who were sisters. Now *that's* a wild story of its own. See Genesis 29.)

Joseph was the confident sort, and his older brothers resented his dreams and aspirations, whether they came from God or not. (Remember, this was a barbaric time.) Joseph's brothers resorted to violence in their rage at their cocky younger brother. While they were in the wilderness together, they beat Joseph and almost decided to kill him. Instead, they settled for selling him into slavery.

This slavery eventually led Joseph to Egypt. He started out in poverty, but despite false accusations and jail time, with some dream interpreting on the side, Joseph became one of the king's most trusted men.

Talk about a twist of fate. Later, when Jacob's land was filled with a fierce famine, he sent his sons to Egypt begging for food. Who do you think was the man in charge of giving out portions? None other than their long-lost brother, Joseph. You can imagine the shuffling feet and wary glances. It was a younger sibling's opportunity for revenge.

But in the end, Joseph knew that his brothers' foolish and violent actions had, in the long run, set the stage for his family's survival in the famine. Eventually the whole family moved to Egypt and established a long-term residence there.

DID YOU KNOW?

An Explanation You Might Need

The historical period Genesis describes is a time in which polygamy (having more than one wife at a time) was accepted. Since it was a culture in which men held the power, there were multiple wives more than multiple husbands. Not only were there wives, there were also concubines (sexual partners, but not marriage partners, who made up a harem). This is difficult to reconcile in today's world, where polygamy exists but is not considered a standard way of living and is often against the law. While polygamy was accepted, throughout history God honored monogamous husband/wife relationships. (After all, He didn't create Adam and Eve and Isabel.)

There are also several occasions listed in Genesis when a woman offered her servant or maid to her husband to bear his children. Sarah tried it with Abraham and brought grief in her family that continues until this day. Leah and Rachel both adopted this practice with their servants. It was so important in that culture to have sons, as many of them as possible, that practices such as this were considered last resorts.

SO WHERE'S GOD GOING WITH ALL THIS?

Since the Bible in its entirety is really about Jesus, even this beginning book lays a foundation. When Adam and Eve disregarded God's one requirement for their paradise living, a snake was involved. We believe this snake to be a force of evil (the devil, Lucifer, the prince of darkness). When God explained the consequences of Eve's, Adam's, and the snake's actions, He said to the snake, "Because you have done this, cursed are you above all the livestock and all the wild animals! You will crawl on your belly and you will eat dust all the days of your life. And I will put enmity between you and the woman, and between your offspring and hers; he will crush your head, and you will strike his heel" (Genesis 3:14–15). This was probably a reference to Jesus' coming to conquer the powers of evil.

Also in God's promise to Abraham was the promise that the Messiah (the Savior, Jesus Christ) would come through Abraham's family line. As soon as people resorted to sin, God began His plan to restore us. So from Genesis 1, God, in the person of Jesus Christ, was the plan.

questions

Q. *What's important about being made in God's image?*

A. *Humans are not replicas of God, but we do share common characteristics with God. God is all-knowing, all-powerful, all-present, perfectly good, holy, and loving. We are not. But like God, we are spiritual beings, rational, emotional, communicative, and moral. We have dignity, purpose, and meaning. And we can experience the bonds of personal relationships.*

Q. *Why did God need to rest on the seventh day of creation (Genesis 2:2)?*

A. *The Bible does not say that God needed to rest, as if from exhaustion, but only that God did rest. God does not lack energy or become fatigued from hard work as we do. But His using the seventh day as rest tells us that rest itself is good. God's rest also helps us understand our own need for a Sabbath (Exodus 20:8–11). God gave us the fourth commandment for our own benefit, but God also put a divine seal of approval on observing a day of rest by doing so Himself.*

Q. *Where was the Garden of Eden? (Genesis 2:8–14)*

A. *No one knows for sure, but the Bible seems to locate the garden near the conjunction of the rivers Tigris and Euphrates, the Fertile Crescent of ancient days. Today that area is in southern Iraq.*

Exodus

IN CONTEXT

Here's the scoop. . .

Written: *around 1450 B.C.*

Written by: *Moses*

Writing style: *a chronological historical account*

One-liner: *In Egypt, Abraham's descendants grew into the Hebrew nation; then they headed back home.*

POST-GENESIS

The book of Exodus picks up the story line where the book of Genesis ended. At the end of Genesis, the twelve sons of Israel (the man who had been named Jacob, remember) had come to live in Egypt. They did this because of a famine in their own land. They were able to do this because one brother, Joseph, had built his home and a great reputation in Egypt, so his brothers were welcome.

Once there, the family of Israel grew and grew. They became a small nation among the Egyptians, and that was nerve-racking for the Egyptian king. What if they decided to overthrow the government? Because of his fears, he made the Israelites slaves. This began the first of many very dark times in Jewish history.

Even as slaves, the Hebrews (another name for the nation of Israel) continued to grow. (This had been promised by God to the very first ancestor of the Jewish nation, Abraham. See Genesis 17.) Pharaoh tried another form of population control: He let the female infants live but destroyed the male infants. In the midst of this tragedy, God raised up a leader named Moses, who would eventually stand up for his people and lead them to freedom.

MOSES

Moses is the main character in Exodus (after God, that is).

Moses was born into a courageous family. When he was born, there was a decree from the king that all male babies should be destroyed. Moses' mom hid him for three months, then made a floating basket and hid him in the basket at the banks of the Nile River. His sister, Miriam, stood watch.

When the princess came to bathe in the river, she found the basket and adopted the bootleg Israelite baby. She gave him the name Moses (which means "out of the water"). Moses' sister, Miriam, showed quick wit and great timing. When the princess found baby Moses, Miriam immediately offered to go and find a Hebrew "babysitter." Of course Miriam brought back her own mom.

Moses grew up in the palace but as a young man was exiled from Egypt. (He killed an Egyptian for mistreating a Hebrew.) It was during this time of exile that God carved out Moses' life's mission: to free his people, to lead them back to Canaan, their promised land, and to establish the Ten Commandments on the way. Easy enough? You thought *you* had it rough. . . .

Sure enough, Moses did lead the people out of Egypt and to the border of their homeland. It took him over forty years to do it and stress points galore, but he died a man who had stood at the edge of God's promise coming true.

THE PASSOVER

The Passover is one of the most significant rituals of the Jewish faith. It finds its origins in the last plague God sent to Egypt to convince the king to set the Hebrews free. During the plague, the angel of death swept through Egypt, taking the lives of the firstborn sons. The Hebrews were instructed to place the blood of a lamb on their doorposts. If they did so, their firstborn sons would be spared. There is a special meal associated with the Passover. Today we often call the celebration of that meal a "seder" (SAY-dur).

The Passover was a symbol of God's salvation through the blood of an innocent life. It was an accurate picture of Jesus Christ's sacrifice for the sins

IN CONTEXT

Most of Exodus is about that journey to freedom from Egypt, through the desert, to the Promised Land. The journey of the Israelites was a lot like the journey of modern believers: We leave the slavery of sin, we travel through an often difficult desert of a life, and finally we get to our real home, heaven.

of His people. He was innocent, He was a firstborn, and He shed His blood. The last meal that Jesus shared with His disciples before His crucifixion was a Passover meal.

STORIES FROM THE ROAD

A lot of amazing things happened to the Israelites along their journey. Here are some favorites among the "remember whens."

The Red Sea. Just as the people left Egypt, the king changed his mind and sent his armies to bring them back. The people stood between chariots and spears and the Red Sea. God parted the waters so they could make their escape on dry ground (Exodus 14:15–30).

Bread from heaven. The people were in a desert for much of the trip. Each morning a breadlike substance would be lying on the ground like snow. This is what they ate (Exodus 16:2–4).

The quail. Once when the people were craving meat, quail came "out of nowhere" to supply a BBQ feast (Exodus 16:13).

Water. Once it came from a rock (Exodus 17:2–6), and once a bitter stream turned sweet just for the Israelites' drinking (Exodus 15:22–25).

Navigation. The people were led by a cloud by day and a pillar of fire by night. No need to ask directions when God is leading (Exodus 13:21–22).

The Ten Commandments. God Himself wrote these on stone. Remember, this was before printing presses and electricity. Writing ten commands in stone was no little feat (Exodus 20).

Moses' glow. After Moses had spent time with God on the mountain, his face literally glowed. He had to wear a veil so the people could deal with him without being distracted (Exodus 34:29–35).

questions q&a

Q. *Is violence okay when fighting violence? (Exodus 2:11–17)*

A. *Moses learned an important lesson about violence and anger. In the first case, he observed violence against a fellow Israelite and responded by killing the perpetrator. Clearly, other options were open to him: reporting the misdeed, using his position to bring the power of the state to bear against the perpetrator, advocating a change in state labor laws.*

In the second case, he intervened when some annoying shepherds pestered a group of young women. This time he did not kill but simply drove off the nuisances.

The lesson he learned was appropriate response. Surely in the latter case, some violence was involved (else why would the bullies retire?). Moses was "getting a grip" on his own temper, restraining his sense of outrage, and calculating his response to achieve just results without letting the situation escalate into vengeance. That principle works just as well between states as between people. If you would reduce violence, keep your response to it firm, calm, and under control.

Q. *Why did God give Moses and the Israelites so many rules to follow? (Exodus 20)*

A. *God's holiness requires that those who serve and worship Him do so with great care. God's laws point to God's purity. "You shall be holy to me, for I the Lord am holy, and I have set you apart" (Leviticus 20:26 TLB). God wanted the redeemed Israelites to stand out and be different from pagan nations around them. By carefully adhering to the standards of the covenant, Israel would be a light to the rest of the world, demonstrating the blessing of knowing and serving Yahweh (the Old Testament name for God). Many of the rules were given to protect the people from harm, such as laws regarding sexual purity, and to provide them a life full of good things.*

Leviticus

IN CONTEXT

Here's the scoop. . .

Written: *around 1450 B.C.*

Written by: *Moses*

Writing style: *a book of guidelines*

One-liner: *God gave the Hebrews guidelines for worship and sanitation to survive their journey.*

A HOLINESS INSTRUCTION MANUAL

You can imagine that as a whole nation of people left Egypt to travel in the wilderness, there was a great need for organization. They were organized into tribes. They were also organized into roles: some were administrative assistants, others were ordained priests, and so on. One family, the descendants of Levi, was assigned to be priests. They cared for the tabernacle (a portable temple). They helped with the sacrifices. They "kept house." They cared for the precious artifacts that reminded their people of the journey to freedom.

The book of Leviticus is mostly a how-to manual for Israel's priests. It is a detailed instruction booklet for just about any situation that might arise. Keep in mind that the Israelites at this time could have been described as vagabonds: They lived in tents, and they moved often. Sanitation was a big concern. The priests were responsible for teaching the people what was "clean" and what was "unclean." There were guidelines regarding mildew, leprosy, disease, food, sin, sacrifices, and even holidays.

HOLINESS

The information found in Leviticus kept the people healthy and clean, but it also taught them something about God. It taught them that God is holy. The Bible doesn't actually say "cleanliness is next to godliness," but Leviticus does make a connection between God's holiness and our cleanliness. That connection probably saved the life of a wandering nation.

IN CONTEXT

Leviticus is a practical treatise on how to worship, how to live in community, and how to stay alive. Don't let the fancy-shmancy Latin-sounding name fool you. In the situation for which it was written, Leviticus is the most practical of books: sandal-meets-the-dirt-road kind of stuff.

SACRIFICES

From the earliest historical records, animal sacrifices were a part of religious life. The concept of an innocent shedding its blood to atone for someone's bad deeds was a part of Jewish and Gentile history alike. (See Genesis 4:4–5.)

Leviticus gives specific guidelines for sacrifices: What animals? What kind? When? How? Sacrifices involved blood and a certain amount of brutality. They were a picture of the sacrifice that Jesus Christ eventually made for all of us; He in His innocence shedding His blood for our bad deeds. The sacrifices were an appalling demonstration of just how seriously God regards our sin.

questions

Q. *Why was Israel commanded to observe so many different offerings and sacrifices? (Leviticus 1:2)*

A. *Leviticus is all about sacrifices that offer penance for sin and restoration of a relationship with God. This is the meaning of the Hebrew term for "sacrifice"—to draw near or approach. Sinful people needed some way to draw near to the infinite, holy God with assurance of acceptance.*

Each of the five major sacrifices carried special significance. The sin and guilt offerings cleansed from sin and compensated for wrongs done to God and others. Burnt offerings showed devotion to God by burning the whole animal as an act of worship. The fellowship offering symbolized peace with God—the only sacrifice in which all parties (priest, offerer, and God) participated. It was a meal eaten in the presence of God. Eating a meal with someone, to the Hebrew person, meant friendship. The grain/meal offerings committed one's work to God. The important sequence points to a specific goal: fellowship impossible without first dealing with sin and then dedication to God.

Numbers

IN CONTEXT

Here's the scoop. . .

Written: *around 1450 B.C.*

Written by: *Moses*

Writing style: *a mixture of stories and official logs or records*

One-liner: *Because of their lack of faith, the Hebrews took a forty-year detour through the desert.*

A CAPTAIN'S LOG

Numbers is a book of facts, figures, and events. It is a record, kept by Moses, of thirty-eight years of wandering.

Remember, the Hebrews had been delivered out of Egypt by God through miracle after miracle. (For instance, food that came like dew every morning and water that gushed out of rocks.) After two years of miracles and hardships, it looked like their journey was about to come to a wonderful end—then it happened.

The Israelites sent twelve spies into Israel to scope out just how big a task lay ahead in reclaiming the land. When the spies returned, ten of them were overwhelmed with fear. Only two of the spies, Joshua and Caleb, remembered what God had already brought them through and said, "We can do it with God's help."

After all God had done, the people doubted Him and were afraid to enter. Because of their lack of faith, God sent them back into the desert. There, they wandered for forty more years before trying again. In fact, everyone who was over twenty when they left Egypt died before entering Israel—except Joshua and Caleb.

NUMBSKULL AWARDS

In many ways, Numbers is a book about failures: foolishness, acts of indiscretion, lack of judgment, poor choices, and just plain old sin. Here are the top five winners for foolish choices recorded in Numbers:

5. *Korah (Numbers 16)*. Korah got two buddies and 250 henchmen and staged an insurrection against Moses. Know what happened? The earth swallowed up Korah.

4. *The prophet Balaam (Numbers 22–24)*. Balaam was paid by King Balak (honorable mention in the Numbskull Awards) to put a curse on Israel. God interceded even to the point of making Balaam's own donkey try to reason with him. Can't get much worse than that.

3. *Miriam and Aaron (Numbers 12)*. Leave it to family. Moses' own sister and brother decided they wanted a bigger piece of the power. Instead, Miriam got a temporary case of leprosy and they both got a bigger piece of humble pie.

2. *The ten fearful spies (Numbers 13–14)*. These men were the leaders of their clans. They had witnessed God's provision. Yet they turned chicken when they were within reach of what God had promised. They used their influence to destroy the faith of their people.

1. *The people (Numbers 11, 13–14)*. The all-time prize has to go to the Israelite people. Sure, it's not easy to trek through a desert, but God had been faithful. Out of 600,000+, all but two of them doubted God. They worshiped idols; they wished for captivity; they figuratively spit in God's face. These tactics didn't work well for them.

questions

Q. *How did God speak to Moses? (Numbers 1:1)*

A. *A news reporter on the scene might have heard an audible voice, for certainly the Bible contains many occasions in which God is said to speak and God's voice is said to be heard. In this case, however, perhaps not.*

God speaks sometimes through a person's conscience or intuition or through a person's emotive longing to know God better. In prayer we commune with God with unusual personal closeness and sometimes feel as if God were speaking to us, though not audibly, as we pray or meditate on His Word.

If God did provide Moses an audible message here, it had the unusual quality of detail. Several individuals are named and selected as assistants for the upcoming census.

God uses many means to speak to His people. Indeed, the great Christian leader Augustine believed that God had spoken to him emphatically through the voice of a small child. The result was Augustine's conversion and his considerable influence on the church even today.

Moses was an unusual person. He was given a very special mission by God, even though he considered himself a mediocre candidate for it. Given Moses' mission, God no doubt needed a channel to Moses' mind that involved less confusion.

The mission of God today is the worldwide announcement that salvation has come in Jesus Christ, His Son. That good news is conveyed through many channels and means, and it bears implications for every person and profession. It's such an important mission that Christians worldwide testify to the fact that God still speaks, even as He did centuries ago.

Q. *Why were women, children, and teenagers omitted from the census recorded in Numbers? (Numbers 1:2–3)*

A. *Israel was a patriarchal culture. Men were leaders, warriors, and priests, while women took responsibility for child-rearing and homemaking. Egalitarian notions typical of the modern era can be seen through the protection of law accorded women and children, but not through equal opportunity for education and social status.*

Obviously women and children were vital to the survival of the Israelite people and to the accomplishment of the conquest of Canaan. Their omission from census numbers does not diminish this importance. On a practical level, the technology for counting large quantities was quite unsophisticated in Moses' day, and a census would be easier to produce if certain mathematical assumptions were applied to a head count of adult males only. In Israel's case, since adult males controlled the culture's technology, it is not surprising that they would count themselves, and only themselves, as a means of calculating the total population.

Deuteronomy

IN CONTEXT

Here's the scoop. . .

Written: *around 1450 B.C.*

Written by: *Moses*

Writing style: *a mixture of stories and sermons*

One-liner: *Moses said good-bye, gave a history lesson, and gave some guidelines for loving and worshiping God.*

FAMOUS LAST WORDS

This book was written at a significant time. The Israelites had traveled for *forty years* in the desert. They did this knowing that one day they would enter the land that had been promised to Abraham, their ancestor. When they had left Egypt (where they were slaves), there were 600,000+ people in the group over the age of twenty. By the time that Deuteronomy describes, just before they entered the land, only three of those people were still living (Moses, Joshua, and Caleb). A whole generation, the ones who had seen God's provision and heard His laws, had passed away. A new generation (or two) had arisen who only knew what they had heard second- or third-hand.

The people were finally at the border. Moses knew he wouldn't get to enter the land with them, and so he shared his heart before he said good-bye. It was his last chance to remind his people of God's miraculous provision and of the journey on which He had led them. Moses' last words to his people make up the bulk of Deuteronomy.

PUT YOURSELF IN THEIR SANDALS

Think about it! A whole generation passed while they were traveling in this gypsy type of environment. Here's one way to look at it.

Let's say you were eight years old when the people left Egypt. You would have left Egypt with your parents and grandparents. By the time you were ten, you would have traveled to the border of your destination. Then, when

IN CONTEXT

Playing the Game of Remember when. . .

You know how it is. You sit around with friends and tell stories you have all lived through, just for the fun of reliving them. Remember when we thought we were buying plaster to fix the wall and it was cement instead? Remember when Uncle Dan dressed up for a masquerade party as a go-go dancer and construction workers whistled at him? Remember when we got goofy at the wedding reception and laughed punch right out of our noses?

The remember whens for the Hebrews were on a somewhat grander scale, but Moses was still creating the same effect. Remember when God did this for us?

- Remember when the angel of death swept through Egypt but our sons were saved because of the lamb's blood on the doorposts?

- Remember when God literally pulled back the waters so we could cross the Red Sea?

- Remember when we needed food and it appeared like dew on the ground every morning?

- Remember when we needed water and it gushed right out of a hard rock?

- Remember when Moses came down from the mountain and his face glowed from God's presence?

- Remember when we made that gold calf idol and Moses was so angry he threw down the Ten Commandments tablets and broke them?

- Remember when we whined and complained and began to die of poisonous snakebites?

- Remember when we heard the report of the spies and were too scared to enter the land?

everyone got scared to cross the border, you would have started traveling again, like nomads in the desert. You would grow to be a teenager, enter your twenties, possibly marry and have kids, then enter your thirties, then your forties, losing your grandparents and parents along the way.

Finally, when you are getting close to fifty years old, you return to the border of that land. You are an adult now and are back at the same place you were when you were ten years old. And somehow you have to keep from making the same mistakes your parents did.

It *does* sound like a good time for a book like Deuteronomy, a book that says, "Okay, this is where we've come from and what we are about and where we are going. We've spent forty years making mistakes. Let's regroup and move ahead."

THE PROBLEM WITH THE ISRAELITES

The Israelites had a once-in-a-lifetime experience. There is probably no other time when God's presence was more evident every day. A pillar of fire and a cloud led the people. They saw miracle after miracle: food on the ground every morning, quails out of thin air, water out of rocks, divine plagues and punishments. God was obviously present and working.

Yet the Israelites continued to doubt.

It would be easy to judge these people, to say they had it easy. After all, they didn't have to have a lot of faith; they could see God's actions right before their eyes.

The Israelites show us what we all are capable of: not trusting God even after He's proven Himself, and continually asking Him to prove Himself over again.

IN CONTEXT

It might have been easier to see God work, but the Israelites only show us basic human nature. Most of us have experienced some kind of answered prayer, only to worry during the next time of trouble whether God will answer us. Most of us have seen God work in some way, whether we called it a miracle, guidance, or intuition. Yet we didn't trust that we'd ever see Him work again.

MOSES' DEATH

Moses led an amazing life. He was one of the few Hebrew males his age to survive a royally decreed slaughter. He was raised in a palace when he should have been a slave. He spent forty years living in the desert in preparation for this journey and more than forty years wandering the desert during the journey.

He spent his life following God's call and leading his people from slavery to freedom and a land promised to them. But at the end of it all, he never set foot in that land. He first knew this would happen when God gave him a simple set of instructions and, for once, Moses didn't obey them. The people needed water, and God told Moses to speak to a rock and water would come. In frustration and anger, though, Moses didn't just speak to the rock; he violently and angrily struck the rock. He took on himself what was only God's to do. He lost perspective.

We don't know for now why a man who did so many good things still had this one thing held against him. It's one of the questions we won't have answered for us in this life. But Moses lived a good life and was an honorable man. The Bible calls Moses the humblest man on earth.

questions &a

Q. *What does "Deuteronomy" mean, and why was the book written?*

A. *The book of Deuteronomy was written by Moses. The word means "a copy of the law" or "a second giving of the law." The law was first given by Moses to the Israelites soon after their deliverance from slavery in Egypt. This second telling of the law was written at the end of Moses' life, forty years after the exodus, and recounts all that God had done for the chosen people.*

As Moses prepared to die, he said, "Take to heart all the words I have given you today. Pass them on as a command to your children so they will obey every word of this law. These instructions are not mere words—they are your life! By obeying them you will enjoy a long life in the land you are crossing the Jordan River to occupy" (Deuteronomy 32:46–47 NLT).

This book of law contains truth that guides relationships with God and neighbor. Moses hoped the people of Israel would remember all God had done for them and pass this truth to the next generation.

HISTORY BOOKS

If the history books of the Old Testament were a movie series, they would be rated at least PG. It was a rough time for humanity. War was the way to gain land, and power meant right. But even in the midst of the rough-hewn society of that day, God was working and people turned their hearts to Him.

These books show you a slice of life that historians call the Bronze Age and the Iron Age. It was a time of great advances but a time very different from our world of roadside trash pickup and orthodontia. It was a time before anesthesia was developed or doctors had figured out that they needed to wash their hands to keep down infection. In the midst of all these differences, it is amazing to note that people still dealt with the same issues: faithfulness in marriage, fear that they weren't hearing God right and asking Him for confirmation, civil unrest, and disobedience. What you find in these pages when you look past the technological and sociological differences is that we still have a lot in common with these people and can learn from the situations they faced.

IN CONTEXT

The Old Testament History Books

- Joshua

- Judges

- Ruth

- 1 and 2 Samuel

- 1 and 2 Kings

- 1 and 2 Chronicles

- Ezra

- Nehemiah

- Esther

Joshua

IN CONTEXT

Here's the scoop. . .

Written: *around 1370 B.C.*

Written by: *Joshua with the help of someone else*

Writing style: *a chronological collection of true stories (war stories, mostly)*

One-liner: *The Hebrews resettled their land after more than four hundred years away by facing down the squatters in every city.*

JOSHUA THE SOLDIER

After nearly forty more years of wandering, the Hebrews faced the border of their homeland for the second time. This time, though, they had a different kind of leader. God had given them Joshua, a soldier and a strategist.

The book of Joshua is about the battles the Israelites waged to recapture and resettle their land. It involves a lot of force and a lot of blood. It involves a lot of actions that our present culture considers barbaric and violent. It was a barbaric and violent time. Basically, it's not a G-rated book. It's pretty violent.

Looking beyond the violence, though, we'll find it is a story of faith. When the people trusted in God's strength and obeyed His commands, they won their battles. When they didn't, they lost (and lost miserably). In this way, the book of Joshua is relevant to the battles we face today in our lives, even though our weapons and our enemies look a lot different.

TRUTH IS STRANGER THAN FICTION

The Israelites won their battles as much by miracle as by strategy. Here are a few miraculous strategies God performed:

- They crossed a river—on dry ground (Joshua 3:9–17).

- The people shouted, and the walls around a city fell down (Joshua 6:1–27).

- God instructed Joshua to fake a retreat and stage an ambush (Joshua 8:15–29).

- God won a battle using a hailstorm (Joshua 10:6–11).

- The sun literally stood still so Joshua's army had more time to fight (Joshua 10:13–14).

questions q&a

Q. Why is Israel called the Promised Land? *(Joshua 1:1–5)*

A. *God established a unique relationship with the ancestor of the Jews, Abram. (See Genesis 12:1–3.) God challenged Abram to leave his old homeland and extended family to follow divine guidance. God also promised to bring Abram to a new land and that divine power would ensure that Abram's offspring became a great nation. So Israel (Abram's primary line of descendants) is as much a promised nation as the land it claims is the Promised Land.*

When Abram packed his bags, he had no children. He did have his wife, Sarah, and God's promises. He didn't know what the future held, but he trusted God with his destination, allowing God to choose a homeland for his family.

Q. How should Bible promises like "You will be successful in everything you do" apply to people today? *(Joshua 1:7 NLT)*

A. *The promise in this verse does not allow for any definition of success. Daily meditation on God's Word will shift our definition of success from power and wealth to service in Jesus' name, from status to disciple-making, from control to friendship and even sacrifice of self for others. Success as a child of God is much different than success in worldly terms. The ultimate measure of success for a Christian will be to hear Jesus say, "Well done" (Luke 19:11–27). The next time you hear someone tout his or her success in terms of property owned, degrees earned, policies sold, or retirement secured, ask yourself whether that measure of success stands up to biblical scrutiny.*

Judges

Here's the scoop. . .

Written: *We don't know.*

Written by: *Maybe Samuel, but we're not sure.*

Writing style: *a collection of true stories*

One-liner: *The Hebrews organized into a nation back in their homeland and were led by wise judges.*

THE BOOK OF JUDGES

Before the Hebrews were slaves in Egypt, they were just a large family with twelve sons led by their father, Israel. When they left Egypt after generations of slavery, they were a people of 600,000+ adults led by a countryman, Moses. As they were settling into their homeland, they were led by a soldier, Joshua. Once they settled, they spent some time without any leadership at all. It is this period of time that the book of Judges describes.

The era of the judges was an era of repeated cycles in the lives of the Israelites. They would fall away from God and fall prey to their enemies. When things got bad enough, they would turn back to God and He would raise up a leader, called a judge (often a military leader), who would rescue them from their current dilemma. But as the cycle continued, the people would fall away again as soon as that judge died or lost his influence. This cycle repeated itself through at least twelve different judges.

DEBORAH

Deborah is one of the most famous judges and the only one we know of who was a woman. She was wise and discerning and a prophet of God. She was known for holding court and settling disputes under a palm tree.

One day she informed Barak, a military leader, that he was to organize ten thousand men to wage a war. Barak refused to go to war unless Deborah accompanied him. Deborah's response was very interesting. She reminded Barak that if she went with him to war, the word would be spread that a woman won the battle. (Remember, this was a *very* sexist era. This interchange alone required Deborah and Barak to live above the culture of their day.)

Deborah did go to battle with Barak, and they were victorious. Their song of victory is recorded in Judges 5.

GIDEON

Gideon was an unlikely leader. He wasn't a member of an important family and he wasn't even an important member of his own family. But God called him to lead, and he obeyed.

Gideon started with thirty-two thousand men. Through God's leadership, he pared them down to just ten thousand. Through testing that ten thousand, he pared them down to just three hundred men. With just three hundred men, Gideon accomplished God's purposes.

At one point in Gideon's life, he needed to know God's direction, so he created a little test. He put a fleece of wool out on the ground overnight and asked God to let dew fall on the fleece but not on the ground. God did it. The next night Gideon asked God to let dew fall on the ground but not on the fleece. God did it. Today people still talk about putting a fleece out before God to determine a specific answer or to "find His will" about something. When they do, they are referring to Gideon.

SAMSON

Samson was, perhaps, the most famous judge. He grew to be the strongest man in the country. His strength was founded on a special commitment he had made to God, called a Nazirite commitment. Part of this promise required that the Nazirite never cut his hair. As long as Samson kept this commitment, his strength stayed with him.

He got involved with a woman named Delilah, though, who tricked him into cutting his hair. Samson's life went from bad to worse from then on. He was blinded and kept as a slave. He eventually killed his captors, but he died along with them.

questions

q&a

Q. Who is Baal? (Judges 2:11)

A. *Baal was one of the main local gods in the land of Canaan. God had instructed the Israelites to stamp out everything in the land that had anything to do with such things as Baal. However, the Israelites ended up joining the Canaanites in their worship of Baal.*

One interesting note is that the word "Baal" has an additional meaning in Hebrew; it means "husband." You could say that, by their worship of Baal, the Israelites "married" a foreign god.

Q. Why did God "test" Israel when the outcome of such a test was almost certain failure? (Judges 2:22)

A. *God wanted perfect obedience from Israel; He wanted a holy nation. And yet He had to give them the choice of not choosing Him. After all, if God compelled Israel to be obedient and holy, if they had no choice in the matter, such obedience and holiness wouldn't be worth much. In fact, it would probably end up like the obedience that a robot might display.*

We are tested in our own lives, tested by having to live in a sinful world and having to deal with our own sinful natures. Like Israel, our own outcome is almost certain failure. However, the difference is that we are offered forgiveness through Jesus Christ.

Ruth

IN CONTEXT

Here's the scoop. . .

Written: *around 1350 B.C.*

Written by: *Some people think Samuel wrote part of it, but we don't know for sure.*

Writing style: *a true story about a Jewish family*

One-liner: *One family's story about God's provision.*

A LOVE STORY

The book of Ruth is about love on a lot of different levels. The story opens with a woman, Naomi, her husband, and her two sons leaving their home because of famine. They settled in a land called Moab. There the two boys married. (Their wives were named Orpah and Ruth.) Naomi, Orpah, and Ruth all became widows. After the deaths of her husband and her sons, Naomi decided to go back to her hometown and freed her daughters-in-law to go and make their own lives in their own land.

After much protesting, Naomi finally convinced Orpah to leave, but Ruth would not budge from Naomi's side. She committed to building her life with Naomi. Together they traveled back to Bethlehem. Their experiences there are told in the book of Ruth.

THE REST OF THE STORY

After settling in Bethlehem, Ruth went out to gather leftover wheat from the fields surrounding Bethlehem. She was noticed by a distant relative of Naomi named Boaz. According to Jewish laws, he could marry Ruth and at the same time actually be honoring a family obligation.

That's exactly what happened. Ruth and Boaz married and gave Naomi a grandchild. And (get a load of this) it was through their family line that the famous King David, as well as Jesus Christ, was born.

questions q&a

Q. *What is a "family redeemer"? (Ruth 3:12)*

A. *Often called a kinsman redeemer, this person was responsible for protecting members of the extended family—a big brother, so to speak. If death created a widow, the family redeemer would take over a husband's duties. The same for orphans.*

Boaz was not the first redeemer in line to care for Ruth, so he secured the permission of the first man in that line, with public witnesses, and then filled the role, encouraged to do so by Ruth's own expression of interest in becoming his wife (Ruth 3:7–11).

1 samueL

IN CONTEXT

Here's the scoop. . .

Written: *during King David's reign*

Written by: *Samuel, Nathan, and Gad*

Writing style: *a historical account*

One-liner: *Samuel led Israel, then anointed King Saul, then anointed King David.*

FIRST, THE STORY OF A PRIEST

Samuel was a miracle baby. His mother had been infertile and prayed long and hard for a child. Because she was so aware that her child was a gift from God, when he was old enough, she sent him to live at the temple to be raised and apprenticed by Eli, the priest.

When Samuel grew up, he was the leader of Israel. But what Israel wanted was a king. A king! This would change everything about Israel's government. They had only been ruled by God and then a few judges. (See the book of Judges.) Samuel tried to dissuade them, but Israel persisted. They wanted to be like all the other countries around them (a logic you might recognize from an argument with a middle schooler). So it was Samuel who anointed their first and second kings.

THEN THE STORY OF A KING

The first king of Israel was a young man named Saul. He had a lot going for him and did many great things for Israel. He was committed to God. . .at first. Then he wavered, fell, and literally went insane.

During King Saul's most troubled moments, he was calmed by a young musician named David. (Do you remember that old spiritual "Play On Your Harp, Little David"?) David became best friends with Jonathan, Saul's son. Little did Saul know that because he had stopped obeying God, he would one day be replaced by David.

As Saul began to realize David's growing popularity, he became jealous and angry and increasingly distressed. He treated David like an outlaw. King Saul finally died in a battle along with his son Jonathan.

THEN THE STORY OF ANOTHER KING

David was anointed future king while he was still a young and very unlikely candidate. He was anointed by Samuel after God rejected Saul as the rightful king.

Soon after, David was honored with the opportunity to play music before King Saul. The king was so impressed with him that he made David an armor-bearer. This is how it came to be that David was at the camp when Goliath made his challenge. You probably remember the story about little David taking his slingshot out to meet the giant, Goliath, and killing him with one stone.

This was the beginning of David's leadership, but it was the beginning of the end for Saul's. As the story of David and Goliath grew, the people of Israel started comparing David and Saul. Eventually Saul resented it so much that David was left a refugee, an outlaw, wandering from cave to cave trying to survive against Saul's anger and his armies.

When Saul was killed in battle, David sincerely grieved for him. Then David took over the throne.

questions *q&a*

Q. *Did the kings help or hurt Israel as a nation? (1 Samuel 8:6–7)*

A. In demanding a king, Israel became like every other nation on the block. Instead of asking God for relief from counterfeit spiritual leaders, they cried, "Give us a king!"—rejecting God's rule in favor of human leadership.

Moses had written about the danger of human monarchy (Deuteronomy 17:14–20). He had warned future kings against having large stables, trading horses with Egypt, collecting many wives, and accumulating wealth. The lives of Israel's kings appear to be an effort to do exactly what God had warned against.

2 samuel

Here's the scoop. . .

Written: *just after King David's reign*

Written by: *Probably by Nathan and Gad. Possibly other writers contributed.*

Writing style: *a historical account*

One-liner: *King David reigned and his family suffered.*

STORY OF A MONARCHY

The book of 2 Samuel is a continuation of the story begun in the Book of 1 Samuel. At the end of 1 Samuel, King Saul had been killed in battle and King David had taken the throne. Second Samuel is all about King David's monarchy.

THE RISE OF DAVID

David was an interesting character. The only other person the Bible has more stories about is Jesus Christ. David was a great man but not always a good one. He often stood for right, but he often failed as a husband and father.

The first ten chapters of 2 Samuel are about the great things that King David did. He built a strong and prosperous kingdom. He returned the ark of the covenant to the tabernacle. He made plans to build a temple. He kept a lifelong promise to his best friend, Jonathan (who died mid-battle with King Saul) and took care of Jonathan's physically challenged son.

THE FALL OF DAVID

David's most famous mistake (and the beginning of his fall from power) was an affair he had with a married woman named Bathsheba. First, David pursued her, slept with her, and then found out she had become pregnant. Next he tried to get her husband, Uriah, home from war so it would look like the baby was his. Poor Uriah (besides having an awful name by today's standards) so revered the king that he wouldn't even go home and enjoy being with his wife while he was on leave.

Next, David set Uriah up to be killed in battle. So David was guilty of adultery, attempted paternity fraud, and murder—all from seeing someone bathing and giving in to temptation. This is a king?

David ended up making Bathsheba his wife, but the baby died. They later had more children—including the future king, Solomon.

DAVID'S DYSFUNCTIONAL FAMILY

After David's affair with Bathsheba, his life only went from bad to worse. His children by his first wives were out of control. One son, Amnon, raped his half sister, Tamar. Another son, Absalom (who had supermodel good looks and long hair), killed Amnon because of the rape. Eventually Absalom rebelled against his father. He was killed by King David's men when they found him hanging from a tree limb by his hair. His mule had ridden under the tree, and when Absalom's hair caught in the limbs, the mule just kept on going (yes, it really happened).

David's throne was succeeded by his son Solomon. Solomon was the second-born son of Bathsheba and grew to be a wise and wealthy king.

THINK ABOUT IT THIS WAY

One of the most important things to know about David is that God called him "a man after his own heart" (1 Samuel 13:14). As you have read, David's life was far from perfect. Because of that, he is a great example to us that God desires our faith, and it is on the basis of that faith that He approves of us. Then He walks with us through our mistakes and failures, redeeming us on the basis of that faith.

questions

Q. *How can God be like a rock? (2 Samuel 22:2)*

A. *Rocks are inert, lifeless, and do not speak. Rocks cannot respond to human sympathy, cannot shape themselves into anything useful (except by accident of nature), and eventually erode into gravel. Is this what God is like?*

Obviously, any metaphor from nature cannot be 100 percent descriptive of the sovereign God. Nothing is like God in each and every way. In this case, David's life seemed to be crumbling around him, his kingdom in a shambles, his army confused, his priests divided. Indeed, his own family was against him, at least in part. In the face of this chaos, perhaps the stability and weightiness of rocks were exactly the picture that David needed to assure himself of God's unchanging, stable love.

Build a fortress out of rock and many rains won't wash it away. God's love endures through the storms and upheavals that David was feeling, and in that sense, comparing God to a rock seemed like just the assurance he needed.

Praise God for the imagination to find spiritual meaning in the humblest of God's creative works.

1 kings

IN CONTEXT

Here's the scoop. . .

Written: *We don't know.*

Written by: *Perhaps a group of people, but we don't know for sure.*

Writing style: *a historical account*

One-liner: *King Solomon ruled Israel, and then the kingdom divided into the northern and southern kingdoms.*

THE STORY LINE

The book of 1 Kings opens with the death of the great King David. Before he died, David named one of his sons—Solomon—as his successor. The first half of 1 Kings is about Solomon's establishing his kingdom, building the temple, and amassing his *unimaginable* wealth.

The second half of 1 Kings is about the kingdom after Solomon. Things get a little complicated here, so hang on tight. The one kingdom of Israel divides into two kingdoms—Israel (the northern kingdom, later called Samaria) and Judah (the southern kingdom). It was an ongoing civil war.

KING SOLOMON

Solomon was known for his wisdom. In fact, God appeared to Solomon in a dream and told him to ask for anything he wanted. (Who wouldn't love to be in that dream? The God of all creation offering you anything. . .) Solomon's request was a surprising one. He asked for wisdom to rule well and to know right from wrong. God rewarded such a request by giving Solomon not only wisdom and understanding, but also the wealth and honor that he could have asked for but didn't.

One of the first things Solomon did as king was build a beautiful temple. Solomon then built his own palace (took thirteen years) and continued to amass amazing wealth. Sounds great, right? Well, there was one little problem.

ONE LITTLE PROBLEM

Way back when, Solomon had married a foreigner, a girl from Egypt (where his forefathers had been slaves, you might note). Along with this wife came her religious practice of worshiping idols. He also married many other women who worshiped other gods. Wouldn't you know it, while things were going great for Solomon, he became more and more tolerant of these idol-worship practices until he was worshiping false gods! It was like spitting in the face of God Almighty.

By the end of Solomon's life, he was a disillusioned old man. He had let go of his foundation, and his kingdom went downhill after him.

THE DIVIDED KINGDOM

You might remember that the origin of the twelve tribes of Israel was the twelve sons of Jacob, whom God renamed Israel. They all traveled to Egypt and then traveled back to the land of, you got it, Israel. One tribe, the descendants of Levi, were given no land because they were the priests and would work in the temple rather than working the land. The land was divided among the other tribes.

After Solomon's death, a civil conflict broke out. The northern tribes followed a man named Jeroboam. The southern tribes, Benjamin and Judah, continued to follow Solomon's son Rehoboam. They never reunited.

AHAB AND JEZEBEL

One of the most famous kings of the northern kingdom of Israel was Ahab. You've probably heard of King Ahab and his wife, Queen Jezebel. You may have even heard of someone referred to as a jezebel. If so, you probably steered clear of her. Jezebel was a mess. She was the Cruella DeVille of her day. If she had lived in the southern kingdom, she'd have probably been called a "floozy." Ahab wasn't a lot better, but he didn't come across as quite so conniving. You know. . .behind every bad man, there is usually a worse woman.

Ahab reigned for twenty-two years. The Bible says he made the sins of the former kings look trivial. In fact, the Bible says that Ahab did more to provoke God's anger than all the kings before him. He and his wife reveled in the worship of Baal. They were downright zealous about it. Basically they

IN CONTEXT

It might sound like things had really changed for the people of Israel (who are now known as the people of Israel and the people of Judah), but in reality it was the same song, second verse. They still fell away from God until they got into trouble and then ran back to Him for help. God forgave and helped them, but He didn't protect them from consequences, and by the end of the story, those consequences were pretty grim.

encouraged evil as much as they could.

There was one man who stood in their way. An important player in the story of 1 Kings is the prophet Elijah, a beacon in that dark day and an aggravating flea in Jezebel's proverbial mane.

ELIJAH

Elijah was a Tishbite (funny word—say it out loud). He was from a place called Tishbe. He first appeared when he announced to King Ahab that God was about to declare a drought.

Elijah didn't always come out on top. Once in particular he got the "poor-me willies" when he had worked really hard to confront evil and all he got for it was run out of town. But most often Elijah had great faith and God used him and provided for him in miraculous ways. He was fed by ravens once. Another time, a widow's flour and oil were miraculously replenished because she fed him. It was even through Elijah that a woman's son was brought back to life. But there is definitely one miracle that is Elijah's all-time claim to fame.

THE BIG SHOWDOWN

Elijah invited Ahab and Jezebel's false religion to a showdown once. It was on top of Mt. Carmel. He instructed the prophets of the idol Baal to build an altar, place a sacrifice there, and pray to their god to send down fire to light the altar. Elijah built an altar, too, and soaked it in barrels of water.

As you can imagine, the prophets of Baal prayed and danced and shouted and even (yes, really) cut themselves to show their fervor and sincerity. But when you are praying to nothing, nothing happens. No fire from heaven. Only a lot of bleeding prophets and some very raw meat.

Then Elijah prayed over his wet, soggy sacrifice. God responded. Fire came down from heaven and consumed that altar, the sacrifice, and the water.

It was a good day for God's people. It was a bad day for Baal's prophets (who were chased down and killed). And, boy, was Jezebel mad.

questions q&a

Q. *What's the point of reading about all these ancient kings?*
(1 and 2 Kings)

A. *The books of 1 and 2 Kings trace the history of Israel during the four hundred years from the death of King David to the destruction of Jerusalem. Each king is judged on whether he was obedient to God or did evil in His sight.*

Many lessons follow from these stories. We learn what motivates people to reject God. We observe sin's consequences. The primary message is that Israel's tragic descent from David to captivity was the result of unfaithfulness. If those people had only known—could have only seen! And us?

Q. *Despite all of his courage in battle, was David a wimp as a father?*
(1 Kings 1:6)

A. *Just because someone is good at one thing does not necessarily mean he or she will be good at another. Just because David was a courageous and skilled warrior does not automatically mean he did well as a father. If such a correlation were true, then we would be able to read interesting and impressive statistics concerning the families and children of our own military forces.*

Rather, David seemed to be a failure as a father. Perhaps this was partly because he spent so much time away from home, fighting his wars. The son in question whom he fathered so badly, Adonijah, was very handsome. The Bible hints, in the first chapter of Kings, that David was indulgent of his son because of this very fact. Overlooking a son's faults just because he is handsome is definitely not the sign of a good father.

2 Kings

IN CONTEXT

Here's the scoop. . .

Written: *No one knows.*

Written by: *We don't know for sure. It may have been a group of writers.*

Writing style: *a historical account*

One-liner: *The story of the divided kingdoms of Israel and Judah during the time of Elijah and Elisha before exile to foreign lands.*

A NATION DIVIDED

The book of 2 Kings is a sequel to 1 Kings. Israel had divided into two kingdoms (northern: Israel; southern: Judah) with their own separate kings, separate economies, separate worship, and separate problems.

Throughout the different governments, God sent prophets to call the people back to obedience. Unfortunately, they continued to return to idolatry. In the end, each kingdom fell. The northern kingdom fell to the Assyrians, and the southern kingdom fell to the Babylonians.

TWO GOOD KINGS

Two kings in the southern kingdom tried to get their country back in line. The first was Hezekiah. One of his first official acts was to restore and open the temple and to destroy the idol altars and worship center. One of his biggest contributions was to create an aqueduct system so that water came within Jerusalem's city walls (so that during battle they could survive without having to leave the city).

The second righteous king was Josiah. Josiah was crowned king at the age of eight. He also restored the temple and, in doing so, found an old copy of the Book of the Law (probably Deuteronomy). Because of this book, Josiah called himself and his people to a new level of understanding and obedience. Josiah was killed in battle at only thirty-nine years of age.

PROPHETS

During Israel and Judah's time of falling away from God, they were consistently reminded of their mistakes by prophets. These men sometimes foretold the future but also just told the truth. They spoke with the kings. They were known throughout the land. Often they were respected as well as abused.

One of the most famous prophets was Elijah. Elijah left the earth not through death but through a chariot of fire (a story you allude to every time you sing "Swing low, sweet chariot, comin' for to carry me home").

Elijah's apprentice prophet was Elisha. Elisha lived an honorable life and even established a school for prophets.

IN CONTEXT

The work of some of the other prophets of that era is recorded in actual books of the Bible such as Isaiah, Micah, Hosea, and Jeremiah. God showed His love by never giving up on His people. He kept calling them back through the message of the prophets, but they never got it together enough to follow Him consistently.

questions

Q. Was Elijah taken up to heaven? (2 Kings 2)

A. Elijah was a faithful prophet who had put the word of God before his own life in condemning Ahab, king of Israel. Elijah's faithfulness was rewarded first by God's telling him when he would be taken from earth and then by God's sending the whirlwind-chariot, sparing Elijah the pain of a normal death experience.

This incident bears similarity to the mention of Enoch in Genesis 5:21–24. Enoch enjoyed a close relationship with God throughout his life. Then suddenly he disappeared when God took him. Like Enoch, Elijah was a faithful servant whom God swept into heaven by divine means.

Q. God promised David that his dynasty and kingdom will continue for all time (2 Samuel 7:16 NLT), but later the Lord tore Israel away from the kingdom of David (2 Kings 17:21 NLT). What happened to the promise?

A. At this point in Israel's history, God was tearing away the northern kingdom, Israel's ten tribes, from Judah. Despite all that God had done for Israel, including repeated warnings through His prophets, Israel would not listen. They were stubborn and refused to believe (2 Kings 17:14). So God rejected the descendants of Israel.

Leading Judah (the southern kingdom) at this time was King Hezekiah, a descendant of David. When Judah was taken captive, a remnant of Jews remained faithful to the Lord.

Jesus, also in the family of David (Matthew 1:17), fulfilled the promise to David by inaugurating a new kingdom that will last forever, a new chosen *people who believe in Jesus Christ as Lord and carry His name before all the nations of the earth.*

Notice the shift from a political kingdom under David to a spiritual kingdom under Jesus Christ. Jesus leads a new Israel, the church (1 Peter 2:10).

Q. **King Hezekiah seems so wise in dealing with Sennacherib from Assyria, yet so foolish in dealing with envoys from Babylon. How could he be so smart and yet so dumb? (2 Kings 18, 20)**

A. *At the beginning of his reign, Hezekiah was strong in faith. Confronted by enemies, he went into the temple of the Lord and prayed. The Lord honored his faith and sent an angel to destroy the Assyrian military encampment. When Hezekiah became ill, he prayed and was healed. Hezekiah repeatedly trusted in the Lord, and God delivered him.*

Yet when the king of Babylon appealed to Hezekiah's sense of importance with letters and gifts, Hezekiah took the bait, showing off his palace and wealth. Confronted by the prophet Isaiah, Hezekiah seemed unaware that his pride was showing—a warning to all of how quickly we can be inflated with arrogance and self-congratulation.

1 chronicles

IN CONTEXT

Here's the scoop. . .

Written: *around 400* B.C.

Written by: *Ezra, according to Jewish tradition*

Writing style: *historical accounts and lists of genealogies*

One-liner: *Israel's story from David's reign until the exile into Babylon, from a spiritual rather than political perspective.*

A SENSE OF ROOTS IN A DARK TIME

The book of 1 Chronicles was written at a time in Israel's history when the people had been physically displaced from their homes. After their exile, they came back home to find that their land had been settled by foreigners. They needed to reunite as a people and reconnect with God. First Chronicles was written to help them do that.

GENEALOGIES

The Book of 1 Chronicles opens with list upon list of genealogies. In fact, there are eight chapters of these lists. True, they are not enthralling bedtime reading fare, but look at them through the eyes of the original readers. This was a culture in which individuals defined themselves by their family history. Their land was even parceled out according to which of the twelve sons of Israel their family descended from. Their whole identity was in genealogies. Their way of life, for the most part, was passed on through stories, oral traditions, feasts, and holidays that found their origin in the great deliverance from Egypt. (See Exodus on page 96 for clarification on that one.)

IN CONTEXT

While you may not read all of the genealogies in I Chronicles word for word, understand that to these people these lists were the only roots they had. Their homes were reinhabited; their land was full of squatters. All that defined them as a nation were the names you see in I Chronicles and the lives those names represented. First Chronicles gets a bad rap for having some yawn material, but when you understand where these people were as a nation, you understand that they weren't yawning when they wrote it.

ISRAEL'S FAMILY HISTORY

The largest part of 1 Chronicles is a different kind of history. It describes many of the same events you find in 2 Samuel and in 1 and 2 Kings. There is much different perspective on those events, though. First Chronicles was written many years after these events. Whenever you look at a period of time from the vantage point of "many years later," you see things differently. You see more of the highlights than the details. You see the significance rather than just the events themselves. First Chronicles really describes the history of worship in Israel, the history of their relationship with God, rather than just who ruled when and for how long.

KING DAVID

David is the central character in 1 Chronicles. As a king, David did many things, but this book describes in detail his temple preparations.

David focused the pre-exile Israelites on worship. Because of this, it was a good thing for the post-exile Israelites to look back again on David's role in history so they could once again make worship a priority. Their temple lay in ruins. Their homes weren't much better. In 1 Chronicles they could find a pattern to follow to find their roots in their family and in their religious commitment.

ACCOMPLISHMENTS

When we look back on our lives, or anybody's life, we can see a clear path of what we accomplished. But when we are in the middle of living our lives, sometimes the path is not so clear. We can't know what King David was thinking about worship in his day, but looking back, it's as if he had this plan in mind:

- Recapture Jerusalem so I can put the temple there.
- Return the ark of the covenant (the holiest thing in Jewish history, sort of like a holy time capsule) to the tabernacle. (The tabernacle was the portable precursor to the temple.)
- Write songs for the tabernacle choir to sing, and work with the choir director, Asaph.
- Organize the priests, the worship musicians, and the guards.
- Gather together building supplies and equipment so that when the time is right, Solomon, my son, can build the temple.

If David had a to-do list, it must have looked something like this, because this is exactly what he did.

questions q&a

Q. *Who wrote the Chronicles? (1 Chronicles 1:1)*

A. *According to Jewish tradition (the Talmud), Ezra the priest authored 1 and 2 Chronicles. Other evidence supports this belief. The books' emphasis on the temple, the priesthood, and the judgment and blessing of God carries the perspective of a priest. The books' writing style resembles that of Ezra. In addition, the conclusion of 2 Chronicles (36:22–23) is very similar to the beginning of Ezra (1:1–3). Some scholars speculate that the books were intended to be read as one consecutive history, similar to Luke and Acts.*

Q. *Why does material in 1 Chronicles repeat material in 1 and 2 Samuel?*

A. *The books of 1 and 2 Chronicles cover the same period of Jewish history as 1 and 2 Samuel; however, the difference is one of perspective. First and 2 Samuel focus on Israel and Judah's political history, whereas 1 and 2 Chronicles offer a religious commentary on the history of the Jews. Samuel's books were written from a prophetic viewpoint. Ezra's books were written from a priestly viewpoint.*

Since the books of Chronicles (probably one unified work when first written) were composed for the returning exiles, they have a distinctly positive tone. By looking back to the beginnings of the Jewish nation and by concentrating on the temple, the messianic line, and the spiritual reforms needed, Ezra hoped to encourage the people to rebuild their spiritual heritage.

2 chronicles

Here's the scoop...

Written: *around 400 B.C.*

Written by: *Ezra, according to Jewish tradition*

Writing style: *a historical account*

One-liner: *Israel's story from Solomon's reign into the divided kingdom from a spiritual rather than political perspective.*

A NATION IN REVIEW

The book of 2 Chronicles is a continuation of 1 Chronicles. So, like 1 Chronicles, it is a recounting of the historical events listed in 1 and 2 Kings, but from a very different perspective. Second Chronicles was written many years later (than Kings) and in the rearview. The Jewish people have been away from their land in exile and are just returning. They have been lost and wandering with no roots and no familiarity.

The writer of the Chronicles (probably Ezra), set about to give the people a sense of history and identity. In light of this, the Chronicles place more emphasis on the positive aspects of the historical characters. There were many wicked and idolatrous kings in the history of Judah, but the Chronicles bring out the best in the reign of these men. It is a deliberate attempt to remind Israel of what they can be proud of and hold on to about their history. It is also a reminder of how their forefathers served and worshiped God so that they can start their new life at home on the right foot.

IN CONTEXT

Tabloids

Here are some of the headlines you would read if 2 Chronicles had a tabloid following:

- Great King Solomon reduces silver to the worth of a stone (2 Chronicles 1).

- Royal grandmother kills all her descendants so she can become queen (2 Chronicles 22).

- Child-king crowned at the age of seven (2 Chronicles 24).

- Ahaz, national leader, involved in child sacrifice (2 Chronicles 28).

- King Jehoahaz sets record for shortest reign (2 Chronicles 36).

SOLOMON

The reign of Solomon takes up the first portion of 2 Chronicles. Solomon was wise. He was wealthy. He was influential. He had many wives. He had it all. In his younger years, it served him well. In his older years, it disillusioned him. In fact, he wrote a book of the Bible named Ecclesiastes in which he says he had it all and, without God, "all" means nothing.

THE KINGS OF JUDAH

After Solomon's reign, the kingdom was divided into the southern kingdom, Judah, and the northern kingdom, Israel. Second Chronicles concentrates on the rulers of Judah. Of those rulers, 2 Chronicles draws a direct correlation between their commitment to God and the success of their kingdom. Throughout their history God told them, "Obey Me and I will bless you; disobey Me and you will not succeed." Second Chronicles reveals in hindsight that what God said was true.

questions

Q. *Does God give open-ended promises today, as God did to Solomon?*
(2 Chronicles 1:7)

A. *This raises one of the most important questions we face in understanding
God: To what degree can we count on real help from the outside? Or is God
like a banker, helping the successful to become more so—in other words,
divine help blended with human ingenuity in a fashion that makes the
divine part difficult to distinguish?*

*The New Testament is filled with seemingly open-ended offers of divine
assistance if not downright provision. In Matthew's Gospel, a comparison
of Jesus' offer to the disciples and God's offer to Solomon makes the latter
recipient appear to be a disadvantaged person (Matthew 6:29).*

*Yet these offers of help are not completely open-ended, and neither was
the offer to Solomon, who could not expect God's help if he did not also obey
God's law. Solomon clearly knew that the covenant under which he would
prosper carried significant responsibility (2 Chronicles 6:16). This was no
free ride. Solomon would be obliged to live in a manner honoring God if God
would continue to bless his reign.*

*Likewise, God's promises today are not free rides. While we cannot earn
God's favor, we are responsible to live in faith and obedience to God. Good
works will not increase God's generosity to us; obedience responds to God in
love and gratitude.*

Ezra

IN CONTEXT

Here's the scoop. . .

Written: *around 400 B.C.*

Written by: *probably Ezra*

Writing style: *a historical account*

One-liner: *The Hebrews returned from exile in Babylon and rebuilt the temple.*

THE MAIN GIST

You may or may not remember that at the end of 2 Chronicles the Hebrews had been exiled to Babylon. When the Persians then invaded Babylon, the Persian leader, Cyrus, let the Jewish people return home. This was a good and a bad thing. They had been in Babylon for *seventy years*! Many of the people who first came had died. More than a whole generation had made their home in Persia. Jerusalem, their hometown, was nine hundred miles away, and this was before automobiles. (Even in a car on a highway, nine hundred miles takes around fifteen hours. Can you imagine on foot?) There was a reluctance among many Hebrews to take Cyrus up on his offer.

EXILES RETURN WITH ZERUBBABEL

Out of two million, about fifty thousand did choose to travel back to their homeland with a man named Zerubbabel (zuh-RU-buh-bul). Their priority when they got there was to rebuild the temple. The significance of this act was more than just having a place to worship. It was an act of restructuring their relationship with God.

There was a great celebration when the builders completed the foundation. There were music and cheering and worship. And there was sadness, too. The senior citizens who had returned with Zerubbabel could remember the grand and glorious temple that Solomon built. They wept at how far they had fallen away from those days.

IN CONTEXT

The history of these people had included a very on-again, off-again style of worship. The fact that they traveled home and rebuilt the temple was a sign that they acknowledged God's leadership in the life of their nation. This was a big step.

EXILES RETURN WITH EZRA

After the temple had been rebuilt, Ezra returned to Jerusalem with about two thousand more people (many of them priests). What he found disappointed him. The temple was together but was much less grand than before.

Ezra's main concern wasn't the building, though. The temple's poor condition was just a reflection of the poor condition of the people's hearts. This really grieved Ezra. He had a vision for restoring his people. He tore his clothes (which was a sign of grief and despair in those days). He preached his heart out. And it worked! The people renewed their relationship with God.

THERE'S ALWAYS A SNAG IN CONSTRUCTION

Even as long ago as this book records, people used paperwork to delay construction. Observe this scenario from Ezra 4.

- Now, remember, there was no e-mail, no fax, no phone, no carbons, no copiers, not even any postal service. There were only camels, chariots, and messengers. And there were nine hundred miles between the building site and the capital city of the government. (You think *you* had delays!)

- Hostile neighbors offered to "help" with construction of the temple. The Israelites refused their help. The neighbors took the attitude of "We'll show them. . . ."

- The neighbors sent messengers or agents with lies about the Israelites. They sent these stories back to King Cyrus as long as he reigned, then King Darius after him. After Darius, they wrote to King Ahasuerus and then King Artaxerxes. They warned the kings that the Hebrews were trouble and if the construction continued, they'd probably stop paying taxes. (Ouch. That must have hurt! Hit 'em right in the tax treasury.)

- King Artaxerxes looked up in his files the history of Judah and Israel and saw their history of rebellion. That wasn't reassuring, so he sent back a demand (nine hundred miles again) for the reconstruction to stop.

- In the midst of this, the Israelites began to fight fire with fire. They began construction again and wrote to the king asking him to look back in his files one more time and find the *original* decree from King Cyrus authorizing the construction. Off went the secretaries to search through the parchment and stone tablets, and there it was, dust and all. (No building permit *ever* took this much work.)

- Construction resumed and the file clerk took a break.

Now *that*, my friends, is bureaucracy—multigenerational bureaucracy.

questions

Q. Why did Cyrus allow the Jews to return to their homeland? (Ezra 1:1)

A. King Cyrus of Persia was basically positive and tolerant toward Israel's faith. He believed it was good for him and his kingdom to allow different groups in his kingdom some degree of independence, especially with respect to religious practice. Above and beyond Cyrus's religious tolerance, God moved his heart to allow the Jews to return to Jerusalem. God frequently "moved the heart" of pagan kings to get a mission accomplished or an individual out of trouble.

Q. Why was it important for Ezra and his followers to restore the temple? (Ezra 1:5)

A. The temple represented the center of Israel's religious life, the glory of Israel, the symbol of all that made Israel special as the people of God. While the temple lay desolate, the people's sense of identity and unity was in disrepair. Until they attended to the house of God, things would not be right in the house of Israel.

Q. *Why was Ezra so upset about mixed marriages? (Ezra 9)*

A. *Israel's greatest problem throughout its history was syncretism—the mixing of pagan religion with worship of the true God. God judged Israel severely for failing to keep worship clean and pure. And one of the easiest inroads to Israel's heart was through intermarriage with pagan peoples. Ezra knew this well, thus his vehement and emotional opposition to taking foreign spouses.*

God's overriding concern was that the nation of Israel be distinct from surrounding nations. As Israel obeyed the Lord's commands, they witnessed to other nations of the glory of God above all other gods. So the injunction against intermarrying was to prevent the loss of witness to the truth, as with Solomon, whose several foreign wives were said to turn his heart from God (1 Kings 11:1–13).

The prohibition against intermarriage was not absolute. Deuteronomy 21 contains regulations for marrying women taken captive in war. Examples of interracial marriage include Moses and a Midianite woman, Boaz and the Moabite Ruth. The key issue is faithfulness to Christ. Any marriage that jeopardizes faith is wrong.

Nehemiah

IN CONTEXT

Here's the scoop. . .

Written: *around 400 B.C.*

Written by: *Ezra and Nehemiah may have written this together.*

Writing style: *a historical account*

One-liner: *More Hebrews returned from Babylon and rebuilt Jerusalem's wall.*

NEHEMIAH TAKES A RISK

Talk about a career strategy. Nehemiah was a man who believed in a creative job market. As the story opens, Nehemiah is a cupbearer to the king. Part of his job was typical administrative assistant kind of stuff, and part was butlering. But part of his job was, literally, to taste the king's wine. One reason was quality control. The other was poison control. Talk about living on the edge!

The good thing about Nehemiah's job was that it gave him opportunities to talk directly with the king about his concerns. Nehemiah had heard from a friend that the Jewish people who had left Babylon to rebuild Jerusalem were having a bad time. The city walls had been destroyed, leaving the city open to attack. This news broke Nehemiah's heart.

When the king asked why Nehemiah seemed so sad (a sensitive boss!), there was a ready response. Nehemiah asked for a leave of absence to help build the wall. He got the time off from work and headed to Jerusalem.

NEHEMIAH BUILDS A WALL

A couple of days after his arrival, Nehemiah snuck out at night and surveyed the wall. It was a mess.

To understand why he had to sneak around, you have to understand that this land had been inhabited by so many people that there were mixed feelings in regard to the Hebrews' reinhabiting the land. There were also government officials who were very sensitive to any independence the Hebrews might regain that would cause them to rebel or (tell me no!) stop paying taxes.

Once Nehemiah had seen the wall, he announced his plan. He divided the gates and sections of the wall among different people and set them to work. Most of the people were glad to be working. Then again, there were two characters named Sanballat and Tobiah.

Sanballat and Tobiah were threatened by the whole resettlement thing. They feared they would lose their own power over the people. So their first strategy was intimidation and verbal abuse.

Nehemiah prayed.

Then they tried to discourage the workers.

Nehemiah reminded them of God's help.

Then they sank to a new level of threats of physical abuse.

Nehemiah armed the workers and set up battle strategies with them. Basically the builders had a tool in one hand and a weapon in the other. What a way to build a wall!

Finally, Sanballat and Tobiah threatened to assassinate Nehemiah.

Nehemiah prayed again, but he didn't back down.

Believe it or not, those builders finished that wall in less than two months (actually fifty-two days, about seven weeks). This was no small feat considering that it was such a sturdy, wide wall that when they finished, they marched on top of it around the city to celebrate. (Can you imagine that party scene?)

REVIVAL MEETING

After the completion of the wall, Ezra (same guy from the book of Ezra) read the Law of God to the people. Together they confessed their sin and recommitted themselves to follow God and to worship Him, to take care of the temple, and, basically, to clean up their act.

Nehemiah worked for a long time to help the Hebrews renew and maintain their commitment to God's way of doing things.

THINK ABOUT IT
THIS WAY

speaker for Hire

If Nehemiah were living today, he would be a prime candidate to speak at leadership conferences. He was an excellent leader and administrator. If he gave you a handout, his main points would look something like this:

- Pray for wisdom about decisions and opportunities.
- If at all possible, work through the powers that be, the chain of command.
- Survey your task well before beginning work.
- Divide your task into manageable segments and assign them to people who have an interest in its completion.
- Don't give in to bullies.
- Don't let someone threaten your reputation. Stand on your own integrity.
- Confront problems and people head-on.
- Know what the Bible says and follow its advice.

questions&a

Q. *How did Nehemiah practice prayer? (Nehemiah 1:4)*

A. *Nehemiah is an example of a person who lived by prayer. He responded to difficulty with prayer. He planned in prayer. He prayed before he spoke. When he evaluated his work, he did so in prayer. When others attacked, mocked, or threatened him, Nehemiah prayed.*

Nehemiah didn't become effective in prayer because he had only big matters to pray about. He prayed about everything and became very good at doing it. Nehemiah lived by the principle described by Paul centuries later in Philippians 4:6–7 (NLT): "Don't worry about anything; instead, pray about everything. Tell God what you need, and thank him for all he has done. If you do this, you will experience God's peace, which is far more wonderful than the human mind can understand."

Q. *What was a "cupbearer"? (Nehemiah 1:11)*

A. *The cupbearer was one of a king's most trusted personal staff members—in charge of the quality of everything the king drank. A cupbearer guaranteed with his own life that the beverage in the king's cup at any moment was fit to drink. With that trust came a significant amount of influence. Cupbearers were often unofficial counselors and confidants.*

Q. *Why was Ezra's reading of God's law so powerful? (Nehemiah 8)*

A. *The events that occurred at the Water Gate in Nehemiah's time can be described as a spiritual revival. The people knew that God had made it possible for them to rebuild the city. Now they were ready to hear what else God would say to them. They listened intently. When Ezra opened God's Word, they stood out of respect and anticipation over what they were about to hear.*

Then the people responded personally, corporately, and immediately to God's Word. In the days that followed, they were quick to put into practice what had been read. The Water Gate revival was a time of significant obedient listening by God's people to God's message, a recovery of a vision and a hope.

esther

Here's the scoop. . .

Written: *around 500 B.C.*

Written by: *We're not sure.*

Writing style: *a story of a queen*

One-liner: *The Hebrews survived exile in Persia because of a Jewish "royal beauty contest" winner.*

GENERALLY SPEAKING

Esther is a story that shows God at work in everyday circumstances. It's a story that affirms for us that coincidences, most often, are not a matter of chance at all.

The events of Esther happened in Babylon while the Hebrews were in captivity there. They weren't slaves; they were forced immigrants. They could do business and live their lives, but they weren't citizens of Babylon. They were waiting to go home someday.

QUEEN VASHTI

The story opens with a conflict between King Ahasuerus (also called Xerxes) and Queen Vashti. The king was having a wild and raucous party with his friends and called for his wife so he could show off her beauty. The queen refused to come. *Refused to come!* That might not seem like a big deal today, but in that day, it was a very big deal. In fact, it was such a big deal that the king divorced her and opened up a search, a beauty contest of sorts, for a new queen.

That event set the stage for Esther's story.

ENTER ESTHER

Esther was a beautiful Jewish girl. (Her Jewish name was Hadassah.) She was also an orphan, so her older cousin, Mordecai, was like a father to her. Esther was brought to the palace and then the king's house for the contest. She won and, sure enough, rose above the ranks and married the king. Somehow this all happened without the king's knowing she was Jewish.

Everything went along fine until. . .Haman.

HAMAN'S PLAN

Haman was a Hitler wannabe. He was a power-hungry fellow who would have been happy to exterminate the Hebrews from his country. He was a bigot, a racist, a bully. He particularly disliked Esther's cousin, Mordecai. Mordecai had won the king's favor by uncovering an assassination plot, thus saving the king. Haman didn't like Mordecai's good name one little bit, and it didn't help matters that Mordecai was not a man who bowed down before Haman. Haman made a plan to be rid of the Jewish people with Mordecai at the top of the hit list.

But what Haman didn't realize was that the queen not only was Hebrew but was related to the man he was preparing to assassinate. Mordecai went to Esther so that she could talk to the king on his behalf and save her people. This was a scary thing for Esther (it was against the law to approach the king uninvited), but she did it. In fact, she revealed Haman's plot to the king with Haman right there in the room.

THE END

By the end, justice was done. Haman was hanged on his own gallows. His plan was nixed. Mordecai was honored by the king. Esther remained queen but no longer had to keep her nationality a secret. The Jewish people established a new feast, Purim. Even today when a Jewish family celebrates Purim, they read together the story of Esther and celebrate God's salvation through their very own queen of Persia.

questions q&a

Q. *The book of Esther doesn't mention God, so why is it included in the Old Testament?*

A. *True, Esther doesn't mention the name of God, yet underlying the story are veiled references to God. Mordecai encouraged Esther to go before King Xerxes, saying, "Who can say but that you have been elevated to the palace for just such a time as this?" implying that God might use Esther to deliver the Jews. Esther then asked Mordecai to gather the Jews and fast; she herself fasted for three days (Esther 4:16), showing her petition to God for assistance.*

While not mentioning God directly, Esther does illustrate the provision of God for His people. Sometimes actions speak louder than words. Esther demonstrates God's providence without articulating what would be obvious to the Jewish reader.

WISDOM BOOKS

These books are like poetry. They are writings more than they are books. They are collections of thoughts. They are lyrics. They are creativity from an ancient world. They are right-brainers relating to God and all of us getting to listen in.

wisdom books

• Job

• Psalms

• Proverbs

• Ecclesiastes

• Song of Songs

job

IN CONTEXT

Here's the scoop. . .

Written: *No one is sure, but the story probably happened around 2000 B.C.*

Written by: *Job might have written it, but we don't know.*

Writing style: *an ancient Hebrew poem (although it didn't rhyme)*

One-liner: *Bad times don't change the nature of God.*

A PEEK BEHIND ETERNITY'S CURTAIN

We don't often think of God and Satan sitting down for a chat. We know they were once companions. Satan was an angel, for goodness' sake, but then things changed, not for goodness' sake.

We may not think about God and Satan communicating, but that is exactly the way the book of Job begins. Satan was talking to God about Job. He made the accusation that Job was only faithful to God because Job had a good life. God denied that Satan's theory was true and, in so many words, told Satan to go ahead and give it his best shot.

Then Job began to suffer. He suffered loss and illness and poverty and, worst of all, three well-meaning friends.

JOB'S "FRIENDS"

At first Job's friends sat with him, offering comfort with their presence. But eventually they did what so many well-meaning people do when they are around suffering. They tried to figure out why it was happening. And ultimately they came to the question we all come to: "What did Job do to deserve this?"

Even sick, having lost his children and his wealth, everything except his despairing wife, Job stood firm. He had done nothing to deserve all this. That left them with the only other question they could ask: "If he doesn't deserve it, then why is it happening?" Since there was no answer to that question, they just kept badgering Job to fess up. Then finally God spoke.

GOD'S REASONING

The bottom line of God's response was "Who do you think you are?" (a question we can never answer without first considering "Who do we think God is?"). God reestablished His place in the world, His creation, His sovereignty, His power, and His desire for righteousness from people.

God doesn't answer the question of why there is evil and suffering in the world. Probably because it was answered in the first three chapters of Genesis. (Humanity brought it on by bad choices.) But God does say that He is the same when we are suffering and when we aren't. He is loving when we are blessed and when we are cursed. Our suffering is not a product of His punishment or a way in which His feelings have changed about us. Life is simply a suffering place sometimes.

This is still difficult for us to understand, mainly because sometimes God intervenes and keeps our suffering from us—but sometimes He doesn't. And in the end, whether we understand or not, His being able to make that choice is why we call Him God.

questions

Q. *Why does God allow Satan to wreck a good man's life? (Job 1:12)*

A. *What God allowed in Job's life and what Satan attempted provide a laboratory for examining spiritual warfare, the battle of good over evil being waged behind the scenes throughout history. Job becomes a prototype of every person who seeks to understand justice and of every victim of injustice. Satan wanted to demonstrate the purely pragmatic basis of religious yearning: People will believe when life is sweet but rebel when things go sour. God granted permission for the experiment to proceed, within certain bounds.*

Satan's experiment backfired. Job does not curse God, though he agonizes over the "why" questions. Job is not destroyed—he prospers in the end. Faith is not fraudulent, but strong and sturdy. And the universe is not malicious, but just and merciful, since God's character and not Satan's malice defines the moral life of human experience.

Did Job grow in faith? Painfully and slowly, yes. Did Job discover more about the meaning of personal trust in God? Through coming to terms with his own finitude and culpability, yes. Are these life lessons vitally important for every person? Yes, indeed.

Fortunately, not all of us endure the extent of Job's tragedies, but none of us is far from the taste of grief or guilt. Job emerged with a new understanding of God's care, and so can we. His life was wrecked only in the short term. God redeemed it in the end. Job lived this tragic story so that we see more clearly the extent of God's care and protection.

Q. *What's the right way to help a friend through a tragedy? (Job 2:11)*

A. *Job's three friends helped at the start, but ultimately they failed in the difficult task of assisting someone through tragedy. Their first approach was to identify and share, as much as they could, in Job's grief. They cried with* him, tore their clothing as a sign of sadness, and threw dust on their heads. They just sat with Job for a long time, no words needed or spoken. All this led Job to express his deepest feelings to them. This was good and helpful.

Then things changed. Job's deepest feelings were mixed with too many probing questions for the three friends, who wanted and apparently had an airtight view of God and moral goodness: All bad events are linked to human sin. To this group, Job's tragedy was linked to some hidden fault that Job needed to confess. The friends became accusatory.

We can understand this. If Job was not at fault, who was?

The friends could have admitted their own ignorance before Job's questions. They could have asked God, with Job, for more understanding. Instead, they forced Job's experience into their own grid, insisting that Job's life held the clue to his downfall. They had to assign guilt, and Job was the only candidate.

Personal responsibility must surely be a part of every person's approach to hard times, yet these friends would have been more effective by listening more sympathetically to Job's distress and sharing his immense confusion and pain, not by trying to impose their boxlike theologies onto his well-rounded questions. Sometimes listening is a greater gift than talking. And as a help in suffering, the lecture method is almost always a loser.

Psalms

Here's the scoop. . .

Written: *over a span of time, anywhere from 1400 to 500 B.C.*

Written by: *a variety of authors, including David, Asaph, Solomon, and Moses*

Writing style: *poetry and song lyrics*

One-liner: *Lyric sheets from Old Testament temple worship.*

IN GENERAL

The book of Psalms is a collection of poems. Most of these poems are also lyrics to a song. Some historians call this book the Book of Praises. Others call it the Greek name, *Psalmoi*, which means "twangings" (as on a harp). Still others call it the Psaltery, which comes from "Psalterion" (songs to be played with a harp). Some just call it "the hymnbook of Solomon's temple."

IN SPECIFIC

The topics of Psalms include the following:

- God's goodness
- God's protection
- God's love

- Anger
- Jealousy
- Joy

- Regret
- Enemies
- The wonder of life

- Fear
- Praises
- Funeral dirges

BUT THEY DON'T RHYME

What's that you say? If they are songs, if they are lyrics, if they are poems, why don't they rhyme? Well, since they were written in another language, one might assume that they rhymed in the other language, just not in English. No. The style of poetry at that time in the Hebrew culture and language followed a whole different way of thinking. Their music was not based on three chords and a chorus the way Western music is today.

THINK ABOUT IT THIS WAY

There are 150 songs in Psalms. Some are about God, and some are addressed to God. Some are gloriously happy and worshipful, and some are filled with dejection and rage. The Psalms were what any songbook should be, a collection of the innermost feelings of people. They are honest. They are full of real-life prayers. They are rubber-meets-the-road, real-life thoughts of people who struggled and celebrated the same things that every person does but who in the end remained in God's presence.

Their poetry forms were based on the thoughts in the poems. The first line usually expressed the central thought. Then the second line repeated or built on that thought. Often each line continued to build on that same central thought. For instance, Psalm 27 builds this way:

The Lord is my light and my salvation;
Whom shall I fear?
The Lord is the strength of my life;
Of whom shall I be afraid?
When the wicked came against me
To eat up my flesh,
My enemies and foes,
They stumbled and fell.
Though an army may encamp against me,
My heart shall not fear; though war may rise against me,
In this I will be confident.
Psalm 27:1–3 NKJV

DOES ANYONE HERE PLAY AN INSTRUMENT?

Today an orchestra is made up of strings, woodwinds, percussions, some brass, and so on. A band is made up of drums, guitars, and sometimes keyboards. Musical instruments were used with the Jewish "church services," as well.

Cymbals—There were two types of cymbals: The clashing cymbals were large disks. The resounding cymbals were small disks attached to the thumb and the middle finger.

Flute—Also called a shepherd's pipe. Smaller than the oboe and without a reed.

Harp—This was a twelve-stringed instrument, held vertically and played with the fingers.

Horns—Also called trumpets, these instruments were made of rams' horns or of hammered metal. They called the people to worship. (They also were the instruments used when the people shouted and the walls of Jericho fell down.)

Lyre—Smaller than the harp, with only ten strings and plucked with a pick. Our modern hammered dulcimer is a distant cousin of the lyre.

Oboe—Often translated as "flute" or "pipe," the word *chalil* means an instrument with double reeds, like an oboe.

Rattle—Also called a sistrum. Often these were made of clay with stones inside to make the rhythmic rattling sound. Today similar shakers are made out of plastic or wood and are shaped like eggs.

Tambourine—Round like our modern tambourines, but with no "jingles" on the side. This tambourine was used as a small drum.

DANCING BEFORE THERE WERE DISCOTHEQUES

Not only were musical instruments used in the worship services of ancient Israel, but dance also was an integral part of worship and of ceremonies. David danced before the Lord. Miriam danced during a celebration.

The movements were certainly different and were not sexual in nature, but movement was an important part of celebrating the God who gives life. Go ahead and try it. Think about your blessings and do a little jig.

questions

Q. *Does God get angry easily? (Psalm 2:12)*

A. *Not really. This psalm suggests only that God deserves our submission (the kiss—the ancient sign of submission to another) without delay. We should not spend a long time calculating whether to submit to God. The rightness of doing so should be so apparent that we rush to show God our loyalty and devotion.*

Will God act like a jealous tyrant if we do not? No, God breaks all stereotypes and cannot be compared with ancient rulers. Yet there is an anger in God that will not tolerate indifference or opposition forever. Come to God now and do not tease that anger. Do not expose yourself to something so terrible, the psalm writer is saying. It's so much better to experience God as a refuge than God as a furnace.

Q. *In what sense are people rulers over creation? (Psalm 8:6)*

A. *At creation, God set humankind above all other species to rule and subdue the earth (Genesis 1:28). Conceivably, reason, intelligence, and self-consciousness could have been given to fish or birds, but, in fact, the gift and responsibility settled on humans, by God's design and will.*

People, therefore, do not rule over creation as final authorities. Rather, people are stewards over all God has created. A good manager cares for the property of his employer (Matthew 24:46) and is compensated according to the growth of assets in his domain. Whether your vocation is law, plumbing, education, forestry, or ministry, God is pleased when your circle of responsibility is well managed, that is, handled with integrity, virtue, and vision.

Q. *Why does God seem to disappear at crucial times?* (Psalm 10:1)

A. *The Psalms are full of statements that seem to accuse God of falling short of expectations: abandoning people in crisis, failing to hear cries of anguish, slow to intervene to correct a painful situation. All of these statements should be taken to reflect the intensely personal relationship the psalm writer experienced with God and the implicit trust of that relationship.*

When you are angry, who hears your complaints? Probably a best friend or spouse, someone with whom you are intimate. When you need a cry, whom do you call? When grief is too heavy to handle alone, with whom do you "let it all out"? Certainly not a stranger or casual acquaintance.

Likewise, God is not under indictment here. But the psalmist is wrestling with God over matters deeply and passionately felt. The questions are not accusations but pleas for help. The psalmist wants more of God than he presently experiences. He knows that intimacy with God is the key to personal peace, and he longs for intimacy in the face of what appears to be the temporarily superior advantage of wicked people. The psalmist is really quite assured of God's help (v. 16) and of a turnaround in his own fortunes.

Q. *Does full-hearted devotion to God lead to prosperity?* (Psalm 25:13)

A. *Yes and no.*

If the prosperity you're after is colored green, comes in quantities of thousands and hundred thousands, and carries portraits of American presidents, then no. Sorry.

Devotion to God is not a guarantee of financial prosperity. Certainly, there are principles of stewardship that, when followed, enhance financial security, but many, many Christians today (and in the past) have been very poor, yet nonetheless prosperous.

If the prosperity you seek centers on being happy, hopeful, capable of love, sure about life after death, and eager to try activities that present an element of risk and adventure, then answer the question in the affirmative. In faith, all people prosper. People were meant to live in relationship with God, who gives us all the prosperity of servants and friends.

Think of the problem in terms of means and ends. What is money for? What would you buy if you could? What does God offer to all who are living in faith? Now the problem is easy. Be faithful, be prosperous—in all the right ways.

proverbs

IN CONTEXT

Here's the scoop. . .

Written: *around 950 B.C.*

Written by: *several writers, including Solomon, Agur, and Lemuel*

Writing style: *a collection of wise sayings, some in the form of Hebrew poetry*

One-liner: *Nuggets of wisdom for dealing with everyday life.*

SOLOMON'S WISDOM

The book of Proverbs is a collection of wise sayings. It's almost like a bag of godly-wisdom fortune cookies, minus the cookies, plus the wisdom (minus the numbers on the back that nobody knows the meaning of). These proverbs are a good example of Hebrew poetry. Many are couplets (two lines) that express the same thought two different ways. Sometimes they restate, and sometimes they give examples by stating the opposite.

PROVERBIAL EXAMPLES

The fear of the LORD is the beginning of knowledge:
but fools despise wisdom and instruction (Proverbs 1:7 KJV).

(See, the second line is the opposite of the first line.)

My son, pay attention to what I say; listen closely to my words.
Do not let them out of your sight, keep them within your heart (Proverbs 4:20–21).

(The second line restates the first line.)

Many are the plans in a man's heart,
but it is the LORD'S purpose that prevails (Proverbs 19:21).

THINK ABOUT IT THIS WAY

Using This Book

Some people read a chapter of Proverbs every day month after month. Since it's broken into thirty-one chapters, there is a daily reading that correlates with every day of the month.

Proverbs is a hodgepodge of truth, but it is a precious book because you can always find something there that will affect your choices on that very day. It's a book about how you live your life in the details, where things can get the most complicated.

HANDOUTS

If you were teaching a seminar based on the book of Proverbs, here are some of the sessions you might include:

- God's Perspective on Sex
- Having Friends
- Knowing God
- Leadership God's Way
- Loving Things or Loving People?
- Making Sense of Marriage and Family Issues
- Money Management
- Morality and You
- Time Management
- Using Words Wisely
- Working for a Living

questions

Q. What is wisdom? (Proverbs 4:7)

A. Wisdom enables a person to live a life pleasing and honoring to the Lord. It includes knowledge but goes far beyond mere information. Wisdom is the ability to use knowledge to serve God—to blend heart, mind, and will in a unified life of devotion to God.

Q. What is meant by "fear of the LORD"? (Proverbs 9:10)

A. While an element of literal fear is involved, this fear refers more to a loving, reverential respect for God. The man or woman who "fears" the Lord will submit to God's will and care more about God's honor than self-esteem or wealth.

Q. Should women today cultivate the traditional kinds of behaviors honored in the Proverbs? (Proverbs 31:10)

A. The Bible is sometimes accused of supporting a patriarchal culture and a husband-dominated home. Nothing could be further from the spirit and tone of these proverbs. Here, women lead in smart financial decisions, in style and fashion, and in that elusive but nonetheless universally celebrated quality of sexual attractiveness. This ideal wife cares about her family, has a variety of specialized skills to put to the service of people around her, and is not captured by false images of beauty her culture puts forward as the norm. Beauty, in fact, goes much deeper than cosmetics and body shape, this proverb notes well.

Does the woman celebrated here possess those strong inner qualities of wisdom, discernment, care, loyalty, and courage? Is the woman portrayed a *person living to the height and depth of her being?*

Yes, emphatically. Is the woman described here caught in a time warp of traditionalism, tied to her chores, prancing to the drumbeat of men, second-class, and Barbie-dollish? Not a chance. God's advice to men and women is consistent over time: Cultivate the virtues that reflect the love and care God has for all people, and you will find peace, contentment, and passion. That's a message for every decade and era.

ecclesiastes

Here's the scoop. . .

Written: *around 900 B.C.*

Written by: *probably Solomon*

Writing style: *wisdom literature, which means a profound kind of thought-provoking writing, sometimes called poetry*

One-liner: *I had it all, and it didn't mean anything without God. Sincerely, King Solomon.*

THE MAN WHO HAD IT ALL

Remember Solomon? He was King David's son. When he was a young king, God asked him what he wanted, and Solomon said, "Wisdom." God rewarded such a discerning answer by giving him wealth and power as well as wisdom. For many years Solomon lived a life that honored God.

Before it was all over, though, Solomon had slipped. He had gotten a little complacent. He had let some idolatry and disillusionment slip into the royal household (along with hundreds of wives and concubines). It was at this point that it is generally believed that he wrote the book of Ecclesiastes.

FOR EVERY SEASON

You probably remember that famous passage: A time to "this" and a time to "that." Let's see how much of it you really remember. . . .

There is a time for everything, and a season for every activity under heaven:

a time to be b___ and a time to die;

a time to plant and a time to up___,

a time to kill and a time to h___,

a time to tear down and a time to b___,

a time to w___ and a time to laugh,

a time to mourn and a time to d___,

a time to scatter stones and a time to g___ them,

a time to e___ and a time to refrain,

a time to search and a time to g___ up,

a time to keep and a time to t___ away,

a time to tear and a time to m___,

a time to be silent and a time to s___,

a time to l___ and a time to hate,

a time for w___ and a time for peace.

Ecclesiastes 3:1–8

HERE ARE THE ANSWERS

There is a time for everything, and a season for every activity under heaven:

a time to be born and a time to die,

a time to plant and a time to uproot,

a time to kill and a time to heal,

a time to tear down and a time to build,

a time to weep and a time to laugh,

a time to mourn and a time to dance,

a time to scatter stones and a time to gather them,

a time to embrace and a time to refrain,

a time to search and a time to give up,

a time to keep and a time to throw away,

a time to tear and a time to mend,

a time to be silent and a time to speak,

a time to love and a time to hate,

a time for war and a time for peace.

Ecclesiastes 3:1–8

SCRIPTURE BITS

A phrase that is used umpteen times in Ecclesiastes is the phrase "under the sun." ("Umpteen" is a round figure depending on which translation you are using.) Another recurring theme is "everything is meaningless." Solomon should know; he had all the conveniences his culture offered him, and still everything wasn't enough without God.

questions

Q. Why should a man who has everything feel so depressed and despondent? (Ecclesiastes 1:1–11)

A. The teacher in Ecclesiastes has everything; yet he still manages to feel depressed and despondent. The reason he gives for his depression is the apparent meaninglessness of life and the fact that man cannot find satisfaction or contentment. Each new day is just a repetition of all the other days that have gone before. In fact, nothing is actually new; nothing is fresh. In a restless and weary turn of phrase, the teacher coins the well-used quote "History merely repeats itself." According to the teacher's reasoning, there is no worth to be found in doing things that have already been done and seen and experienced by other people.

Depression and despondency are easy pits to fall into. Absolutely nothing in life will bring fulfillment if we do not realize and understand that only God brings validity to our lives. We can achieve the highest statesmanship, amass fortunes, create great works of art, or spend our lives in humanitarian causes. If these things are done in the absence of God as Lord in our lives, however, they will not bring fulfillment; instead, they will only bring emptiness.

Q. *Against so many biblical commands, how can Solomon advise that there is a time to kill, to hate, and to tear down? (Ecclesiastes 3:1–11)*

A. *Solomon's list of times—to weep, to laugh, and so on—must be viewed within the larger context of life and history. He isn't saying, hey, it's twelve o' clock, time to kill—so go out and bump someone off.*

Rather, Solomon insists that human life takes place within a larger framework of events that repeat down through history: laughter, tears, killing, healing, destruction, building, death, birth. We should not be surprised or think it strange if such things happen to us. Such has happened before to countless people and will happen again to countless more—the rhythms of life, joyous and sad.

song of songs

IN CONTEXT

Here's the scoop. . .

Written: *around 950 B.C.*

Written by: *King Solomon*

Writing style: *a love poem*

One-liner: *I'm passionately in love, and I can't stop thinking about her! By Solomon.*

AN APPLE FALLEN NOT FAR FROM THE TREE

Solomon was the son of a musician and a soldier. His father, David, wrote many of the Psalms (which are poems or songs, remember). Solomon came from a creative bloodline. So out of his love for a beautiful woman, one he treasured, came this love poem that is inspired not by Cupid's arrow but by God Himself.

THINK ABOUT IT THIS WAY

A PG-13 RATING?

It might not always seem like it at first glance, but the Bible is a very practical book. It deals with the issues of everyday life. The Song of Songs is a good example. This is romantic love at its most syrupy and, sometimes, at its most seductive.

HOW THE THEOLOGIANS FEEL

As you can imagine, this book of the Bible has created quite a stir through the centuries. For goodness' sake, parts of it are almost pillow talk. (Young Jewish boys were not allowed to read this book until they were thirteen years old.) Because of that, many have been uncomfortable with the interpretation. After the dust has settled, most agree that Song of Solomon is a literal love poem about real people.

But most also agree that this book is a great picture of how Christ feels about the church. The New Testament calls the church the "bride of Christ." In this way, the desire and passion that the king in this book shows for his bride are akin to the desire and passion that Christ has toward us, His body, His church. We are valued. We are prized. We are an object of desire. We bring Him joy.

questions q&a

Q. *Should people be talking about these kinds of things in public?*
(Song of Songs 3:1)

A. *Perhaps not in public-public, because that makes a market out of intimacy and tends to turn true love into pornography, gratifying not heart needs but the needs of a person's hormonal drives pure and simple. Too much public talk makes sex more the activity of animals and less the activity of gifted human beings living before a God of love. The most intimate of all human encounters should be protected from too much public exposure, lest intimacy be lost and the dynamic of love itself be prostituted.*

But in many Christian circles, the opposite problem is the norm: not enough discussion about sex as a gift from God. How futile! Christians who think that silence will suppress the topic are kidding themselves. From the start of sexual feelings in puberty to the quieting of sexual drives in older age, the topic should be given a lot of talk in the family and in the church. We need to understand this remarkable part of our being, and our understanding needs to be, like every other important question, informed by God's Word and repaired (because often it's broken) by God's saving love.

PROPHETIC BOOKS

The prophecies of the Old Testament include a lot of different kinds of information. They include stories (as in Daniel), wild visions (as in Ezekiel), sermons (as in Isaiah), and some future-telling. They are the writings of men who were plucked from their lives by God and were given a message. Their responsibility, then, was to get that message out. They came from a lot of different backgrounds. If you remember Jonah, then you remember that they were not all completely comfortable with God's call on their lives. But they all responded to it, and some of them quite creatively. Hosea was asked to marry a prostitute to show a picture of how God had loved an unfaithful Israel. Ezekiel gave part of his prophecy through pantomime (no record of white gloves or weird suspenders, though). Jeremiah wrote some of his message as funeral dirges.

Their writings are about as diverse as any collection you'll find. But they were the Billy Grahams of their day. They were the voices calling out to their country, "We're missing the point here! God wants to relate to us in a different way!" Because of that, their messages still have something to say to us today.

We have even greater confidence in the message proclaimed by the prophets. Pay close attention to what they wrote, for their words are like a light shining in a dark place—until the day Christ appears and His brilliant light shines in your hearts. Above all, you must understand that no prophecy in Scripture ever came from the prophets themselves or because they wanted to prophesy. It was the Holy Spirit who moved the prophets to speak from God. (2 Peter 1:19–21 NLT)

Major prophets	Less major prophets	
• Isaiah	• Hosea	• Nahum
• Jeremiah	• Joel	• Habakkuk
• Lamentations	• Amos	• Zephaniah
• Ezekiel	• Obadiah	• Haggai
• Daniel	• Jonah	• Zechariah
	• Micah	• Malachi

isaiah

IN CONTEXT

Here's the scoop...

Written: *around 700 B.C.*

Written by: *Isaiah*

Writing style: *a collection of sermons and prophecies*

One-liner: *Pay attention. God has a master plan in the works, and we need to be a part of it.*

A PROPHET'S PROPHET

Isaiah preached to the Jewish people at a time when they didn't have much of a leg to stand on. They had refused to be faithful to God in worship. They had mixed and mingled their culture with the cultures of those around. They were a spear's throw from being taken to Babylon as exiles, thus completely losing hold of home.

How would you like to prepare a message for that crowd? What would you say? What Isaiah said was, essentially, "Let's examine the details of our lives, but let's find hope in the big picture. We might have messed things up royally, but God has a bigger plan to redeem the world. Let's hold on to that."

THE FIRST PART OF ISAIAH

The book of Isaiah divides easily into two parts. The first thirty-nine chapters are about judgment. They refer to events current to Isaiah's day as well as events that haven't even happened yet today. You'll find that's true of much of the prophecy in the Bible. There was truth for the people then and there, but the prophecies also reflected a greater event in the more distant future.

God spoke through Isaiah with compassion and with an in-your-face-but-because-I-love-you kind of voice.

THE SECOND PART

The last twenty-seven chapters of Isaiah (40–66) are often called the "Book of Consolation." They address Jesus' appearance in the New Testament. Isaiah 53 is one of the most famous and most picturesque prophecies about Jesus' birth, life, and death.

> *He was oppressed and he was afflicted, yet he never said a word. He was brought as a lamb to the slaughter; and as a sheep before her shearers is dumb, so he stood silent before the ones condemning him. From prison and trial they led him away to his death. But who among the people of that day realized it was their sins that he was dying for—that he was suffering their punishment? He was buried like a criminal in a rich man's grave; but he had done no wrong, and had never spoken an evil word (Isaiah 53:7–9 TLB).*

No one knew better than Isaiah that when Christ came to earth, He would suffer greatly so that we would not have to.

DID YOU KNOW?

isaiah put to music?

Have you ever heard Handel's *Messiah*? It's a classical choral piece performed often around Christmas. The most well-known song from the collection is the "Hallelujah Chorus," which has appeared in everything from church sanctuaries to sitcoms and commercials.

Anyway, if you've heard Handel's *Messiah*, you've heard parts of Isaiah put to music. Check out these scripture lyrics and see if they ring a bell or two. The scriptures listed below are from the King James Version of the Bible, which uses an older style of English. It is the version Handel quoted.

"Every valley shall be exalted, and every mountain and hill shall be made low: and the crooked shall be made straight, and the rough places plain" (Isaiah 40:4). *This verse describes God's truth revealed in Jesus Christ.*

"For unto us a child is born, unto us a son is given: and the government shall be upon his shoulder: and his name shall be called Wonderful, Counsellor, The mighty God, The everlasting Father, the Prince of Peace" (Isaiah 9:6). *Many songs have been based on this verse in one version or another.*

"He is despised and rejected of men; a man of sorrows, and acquainted with grief: and we hid as it were our faces from him; he was despised, and we esteemed him not" (Isaiah 53:3). *Jesus was not accepted among his peers. He wasn't recognized for who He was.*

"He was wounded for our transgressions, he was bruised for our iniquities: the chastisement of our peace was upon him; and with his stripes we are healed" (Isaiah 53:5). *Jesus died for our sins. The stripes refer to the flogging He received before He was killed.*

"All we like sheep have gone astray; we have turned every one to his own way; and the LORD hath laid on him the iniquity of us all" (Isaiah 53:6). *This is the bottom line of the gospel: Jesus sacrificed Himself for our sin. (That's what iniquity is.)*

questions

Q. Why did God say He was sick of the sacrifices being offered by the Israelites (Isaiah 1:11–14)?

A. *The people of Israel were outwardly religious but inwardly rebellious. Rather than obeying God from their hearts and faithfully keeping His covenant, they modified their religious practices to suit their own desires. The result was an eclectic, idolatrous hodgepodge in which the Holy One of Israel (the prophet's favorite name for God) was barely acknowledged. God's strong indictment (delivered through the prophet) read "They honor me with their lips, but their hearts are far away. And their worship of me amounts to nothing more than human laws learned by rote" (Isaiah 29:13 NLT).*

For these reasons, God told the Israelites to stop their useless, hypocritical behavior.

Q. Did Isaiah really go naked for three years at the command of God? (Isaiah 20:1–6)

A. *God's instruction to Isaiah uses the same language as found in Genesis 2:25, which speaks of Adam and Eve in their innocence, naked and without self-consciousness or shame. If Isaiah understood the command as requiring literal nakedness, he must also have understood what his attitude was to be.*

On the other hand, going naked may refer to walking about stripped of outer garments (prophets often wore a covering of sackcloth), covered only in a loincloth.

Whatever the degree of nakedness intended here, Isaiah got the attention of his Egyptian and Ethiopian audience. The Assyrians would soon invade and humiliate those who assaulted Israel.

Q. *What can we say for sure about the so-called "new heavens and new earth"? (Isaiah 65:17 NLT)*

A. *Here God says, "Look! I am creating new heavens and a new earth—so wonderful that no one will even think about the old ones anymore." The same phrase appears again in Isaiah 66:22–23; 2 Peter 3:13; and Revelation 21:1 (referred to there as "new heaven," singular), yet few details are known. All that can be said with certainty is that God's recreated cosmos will be marked by the sure rule of God and that the inhabitants of this eternal state will experience safety, peace, prosperity, and joy. It is with good reason that the final two chapters of the Bible have been a great source of comfort to so many saints down through the ages!*

Jeremiah

Here's the scoop. . .

Written: *around 600 B.C.*

Written by: *Jeremiah*

Writing style: *a prophecy or message from God*

One-liner: *Prepare to face the consequences of living apart from God. Know that God's plan is still in place.*

WEEPING AND WAILING

Jeremiah had a life that few of us would wish for. He experienced a lot of rejection. He spent most of his whole life and certainly all of his adult life grieving for the mistakes of his fellow citizens. He was a prophet who didn't get a lot of glory.

Jeremiah preached mostly in Judah, the southern kingdom of Israel. Like all of Israel, these people had drifted farther and farther from God's way of doing things. At first Jeremiah's prophecies were warnings, such as "You know what *always* happens when we don't follow God. We get weaker and weaker until some other country takes us over. It's about to happen again."

Later in his ministry, his prophecies were more like this: "Well, you've made your bed now. You need to get ready to lie in it. You've become too weak with sin and idolatry to fight off any enemy at all. Accept that something bad is going to happen."

Still later he gave up on trying to amend the current situation and instead began to prophesy about the long-term salvation that was ahead of them. His message was "We have wasted this time as a nation. But there is always eventual hope, because God promised a Messiah who will fix this mess we've created."

Sure enough, Jeremiah's people did become captives in Babylonia. Sure enough, about six hundred years later, Jesus did come to give them, and us, hope.

questions

Q. *How can God know anyone in advance of such a person being a person? (Jeremiah 1:5)*

A. *God knows us before we are even fertilized eggs in our mothers' wombs. You see, God is the one who thinks up each person, knows and understands each person's individuality, and examines the entire path each life is going to take.*

It is important to realize this, because it is for that reason we can know that each person born is already known, chosen, and cherished by God. Therefore, whether a child is conceived by apparent accident, by violence, or within the love of a family, the fact of foremost importance is that the child was first known by God.

Q. *Repeatedly, Israel is compared to a prostitute. What is the reason for this? (Jeremiah 2:20, 33; 3:1–3)*

A. *When God chose Israel to be His holy nation, He intended them to be solely devoted to Him. Israel was like a beloved bride who had saved herself for one man. Throughout Israel's history in the Old Testament, however, the nation was constantly breaking its commitment with God and making alliances with other nations and other gods. Because of this flirting with and loving other gods besides the Lord, Jeremiah compared Israel to a prostitute.*

Q. *How is it possible to circumcise the heart? (Jeremiah 4:4)*

A. *Circumcision was an act of covenant, of entering into an agreement with the Lord. The physical act of circumcision, however, doesn't necessarily mean that the person actually is in covenant with the Lord. It can quickly become another case of merely going through the motions.*

Circumcising the heart, on the other hand, means that you are entering into covenantal agreement with the Lord where you really live, down among the true motives and desires of your private self. Circumcising the heart means that you are allowing the Lord to enter your heart, to be Lord of your being, Lord of your life, of your desires, will, and thoughts.

Physical circumcision can be easily done by a human being, done in a day and then forgotten. Circumcision of the heart can be done by any person but is not so quickly forgotten, being deeper than physical circumcision.

Lamentations

Here's the scoop. . .

Written: *around 600 B.C.*

Written by: *Jeremiah*

Writing style: *sermons or prophecies in the form of funeral dirges*

One-liner: *What we dreaded has happened. Our sin has destroyed us. My heart is broken.*

NOBODY LIKES ME, EVERYBODY HATES ME, THINK I'LL EAT SOME WORMS. . . .

Think of the saddest song you know, and you'll be in the right mood for reading Lamentations. The book of Lamentations is actually five Hebrew poems. They are so sad that they are considered funeral dirges. Chapters 1 through 4 are actually acrostics in Hebrews—you know, where the first letter of each line spells something. In the case of these chapters, the first letters of each line are the letters of the Hebrew alphabet. (For chapter 3 it's every three verses.) Chapter 5 is the only chapter that is not alphabetical, but it is still a poem.

We spend so much of our lives not worrying about sin that it's hard to understand Jeremiah's getting so worked up about it. Actually, the people of his day felt the same way. They ridiculed Jeremiah. They rejected his message. But that didn't change the fact that what he said came true. He had told them that if they didn't straighten up, they would lose their land again, and. . .guess what? Sure enough, they were taken captive into Babylonia. As far as we know, Lamentations was written for the people while they were captives. It was pretty good of Jeremiah, when you think about it, to warn the people, be disregarded by them, and then write them some sad songs when they needed them. (Sad songs say so much, you know.)

Lamentations could have been a told-you-so book. Jeremiah had, indeed, warned the people about the consequences of their sin. But rather than being a told-you-so book, Jeremiah is a book of sadness that his people were separated once again from their land and disobedient to God, which caused further separation.

questions

Q. *Why does an all-powerful God allow children to suffer? (Lamentations 2:19)*

A. *Of the horrible things that happen in the world, the suffering and death of children may be the hardest to understand. Surely God would not allow those who are so clearly helpless to be hurt.*

The problem often focuses on the innocence of children. But innocence only suggests that children suffer in situations for which they are not directly responsible. Other people, often greedy or malicious adults, make decisions or take actions that result in the suffering of children. Children are caught in the crossfire of others' sin. Innocence disappears when all the facts are in.

To argue that children shouldn't suffer because they are sinless indicates a naive view of human nature. The idea of sinlessness misunderstands sin itself, which is part and parcel of human nature. Sin affects every person and every human institution, and pain is its result.

Q. *Only God can eradicate suffering. God has promised to do this at the end of history. If God can do it, why not now?*

A. *Pushing responsibility for innocent suffering onto God avoids one of the core lessons of life: personal responsibility. No one lives as an isolated individual; decisions and actions always affect someone else. Innocent people suffer when someone chooses to boost his empire, take a foolish risk, or appease an evil appetite. Children suffer because God created a world where decisions really matter.*

Will suffering be vindicated? Will moral justice ever be reached in human experience? Will the suffering of an innocent person, a child, ever be addressed in some court of appeal where restitution is possible? These questions are staggering. Such a process would be the most difficult problem-solving sequence ever tried. Yet God promises just this. In a kingdom to come, tears will be wiped clean in the beauty of God's holiness, the comfort of His love, and the community of His people.

God knows the suffering people experience and has done something about it: Jesus Christ the Messiah, sent to redeem the world. Trust in God's holy Son, and know that suffering is only for a while.

EzekieL

Here's the scoop. . .

Written: *around 550 B.C.*

Written by: *Ezekiel*

Writing style: *a sermon or prophecy*

One-liner: *Here are some visions I saw from God's perspective on how we've lived our lives and of heaven.*

A MAN WITH A VISION

That's Ezekiel. Not just one vision, either. Many visions. The book of Ezekiel is a colorful prophecy. It includes judgment and condemnation. It's almost kicking the people while they are down, since he was preaching to them while they were exiled from their homes. The book also includes visions of heaven and hope for the future.

Because Ezekiel is such an imaginative book, it can seem difficult to wade through at times. Just remember this is the writing of a man to whom God is showing spectacular things. Ezekiel is trying to describe his visions of heaven and of heavenly things in human terms. Basically, that is impossible. So he makes a lot of "It was like. . ." kind of statements. In the end we'll all have to wait until we see God to really understand what Ezekiel saw.

A VISION OF GOD

Sometimes, just as a cute adult thing to do, we ask little kids what they think God looks like. Some responses are hilarious, but none is ever like Ezekiel's view of God. Listen to this:

> For high in the sky above them was what looked like a throne made of beautiful blue sapphire stones, and upon it sat someone who appeared to be a Man. From his waist up, he seemed to be all glowing bronze, dazzling like fire; and from his waist down he seemed to be entirely flame, and there was a glowing halo like a rainbow all around him. That was the way the glory of the Lord appeared to me. And when I saw it, I fell face downward on the ground (Ezekiel 1:26–28 TLB).

And listen to his description of the angels around God's throne:

- Their form was that of a man, but each of them had four faces and four wings.

- Their legs were straight; their feet were like those of a calf and gleamed like burnished bronze.

- Under their wings. . .they had the hands of a man.

- Each of the four had the face of a man. . .the face of a lion. . .the face of an ox. . .also the face of an eagle.

- The appearance of the living creatures was like burning coals of fire or like torches. . . . The creatures sped back and forth like flashes of lightning.

- I saw a wheel on the ground beside each creature with its four faces. . . . Their rims were high and awesome, and all four rims were full of eyes all around. (See Ezekiel 1:5–21.)

THE HOLY MIME

Ezekiel actually acted out part of his prophecy much like a mime would. He went for a long time without speaking. He went for an even longer time lying in exactly the same place. He went to some great lengths to get his point across.

THINK ABOUT IT THIS WAY

Whether we understand Ezekiel's vision or not, we can understand his message that there is reality beyond what we can see and there is hope beyond any difficulty we might face.

DID YOU KNOW?

which Bones?

One of the most powerful images of Ezekiel is the valley of dry bones. The bones represented Israel with no hope. God breathed life into the bones to show Ezekiel that there was hope for Israel and that they would one day return to their land. Do you recognize that story? You might recognize it more this way:

> *Dem bones, dem bones, dem dry bones,*
> *Dem bones, dem bones, dem dry bones,*
> *Dem bones, dem bones, dem dry bones,*
> *Now hear the word of the Lord.*
>
> *The toe bone connected to the ankle bone,*
> *the ankle bone connected to the leg bone,*
> *the leg bone connected to the hip bone. . . .*

(See Ezekiel 37:1–14.)

questions

Q. *What does "son of man" mean? (Ezekiel 2:1)*

A. *The prophet Ezekiel is addressed as "son of man," a title used for him more than ninety times throughout the book of Ezekiel. The title shows the contrast between Ezekiel, a man, and the almighty Lord. This name would portray Ezekiel's human limits and weaknesses in contrast to the glory and greatness of God.*

The term "son of man" is used twice in Daniel (7:13 and 8:17), the only other references in the Old Testament. Daniel 7:13 describes the "son of man" as one "coming with the clouds of heaven" who is "given authority, honor and royal power over all the nations of the world." This is often taken to refer to the expected Messiah.

Jesus' reference to Himself as "son of man" in Mark 2:10 and elsewhere points to His identification with humanity as well as His deity.

Q. Why is Ezekiel told not to grieve the death of his wife? (Ezekiel 24:16)

A. Ezekiel loves his wife, but God tells him not to grieve publicly when she dies. This is to be a living message to the people concerning their abandonment of God. Yes, grief will come to them, the grief of captivity. They will suffer at the hands of Babylonian conquerors, and their homes, lands, and precious temple will be destroyed. Will they be as mute as Ezekiel, or in grief repent of sin and return to the worship of God?

Ezekiel's personal sacrifice must have affected him deeply. Yet obedience to God puts unusual demands on leaders. No Christian is called to be a stoic, tearlessly accepting any and all pain; sometimes, however, for special purposes, Christians are called to endure unusual difficulty for the sake of the mission. Ezekiel knew his assignment, and while others could not understand his facade, he did. It was God's call—God's way for Ezekiel to send a message the people would not hear through any other channel.

Q. "Dem bones, dem bones, dem dry bones," the song goes. What message lies hidden in dry bones? (Ezekiel 37:1)

A. The dry bones symbolize that the nation of Israel was dead and gone, scattered among the nations because the people had grown cold—made their hearts dead—to God.

Ezekiel speaks to the hope that the scattered exiles of Israel will hear God's word anew, draw together, and again find identity as a people committed to God.

DanieL

IN CONTEXT

Here's the scoop. . .

Written: *around 550 B.C.*

Written by: *Daniel*

Writing style: *stories, visions, and prophecies*

One-liner: *Here are the stories of Daniel, a Jewish exile in Babylonia, and his visions of the future.*

DANIEL: THE STORY

The first six chapters of the book of Daniel tell his story. It's like a mini-series set in the midst of the exile of the Jewish people. Daniel was a young adult when his people were taken captive into Babylonia.

First, the Babylonians tried to feed him rich foods that were taboo for a young Jewish boy. He opted for vegetables and fruits. Before you knew it, he had influenced the guards to serve all the boys healthier meals.

Next, he became a servant to the king and even interpreted the king's dreams. Because of this, he was put in charge of all the wise men in Babylonia.

As you can imagine, this did not set well with the Babylonian locals. They set a trap, convincing the king to give an order for everyone, including the Jewish people, to bow down to an idol. Daniel and his friends refused. You've probably heard the miraculous story of the three friends' being thrown into the fiery furnace (a form of capital punishment) and not only surviving, but not even smelling of smoke.

In another attempt to trip Daniel up, a decree was sent out that no one could pray to God for thirty days. Daniel, of course, continued to pray. His punishment was to be thrown into a cave with hungry lions. Believe it or not, not one lion touched Daniel.

DANIEL: THE PROPHECY

The last half of the book of Daniel is made up of Daniel's prophecies. As far as we know, many of those prophecies have already been fulfilled. Some, though, refer to the same time period as described in the book of Revelation (in the New Testament)—the end of the world.

questions &a

Q. *Why didn't Shadrach, Meshach, and Abednego bow down to the golden statue? (Daniel 3:12)*

A. *They knew it wasn't God, so what difference would it make? People salute a passing flag, stand at attention for a presidential motorcade, and put hand over heart for the national anthem. Why not bow to the king's phony idol—just another symbol of national identity?*

Fear is a fertile field that yields a huge harvest of excuses. Daniel's friends could have used several: (1) Pretend by bowing, but don't actually worship. (2) Go ahead and worship this time, then ask God to forgive later—God understands this kind of pressure. (3) If bowing this time is wrong, why would God put us in this position? (4) The king has been good to us, so let's cooperate. (5) If we show the people a little goodwill, maybe they will listen when we tell them about God. (6) Bowing down might not be the best choice, but think of all the worse things our ancestors did, even in God's own temple in Jerusalem! (7) A little bowing won't hurt anybody. (8) If we lose our positions, the king will appoint a pagan and we won't be able to help our people anymore.

Some of these alleged excuses mask compromise better than others, but each is a form of betrayal. Shadrach, Meshach, and Abednego valued their relationship with God more than they valued their lives. To show respect for national symbols was one thing; to worship an idol—even if no one believed in the idol's divinity—was quite another. The three young Jews drew the line at homage. Theirs belonged to God alone.

Q. *Does trusting God mean nothing bad will happen to us? (Daniel 3:19)*

A. *Trust in God is not a bargain we offer in exchange for God's sparing us the pain of persecution or the threat of natural disaster. Trusting God means we don't waver when things are not turning out the way we would plan. Daniel's friends told the king they expected to be rescued from the flames (Daniel 3:17) because they believed God was able to do it. But they also told the king that even death, if God chose, would still accomplish their rescue. Trusting God means we have a reason to hope even when it seems like everything bad may happen to us.*

Q. *Who was the fourth person in King Nebuchadnezzar's furnace? (Daniel 3:25)*

A. *Perhaps this was an early visit by Christ or maybe an angelic companion God sent to protect the three faithful men. Whatever his identity, the fourth person's appearance was different. The king described him as someone who "looks like a son of the gods." When the king called Shadrach, Meshach, and Abednego to step out of the furnace, he failed to invite the fourth person. Apparently Nebuchadnezzar wasn't ready for a face-to-face encounter with whoever he was.*

Hosea

IN CONTEXT

Here's the scoop. . .

Written: *around 700 B.C.*

Written by: *Hosea*

Writing style: *a collection of Hosea's prophecies mixed in with stories about his life*

One-liner: *Ephraim, you are as unfaithful to God as a prostitute to her husband. Turn around!*

THE BIG "HUH?"

If anybody knows anything about Hosea, it is usually that he was the prophet who married the prostitute. Huh?

Why? Because God told him to.

Why would God tell him to do that? So that his life could be a picture of how much God loved Israel whether they loved Him back or not.

Why would God compare Israel to a prostitute? Good question. The answer to that question is the foundation for understanding the prophecy of Hosea. The collective Hebrew people were very much like a prostitute because they were unfaithful to God. God had asked them to worship only Him, no idols, no false gods—a monogamous worship relationship. Sometimes the people would obey God, usually when they needed God's help. But as soon as they were doing okay, they forgot their allegiance and began to worship whatever was the popular idol of the day.

This had been going on for years. It had weakened them politically. It had caused them to lose their homes, their battles, their well-being. It was about to cause them to be taken captive to another land as exiles. That's why God asked Hosea to go to such desperate lengths. Basically God said, "Marry a call girl and let her despicable actions toward you show these people how they have treated me." In other words, Hosea's marriage was another of God's object lessons.

Hosea did it. He married a prostitute. They had three children together. Hosea's wife, Gomer (go figure), constantly broke Hosea's heart by going back to her old life, no matter how much he loved her or how well he treated her.

A MESSAGE TO EPHRAIM

The prophecy of Hosea isn't just a story of his marriage, though. Hosea was a prophet in the northern kingdom of Israel. He addressed his message to the tribe of Ephraim, the largest tribe of that kingdom, but it was a message for all Hebrews. He called their hand on several issues: the instability of their commitment to God, their diluted identity as followers of God, and their spiritual superficiality.

Maybe some of the Israelites listened. We don't know. They didn't repent of their religious prostitution. They kept right on worshiping other gods until they were destroyed as a nation.

questions q&a

Q. *Is the story of Gomer and Hosea real history or allegory? (Hosea 1)*

A. *Why would a holy God order His servant to marry a prostitute? The unlikelihood of such an order has led some to interpret Hosea as a picture of the relationship between God and Israel. However, the first three chapters of Hosea are presented as straightforward historical narrative. Nothing in the text points to anything less than a literal understanding of these events.*

JOEL

IN CONTEXT

Here's the scoop...

Written: *around 800* B.C.

Written by: *Joel, a prophet to Judah, the southern kingdom*

Writing style: *a collection of sermons*

One-liner: *Because of our sin, it's going to get worse before it gets better. But it will get better one day.*

GRASSHOPPERS ON THE LOOSE

In the Old Testament, God's judgment for sin came in the form of many things. In the plagues of Egypt, God's judgment came in the form of death and bugs and sickness and weather.

The book of Joel is a red-flag message to the people of Judah that God had just about had enough of their waywardness and rebellion. Joel was specific, as well. He told his people that their punishment would come in the form of locusts—flying, grasshopper-like bugs that fed off the vegetation of the land.

Punishment by grasshoppers might not sound like much more to us than an inconvenience and a great time to stock up on bug repellant. We need to understand the culture of that day, though. People lived off the land. They farmed; they raised food for their animals. If a huge swarm of locusts came through and destroyed all the vegetation, the people would have nothing. The livestock would die. Everyone would eventually starve.

(Even worse, some people believe that Joel was using locusts as an illustration of Assyrian soldiers rushing to take over Judah. There was no Assyrian soldier repellant.)

When Joel gave this gloom-and-doom prophecy, everything was going pretty well in Judah. It was difficult for the people to think of hard times when they had plenty to eat. That's probably why they didn't listen to Joel. When life is easy, it's not hard to disregard God's warning that sin destroys.

AND IN THE FUTURE. . .

Joel did give a little good news, as well. Like many other prophets, his message included an in-the-future clause. He predicted not only Judah's destruction because of their sin, but also Judah's eventual salvation through God's eventual forgiveness.

People today refer to prophecies of Joel when they discuss the end of the world as we know it. A lot of vision is packed in this three-chapter manuscript.

SCRIPTURE BITS

Joel's words appear not only here in his prophecy, but also in the New Testament. You might remember that at the beginning of Acts, God comes to the church in a new way—as the Holy Spirit. It's a wild time of multiple languages and fire from heaven. In the midst of it all, Peter quotes Joel. Here's part of what Peter said:

"What you see this morning was predicted centuries ago by the prophet Joel—'In the last days,' God said, 'I will pour out my Holy Spirit upon all mankind, and your sons and daughters shall prophesy, and your young men shall see visions, and your old men dream dreams. Yes, the Holy Spirit shall come upon all my servants, men and women alike, and they shall prophesy.'"

Acts 2:16–18 TLB

questions

Q. *Are natural disasters like floods, locusts, drought, and earthquakes God's methods of punishment? (Joel 1)*

A. The Bible cites many occasions in which God used natural disasters as a means of punishment. The little book of Joel, for instance, begins with an impending plague of locusts that will devastate the nation. Along with the warning comes an invitation to repentance. The people are told that a genuine turn from sin may save them, but they cannot assume a reprieve from punishment. The disaster may come no matter what the people do.

The Bible never claims that natural disasters are always God's punishment. Sin will be punished, but the time, place, and manner are not so predictable as simple formulas that equate weather disturbances with divine anger.

Q. *How does Joel's message to Israel apply to anything today? (Joel 2:12–13)*

A. The message of Joel was first given to a specific audience at one time in history. Although all of the message applied to them, it applied in different ways. The same process works today. Application refers to the way God's Word covers us, governs us, and becomes the basis for action.

God's Word covers us when we realize that we are the kind of people described in a passage. When we identify with scripture, the Holy Spirit applies scripture to us, the vivid truth of God's Word for us personally. The people of Joel's day were covered by God's words of warning and hope. We are covered by those same words. Coming dangers may not be swarms of locusts or invading armies, but they are just as dangerous if we face them with unrepentant hearts and spirits that refuse God's care.

God's Word governs us when we take its commands seriously and recognize its authority. God doesn't have to earn the right to give us direction; we should be eager for and attentive to God's direction. The people in Joel's day who benefited from the prophet's words were not those who took it as curious information. Rather, those who heard God speaking through His prophet and listened to obey were blessed and forgiven.

God's Word is meant for action. Verses in scripture can often find an immediate place in our lives. Joel wrote, "That is why the LORD says, 'Turn to me now, while there is time! Give me your hearts. Come with fasting, weeping, and mourning. Don't tear your clothing in your grief; instead, tear your hearts'" (2:12–13 NLT). These words confronted the people of Joel's day with an immediate call to repentance. That same call reaches across the centuries to us. Our persistent tendency is to turn away from God. Instead, we should take every opportunity to learn from God's Word.

Q. What is repentance? (Joel 2:13)

A. Repentance describes the process of sorrow and regret over sin that causes a person to deeply desire forgiveness. Like most human experiences, repentance comes in true and false versions. True repentance affects the deep inner springs of the human heart; false repentance settles for a change in behavior unconnected to any internal transformation. In the Bible, people often would tear their clothes as a sign of repentance. This was an effective demonstration when it conveyed real emotion. Unfortunately, this action became just an act. People discovered the efficiency of tearing clothing without that bothersome inward struggle involved in repentance. To these people, Joel's words stung.

Other people should be able to observe the effects of true repentance, but the real audience for repentance is God, who is never fooled by the mere outward show of repentance but seeks the deep inner connection to our spirits that signals authentic recognition of God's holiness and our wretchedness.

AMOS

IN CONTEXT

Here's the scoop. . .

Written: *around 750 B.C.*

Written by: *Amos, a prophet from Judah (southern kingdom) who preached to Israel (northern kingdom)*

Writing style: *a sermon or prophecy*

One-liner: *By human standards, you're looking okay, but by God's standards, you're failing.*

A LESSON IN IRONY

Amos was a fish out of water in a lot of ways. He was from the southern kingdom, but he preached to the northern kingdom. He was a shepherd, but he preached to rich people. His message was somewhat negative, but he was preaching to people who were having a great time.

The meat of Amos's message was that God was not satisfied with the worship of His people in Israel. They were coming to the temple to worship, then making their living by exploiting the poor of their society. They were doing some of the right ceremonial things, but they weren't worshiping God with the way they lived their lives. For this, God, through Amos, condemned them.

One of the ways in which God directed Amos to warn the people was through an object lesson. God showed Amos a plumb line. A plumb line was a string with a weight that showed a workman whether his work was straight. It was like a vertical level. God told Amos that He was holding a plumb line up to Israel to see if their ways were straight or not. They were definitely not making the grade compared to God's plumb line.

questions q&a

Q. *What is a Nazirite? (Amos 2:11–12)*

A. *The state of being a Nazirite is the result of a vow taken by someone who will thereafter be "separated" or "dedicated" to the Lord in a special way. Nazirites were not priests but were used by God as examples of holiness to the larger population. Among the Nazirites were Samson, Samuel, and John the Baptist. They led ascetic lives, denying themselves many physical comforts, including drinking wine, which was forbidden to them.*

obadiah

IN CONTEXT

Here's the scoop. . .

Written: *around 850 B.C.*

Written by: *Obadiah*

Writing style: *an announcement of judgment*

One-liner: *Attention, people of Edom: You've bullied Israel, and now you'll answer to God Himself.*

YOU'LL GET YOURS

Obadiah is unique in that he didn't preach to Israel or Judah. Instead, he preached on their behalf to the Edomites.

A little background: Many generations before, the country of Edom originated from a man named Esau, whose name later became Edom. Esau was the twin brother of Jacob, whose name was later changed to Israel. In other words, the Israelites and the Edomites descended from twin brothers. Just as Esau and Jacob had their differences (Genesis 25–27), the Israelites and the Edomites had theirs.

Obadiah's prophecy is basically a condemnation of Edom for *not* helping Israel defend itself and for being a bully to Israel. Obadiah prophesied that the whole nation of Edom would eventually die out. By A.D. 70, they had.

TALK ABOUT A SOAP OPERA

The actual skinny about the Edomites and the Israelites reads like a daytime drama.

Esau (later named Edom) and Jacob (later named Israel) were twin boys who, even in the womb, fought to see who would be the better, the first. Esau was born first, which meant he had the family birthright. This birthright became a conflict that lasted their whole lives.

Esau was a rough outdoorsman. Jacob was just the opposite. One day Esau came in from hunting and was ravenously hungry. Jacob talked him into trading his birthright for some stew. Yes, you read it right. Birthright for stew.

The birthright was really nothing without the blessing of their dad (Isaac) to go along with it. When the time came, Jacob dressed up like Esau and went to his dad in disguise to receive Esau's blessing. Isaac was old and almost blind. He mistakenly promised Jacob the bigger part of the inheritance and the leadership role in the family. That might not sound binding today, but in that day it meant everything.

When Esau got back to the house that day, he realized that he had been snookered out of his future as a leader and a rich man. He was left to make his home among foreigners. This is why he ended up in Edom with a huge grudge that he passed down through generations.

Talk about a family feud.

THINK ABOUT IT THIS WAY

You might ask yourself, why is somebody else's "hate" mail a part of the Bible? Obadiah's message is like a coin with two sides. One side is a very fiery denunciation of Edom. But the other side of the coin is a look into the "momma bear" side of God's attitude toward His people. Obadiah reveals to us a side of God that does not sit back and leave us to our enemies undefended. Obadiah's message says that when God steps in, He will have the final word. The one who defends us has the power to get the job done.

questions q&a

Q. *If God will judge whole nations, what good is individual virtue and obedience? (Obadiah 15)*

A. Nations are judged for the courses of action that they follow as a collective whole, the choices that affect and are acquiesced to by the whole society. God judges nations for such choices right down here, in the earthly here and now.

Each person, however, is judged as an individual. It is according to our virtue, our obedience to God, our relationship with Him, that each of us is judged and punished or rewarded. And this particular judgment has eternal consequences.

Besides the reason of individual judgment, there is the fact that God calls us to virtue and obedience. If we are in relationship with God, we should be happy to obey Him. John states that the Christian who loves God will obey His Word (1 John 2:5).

Jonah

IN CONTEXT

Here's the scoop. . .

Written: *around 750 B.C.*

Written by: *Jonah*

Writing style: *the story of Jonah's prophecy to Nineveh*

One-liner: *Jonah unwillingly prophesied to a wicked place and was disappointed at the good turnout.*

A FISHY STORY

The story of Jonah is a classic story of My Way versus God's Way. God told Jonah to go to Nineveh and prophesy. Jonah headed the opposite direction. At first this can seem like a very rebellious thing for Jonah to do. Was he just disobedient? Did he not want to serve God?

Like most human dilemmas, it's more complicated than that. Do you know where Nineveh was? Nineveh was the capital of the country that was the biggest enemy of Jonah's country. To prophesy to Nineveh, Jonah had to violate every racial and political prejudice that was a part of his fabric. He wanted God to judge Nineveh for their cruelty rather than give them an opportunity to repent. Most of us would have felt the same way if we had stood in Jonah's sandals.

Back to the story, Jonah got the call from God and jumped on a boat headed in the opposite direction. The boat ran into a storm—and a bad storm at that. Destruction was soon at hand when the sailors realized that God was after something. Jonah "fessed up" and they *(splash!)* threw him overboard. Jonah was swallowed by a big fish and had three days in a dark, briny belly to contemplate his next move.

Jonah did some praying while he was in the fish, and after those three days, the fish regurgitated him (yuck!) on the beach. God once again told him to go to Nineveh; Jonah went.

Thus far this story is pretty familiar. The belly-of-the-fish part is the famous part. But there is more.

When Jonah got to Nineveh, he preached to the people, and, evil as they were, they responded graciously. They repented of their sin and banned evil from their city.

How did Jonah respond, this great prophet of God?

He was disappointed. He had gone to a lot of trouble and come a long way, and here these people had changed their ways and gotten off the hook. Jonah sat himself down and had a big ol' pity party.

Then God did one of those object lessons that leaves us going, "Huh?" One day a plant grew up around Jonah that kept him in the shade. This was a great thing. But the next day, a worm killed the plant, leaving Jonah back in the sun.

Jonah complained to God. Now, get the picture. Here is a man who spent three days in the belly of a fish, and he's complaining because a worm ate a vine. God gave Jonah a little talking-to.

THINK ABOUT IT THIS WAY

So this is the question: What is the story of Jonah really about? Is it about a wicked town called Nineveh getting a second chance? Is it about a thickheaded prophet who needed to learn some lessons? Is it about a God who wants everyone to leave their self-destructive ways, no matter what they've done or who they are? Is it about a God-follower who would rather see the bad guys get theirs (their just desserts, not their gracious forgiveness) than God get His? We can all find ourselves in a lot of different roles in this story. It's worth reviewing.

questions

Q. *How can a person survive for seventy-two hours in a fish?*
(Jonah 1:17)

A. *The sheer unlikelihood of this event has caused many to interpret Jonah's book as allegory or parable, not history as such. Indeed, no other account exists of a human being surviving such an event. Did it really happen to Jonah, and how did he survive?*

First, consider biblical time periods. "Three days and three nights" could mean one full day and parts of two others, as it did in the case of Jesus' death, which Jonah's experience clearly foreshadows (Matthew 12:40). Jonah's time of food and water deprivation could have been considerably shorter than seventy-two hours.

Second, consider the scientific possibilities. Remote, indeed, are the chances that a large surface-swimming fish without digestive enzymes picks up a human being and hours later dumps the living but limp body in shallows near his intended destination. Very remote.

Third, consider the miracle. God is saying something important about all of human history through the life of this minor prophet. The gospel will come through God's own Son, who will succumb, as it were, to an implausible end: death as a criminal. Yet there is life beyond. God's miracle in Jonah's experience is one of many miracles God has chosen to communicate with the creation He loves. The greatest of those miracles was the incarnation, that is, the coming of God Himself in human form, Jesus Christ, whose resurrection gives hope beyond the certainty of death.

MICah

IN CONTEXT

Here's the scoop. . .

Written: *around 600 B.C.*

Written by: *Micah*

Writing style: *several sermons based on visions from God*

One-liner: *We are immoral at every level and headed for destruction. Only God can deliver us from ourselves.*

GOOD NEWS, BAD NEWS

The prophet Micah was unique in that he preached or prophesied to both the northern kingdom of Israel (called Samaria) and the southern kingdom of Judah. The other prophets preached to either one or the other. But like the other prophets, he did prophesy both good news and bad news. He prophesied of judgment that was coming to the Hebrews and of the future victory that would come through Jesus Christ.

Micah was a down-to-earth prophet who looked around himself and saw a mess. He didn't mince words whether he was describing the evil he saw, the destruction that was coming, or the hope of the future. He called his people back to a heart devotion instead of a faith that just goes through the motions. He foretold their exile from their homes, which did eventually happen. He also foretold the place of Christ's birth, Bethlehem.

SCRIPTURE BITS

Micah had a way of cutting to the chase.

He has told you what he wants, and this is all it is: to be fair and just and merciful, and to walk humbly with your God.
Micah 6:8 TLB

questions

Q. *Why should people listen to God against their personal best interests? (Micah 1:2)*

A. *It appears that the news will be bad. A crime has been committed, and God will be the chief witness for the prosecution (who is also God). The accused, the people, must listen.*

But unlike a normal criminal trial, God never forces people to listen, and these people certainly had a choice. Why choose to hear bad news?

The answer lies in the character of the speaker. God announces no bad news, only the truth about our human condition and His own provision to repair the damage. Yes, this news is not good—people have sinned terribly. Consequences will surely follow, a worst-nightmare scenario of fear and pain. But even then, despite the sin and loss, God has a heart to redeem and save. That's why people must listen. Without God's hope, pain is just pain, but in God's plan, pain recedes into restoration and blessing.

Nahum

IN CONTEXT

Here's the scoop. . .

Written: *around 650 B.C.*

Written by: *Nahum*

Writing style: *a sermon*

One-liner: *No matter how strong evil seems, God will do away with it when He is ready.*

WHO IS GOD?

Nahum was a prophet in Judah. His prophecy was written in a form of poetry. It opens with some strong statements about God's power and goodness. Nahum established God's power to take care of His own. Then when Nahum had made his point, he turned his attention to a force of evil in his day and time—Nineveh.

WHAT IS NINEVEH?

Assyria was Israel and Judah's neighbor to the east, and Assyria was a bully of a neighbor. First, Assyria took over Israel. Once that happened, Judah and its capital, Jerusalem, were under constant threat. Nahum directed his prophecy to Assyria and particularly to its capital, Nineveh.

Remember that Nineveh was the town that Jonah prophesied to after the whole big-fish-regurgitating-a-prophet-on-the-beach fiasco. One of the reasons Jonah hadn't wanted to preach to Nineveh was that they were the enemy. That was also why he was less than thrilled when they repented and God did not destroy them. That was about one hundred years before Nahum's day.

Nineveh did not stay in a repented state. They returned to their evil ways. Nahum faced them with the news that God would punish their evil once and for all. Hands down. No holds barred. Sparing no expense. No questions asked.

questions

Q. Why are the books at the end of the Old Testament called the "Minor" Prophets?

A. The prophets spoke to different audiences over a number of years, but each emphasized common themes: Sin is condemned; holiness is encouraged; judgment is coming; and the pain of God's judgment will be followed soon by the joyous arrival of Messiah.

In the same way that the four Gospels (Matthew, Mark, Luke, and John) describe the life of Jesus Christ but focus on different aspects of His person and work, so the prophets took basic messages to their respective audiences. Overlap and repetition in the prophetic books are the result.

"Minor" reflects size, not significance. The final twelve prophetic books are generally shorter than the five major prophets (except Lamentations, written by Jeremiah and "attached" to his longer work).

Habakkuk

IN CONTEXT

Here's the scoop. . .

Written: *around 600 B.C.*

Written by: *Habakkuk*

Writing style: *a sermon in the form of questions and answers*

One-liner: *God, why don't You stop bad things from happening?*

THE HARD QUESTIONS

Habakkuk was honest enough to ask the hard questions. In fact, that was how his prophecy began. As refreshing as it is to hear a prophet of God ask the questions we have often asked, it's even more refreshing to know that Habakkuk got answers.

Basically God told Habakkuk what a lot of good dads tell their kids: You're going to have to trust Me to take care of this in My own time. God said that punishing evil was up to Him alone. He reminded Habakkuk, though, that evil would not go unpunished in the end.

One of the interesting things about Habakkuk's prophecy is that he began with hard questions, but he ended with worship. That happens a lot when you sit with God long enough to hear His answers and to trust them. After Habakkuk listened to God, he accepted God's control over the situation. He closed with this prayer:

Though the fig tree does not bud and there are no grapes on the vines,
though the olive crop fails and the fields produce no food,
though there are no sheep in the pen and no cattle in the stalls. . .

(In Habakkuk's day this meant, "Though the economy is going to pot and we aren't going to survive. . . .")

. . .yet I will rejoice in the LORD, I will be joyful in God my Savior
(Habakkuk 3:17–18).

Most of us define who God is in our lives according to our current circumstances. Habakkuk looked into the face of the worst of life and still found there God's faithfulness.

COMPARISON

Habakkuk was a lot like David in the fact that he was willing to look through the "hard stuff" to see God. Compare the following writing of David to that of Habakkuk:

But as for me, I came so close to the edge of the cliff! My feet were slipping, and I was almost gone. For I envied the proud when I saw them prosper despite their wickedness. They seem to live such a painless life; their bodies are so healthy and strong. They aren't troubled like other people or plagued with problems like everyone else. . . .

And so the people are dismayed and confused, drinking in all their words. "Does God realize what is going on?" they ask. "Is the Most High even aware of what is happening? . . ."

Then I realized how bitter I had become, how pained I had been by all I had seen. I was so foolish and ignorant—I must have seemed like a senseless animal to you. Yet I still belong to you; you are holding my right hand. You will keep on guiding me with your counsel, leading me to a glorious destiny. Whom have I in heaven but you? I desire you more than anything on earth. My health may fail, and my spirit may grow weak, but God remains the strength of my heart; he is mine forever (Psalm 73:2–5, 10–11, 21–26 NLT).

SCRIPTURE BITS

Habakkuk asks God the kinds of questions we would often like to ask:

How long, O LORD, must I call for help,
 but you do not listen?
 Or cry out to you, "Violence!"
 but you do not save?
Why do you make me look at injustice?
 Why do you tolerate wrong?

Habakkuk 1:2–3

questions q&a

Q. *Why does God make us wait for the answers to our prayers?*
(Habakkuk 1:2)

A. *Habakkuk opens his short book with words heard many times in every life,*
basically "Who's listening to my prayers?" Several psalms echo the same
sentiment. (See Psalms 6 and 10.)

> *Typically we answer this common complaint by observing that human*
time and divine timelessness do not always match well. God is not limited
by time. A delay to us is not a delay to God. This answer fails, however,
because God the Creator established the circumstances of temporality and
understands perfectly how time-bound people feel. God would no more insist
that people disregard feelings about time than that they disregard the law of
gravity. Both are absolute conditions of human experience.

> *The appropriate answer to delayed answers to prayer is that God wills*
it so. God's will is not open to human review or judgment; neither is God
obligated to pick up the phone, so to speak. God hears our prayers by His
own generous will, and He answers likewise. God's wise answer may not
correspond, either in substance or in timing, to our own choice in the mat-
ter. Neither is God likely to debate His will for us, as if His answer or timing
needed justification.

> *The key to prayer is faithful communication with our Creator and*
Redeemer. Pray without ceasing, Paul urges (1 Thessalonians 5:17). In
Habakkuk's case, prayer took the form of a complaint concerning God's will-
ingness to listen, but the complaint itself demonstrates the prophet's underly-
ing faith: There's no point in complaining about prayer, in a prayer, unless
you believe that God hears your prayers. Habakkuk believed this, and so
should we, even when we are impatient for answers.

zephaniah

IN CONTEXT

Here's the scoop. . .

Written: *around 630 B.C.*

Written by: *Zephaniah*

Writing style: *a message directly from God*

One-liner: *God will hold us accountable for our actions. All of them.*

Zephaniah was one of the last prophets to Judah before the people were taken captive into Babylonia. His message, though first to Judah, was to all nations. He reminded the Hebrews that God would hold them accountable for their actions. He reminds us still today.

The first section of Zephaniah, which is the section on judgment, is classic among the prophets. You may have heard the term "hellfire and brimstone" to describe a preacher who is really letting his listeners have it. Zephaniah's message started out that way. Then gradually he moved from a place of condemnation to a place of hope.

Zephaniah actually followed the pattern of many self-help groups today. First, he knew the people needed to recognize just how much they had messed up. Then he could offer them hope that they weren't alone in their situation. The last portion of Zephaniah even points to the coming of Christ as the greatest hope of salvation.

questions

Q. *What will the "day of the LORD" be like? (Zephaniah 1:7)*

A. *According to Zephaniah, it will happen suddenly and will be unavoidable, global in scale, and catastrophic in nature. This coming day of judgment will involve both Israel and the Gentile nations (3:9–20).*

The phrase, in its broadest sense, refers to the absolute and righteous reign of God over His creation. Hints of this day occur in history at various times when God powerfully intervenes to bring about judgment. The most important of those interventions is the first coming of Christ and His conquering of sin, Satan, and death by His own death and resurrection (Luke 10:18; John 3:19).

A more common view sees the day of the Lord (in its fullness) as future—an extended period of time beginning at the second coming of Christ and including all of the events through God's recreation of the heavens and earth (Isaiah 65:17–19; 66:22; 2 Peter 3:13; Revelation 21:1). The terrible judgments associated with the day of the Lord (Zephaniah 1:15–16) are described in Revelation 4–19.

Q. *What's so important about the prediction of Nineveh's downfall? (Zephaniah 2:13–15)*

A. *At the time of Zephaniah's prophecy, Assyria (of which Nineveh was the capital) was the greatest, most powerful empire on earth. For three hundred years, the Assyrians had conquered all peoples in their path. Nineveh, the shining center of Assyrian culture, learning, and technology, was considered invincible with its high walls and state-of-the-art defenses. To predict its destruction was startling and unthinkable. Such a prediction posed the seemingly invincible power of worldly might against a seemingly invisible power of spiritual truth.*

Q. *"How can imaginary ideas bring down an empire?" a secularist would wonder.*

A. *"How can a mere empire stand against the power of almighty God?" a Christian would reply. Mere empires cannot get away with rebellion against God forever. Eventually they meet real power.*

Q. *Why is God (the true and only God) so perturbed at false gods (fakes)? It could seem like a case of self-doubt and insecurity. (Zephaniah 3:8)*

A. *The scriptures describe God as jealous (Exodus 20:5; 34:14; Deuteronomy 4:24; Joshua 24:19) and unwilling to share His glory with another. This has nothing to do with self-doubt and everything to do with righteousness. As the holy and awesome Creator, God alone deserves ultimate honor. To worship what is not God is the consummate perversion. As creatures made by God, we cannot find ultimate fulfillment apart from Him. To give place to false gods is to miss out on the pleasure of knowing and serving God. Because idolatry robs people of the truth and robs God of honor, God hates it—emphatically, certainly, and uncompromisingly.*

Haggai

IN CONTEXT

Here's the scoop. . .

Written: *around 500 B.C.*

Written by: *Haggai*

Writing style: *five short sermons*

One-liner: *Don't ignore what matters most—your relationship with your God and Creator!*

SETTING PRIORITIES

The book of Haggai is about priorities. Unlike the book of Zephaniah, written before the exile from Judah to Babylon, Haggai was written after the exile. The people had returned to Judah but were putting off making God a priority by not restoring their place of worship, the temple. Haggai confronted them with their procrastination: "What are you doing leaving God's house in a mess so you can work on your own?"

Haggai's message can seem a little backward to us. After all, we are always hearing that expression "Charity starts at home." Weren't the people right to work on their own homes first? Well. . .remember two things:

1. *It had been at least ten years since they returned home.* It's not like Haggai was telling them to rebuild the temple before they even unpacked their bags. They had established a pattern of not getting around to it.

2. *The problem all along with the Jewish people, in fact the reason they lost their homes to begin with, was a lack of priority on worship.* God had told them, "Only worship Me." But they hadn't listened. Rebuilding the temple would be a significant step to establishing a new pattern of living. It was about their own attention to their spiritual well-being, not just a building.

Haggai also spoke to the people about the future temple. That meant far in the future, when Jesus would return to earth and the new heaven and new earth would be in place. Coming from Haggai, this served as a reminder that better days were ahead.

questions

Q. *Why was rebuilding the temple so important to the Israelites?*
(Haggai 2:3)

A. *The temple was the center of religious life in Israel since the time of David and Solomon. The ark of the covenant was placed there. The temple represented the presence of the Lord; there the Lord revealed His will to the people. It also was a mark of Israel's unity in the worship of the Lord.*

The temple was destroyed and its contents carried to Babylon when Nebuchadnezzar defeated Judah and took its people into exile. Daniel records that the sacred objects of the temple of God were taken and placed in the treasure house of the god of Babylon. It was as if God had been defeated and taken captive. The temple's destruction was a graphic reminder of God's punishment for the people's rebellion and wickedness.

The rebuilding of the temple was a symbol for the exiles of hope that God was still among them and an affirmation of their commitment to believe in God's promise that the kingdom of David would be forever—that God would continue His covenant relationship by sending a new leader (a messiah) to restore the nation.

zechariah

IN CONTEXT

Here's the scoop. . .

Written: *around 500 B.C.*

Written by: *Zechariah*

Writing style: *two sermons*

One-liner: *Finish the temple and get your relationship with God in working order. The Messiah is coming!*

IT'S ABOUT TIME!

The first part of the book of Zechariah relates most closely to the rebuilding of the temple in Jerusalem. Zechariah wrote to motivate the people. "It really is worth it!" was Zechariah's message.

The second part of Zechariah holds more prophecies about Jesus than any other Old Testament book of prophecy.

- Jesus rode into Jerusalem riding on a donkey a week before He died (Zechariah 9:9).

- Judas betrayed Jesus Christ for thirty pieces of silver (Zechariah 11:12).

- Jesus' side was pierced during the crucifixion (Zechariah 12:10).

- Jesus' blood cleansed our sin (Zechariah 13:1).

- Jesus had scars in His hands and side (Zechariah 13:6).

- Jesus was arrested and deserted by His disciples (Zechariah 13:7).

- Zechariah also prophesied Jesus' second return to reign on earth (Zechariah 14:4; Revelation 11:15).

questions

Q. *How does God compare to a wall of fire? (Zechariah 2:5)*

A. *Zechariah's prophecy was intended to inspire spiritual renewal among Jewish believers who had returned to Jerusalem and faced the rebuilding of the temple. Yet the prophecy greatly expanded that narrow vision. Instead of a temple where God would dwell, the promise was that God would dwell "among you." Instead of stone walls for protection from aggression, the Lord would be their wall of fire. This type of wall accomplished three purposes stones could never do: (1) It kept enemies far away—there's no threatening approach with fire leaping into the sky; (2) it expanded the city at will—a fire wall expands to accommodate more area or protect more people. In this case, people from many nations would join with those Jews protected by the Lord; and (3) it consumed when it turned inward—the people must hear God's message and obey. The tone of the promise here was not to motivate through fear, however, but through faith in God's power to protect and provide. The future was full of possibilities. Be full of faith, the prophet urged.*

maLachi

IN CONTEXT

Here's the scoop. . .

Written: *around 400 B.C.*

Written by: *Malachi*

Writing style: *a sermon in the form of questions and answers*

One-liner: *Worshiping God is not about doing the least to get by. Be wholehearted instead.*

LAST BUT NOT LEAST

Malachi is the prophet who connects the Old Testament to the New Testament. He prophesied about John the Baptist and was the last prophet until John the Baptist. While not all of the books of the Old Testament are in chronological order, Malachi really is. It was the last book written and it is the last book in the Old Testament.

Malachi reminded the people that they were making a halfhearted attempt at keeping God's law. They brought their sacrifices, but they brought the most damaged of their animals and crops. They were living as if God could not see their hearts and know that they didn't really honor Him. They were doing the least they could to still have some semblance of a life of faith.

Malachi also reprimanded the people for the same practice that the Hebrews were guilty of since they came to their land: They continued to marry into families who worshiped idols, and so the Hebrews would begin to mix idol worship into their own worship. In Malachi's day, the men were even divorcing their Hebrew wives to marry foreign wives.

Malachi foretold the coming of John the Baptist as well as of Jesus Christ.

questions

Q. *Is it possible for God to hate a people forever? (Malachi 1:4)*

A. *It is possible, if a people rebel from God and abuse His law. The Edomites had a long history of "hands-off" anything associated with God's people or true worship. The Edomites had grown stubborn, intransigent, and self-willed, never relaxing their guard against the truth. The hate God expresses to such people is not a general hatred of people, for that would contradict God's character. The hate is against their willful rebellion. As God will never relax His holiness, compromise with sin, or negotiate with evil, so the hatred of God against sin stands as long as sin is a people's purpose and priority. The Edomites knew what they were about, and it was wrong. God's mercy, though not explicit in this passage, is everlasting and always welcomes repentant sinners into God's family.*

new Testament Book summaries

The following pages include a little information about each of the books in the New Testament. Just as with the Old Testament, these books are marked off in sections (Gospels, history, letters, prophecy), but they are in the order that they appear in the Bible.

For each book you can read some facts and a one-liner overview, or you can dig a little deeper and read the major stories or points of that book.

Keep in mind that this was a phenomenal time in world history as well as Christian history. The life of Christ changed everything—power structures, world views, and so on. You know how you feel when you are working on a new project that is really important to you? Maybe you're working on a project like building a house through Habitat for Humanity or helping at the homeless shelter. Think of setting out on a project that you really believe in. That is the kind of atmosphere in which these books were written, but it was *life* for these guys rather than a weeklong excursion.

Get a load of this accusation made against the early Christian leaders:

But the Jewish leaders were jealous, so they gathered some worthless fellows from the streets to form a mob and start a riot. They attacked the home of Jason, searching for Paul and Silas so they could drag them out to the crowd. Not finding them there, they dragged out Jason and some of the other believers instead and took them before the city council. "Paul and Silas have turned the rest of the world upside down, and now they are here disturbing our city," they shouted (Acts 17:5–6 NLT).

Turning the world upside down. That's what the New Testament is really about.

The Gospels

There are four Gospels. They are each written by a different person. You've probably heard them called "the Gospel according to Matthew," "the Gospel of Mark," and so on. "Gospel" means "good news." The good news was that Jesus was the Messiah. Each of these men wanted to write about Jesus' life in such a way that he could convince his audience that Jesus really was the one God had promised throughout history.

The Gospels aren't really biographies in that the authors didn't try to write down Jesus' life in chronological order. They each organized what they wanted to say differently. They included different information. Matthew was writing to a Jewish audience, so he included a lot of quotes from the Old Testament. Mark was writing to a Roman (or non-Jewish) audience, so he didn't refer to Jewish history in any big way at all. Each writer brought a different slant to the story. What they had in common, though, was that they desperately wanted their readers to understand that Jesus wasn't just one more martyr, just one more prophet, just one more Christian celebrity. Instead, Jesus was the Messiah the whole Old Testament had wrapped its hope around. Jesus was the fulfillment of God's promise to make an open door between Himself and humanity. Jesus was God coming to us to pay the price for humanity's waywardness.

IN CONTEXT

The Gospels

• Matthew

• Mark

• Luke

• John

Matthew

Here's the scoop. . .

Written: *around* A.D. *60*

Written by: *Matthew*

Writing style: *a biographical narrative, a collection of true stories*

One-liner: *Hebrew friends, Jesus is the Messiah that God promised through the prophets, and here's how I know.*

MATTHEW'S TAKE ON IT

This was Matthew's slant: Jesus is the promised Messiah. Matthew included more Old Testament prophecies than any other writer. He traced Jesus' genealogy back to Abraham, who is the father of the Hebrews. Matthew established Jesus' role as the one his people had been waiting for.

The book of Matthew is the first of four Gospels, or versions, of the story of Christ. Each of the Gospels has a different slant, a different perspective. They tell the stories in a different order or with different details. Each of the writers gives a true but different viewpoint on Jesus' life.

THE PROBLEM

Unfortunately, Jesus' importance was pretty difficult for the Hebrews to swallow. Throughout the Old Testament, they had heard the promise of the Messiah. Each time they were oppressed (even if it was a consequence of their own sin), they comforted themselves by remembering the promise of the Messiah. The problem was, they thought the Messiah was going to be a political and military ruler who would destroy their enemies with a single blast. That was not the kind of messiah Jesus was, at least not this first time around.

As Matthew revealed, Jesus came to die for our sins, not beat up our enemies. He came to show us another way of *living*, not winning. He came to save us from ourselves.

This is why the religious leaders of the day didn't get it. Here was the Jesus they had watched grow up. They knew His parents. They had been to His hometown. He didn't look like anything special to them. And He was claiming to be God? They just couldn't go for that. Add to that the fact that Jesus confronted them on a regular basis about their own hypocrisy, and they were first upset, then resentful, then jealous, then out to get Him.

So after all the dust had settled, after Jesus had lived before Matthew's eyes and worked miracles and died, then come back to life and gone back to heaven, Matthew sat down to set the record straight. He methodically recorded the events and the teachings of Jesus' life so that (in his mind) any reader would know, without a doubt, that Jesus was the Messiah.

A NEW KINGDOM

Jesus had come to establish a new kingdom, all right; it just wasn't the kingdom of Israel. It was a new kingdom in people's hearts. That was a difficult concept to understand. It was easier to reject Jesus and look for someone else who fit the expectations a little better.

Matthew closed his version of Jesus' life with a famous statement that we now call the "Great Commission."

"Therefore go and make disciples of all nations, baptizing them in the name of the Father and of the Son and of the Holy Spirit, and teaching them to obey everything I have commanded you. And surely I am with you always, to the very end of the age" (Matthew 28:19–20).

In other words, Jesus came to establish the kingdom of heaven in the hearts of people. Then He wanted His followers to go and do the same.

questions

Q. *When was Jesus born? (Matthew 1:18)*

A. *Christians around the world celebrate December 25 as Jesus' birth date, but of course no one knows the exact date of His birth, nor are we sure of the year. Based on political information contained in the Gospels, Jesus was likely born in the year 4 B.C.*

Q. *What was the "good news of the kingdom" that Jesus preached? (Matthew 4:23)*

A. *The full answer to this question requires that we start in Genesis and end in Revelation; that is, that we review the entire Bible and all of God's dealing with creation. The good news about the kingdom is simply that God has loved His creation and wills to save it, not destroy it, and that God's will is being accomplished before the eyes of the listeners of this message—both Jesus' immediate listeners and all who hear Jesus' message today. This is the meaning of everything in the Bible from the beginning to the end: God has come, through His Son, Jesus Christ, to seek and to save the lost.*

SCRIPTURE BITS

The Be-a-ti-whats?

The Beatitudes are probably the most famous passage in Matthew. How's your memory?

Blessed are the poor in spirit, for theirs is the. . .
Blessed are those who mourn, for they will be. . .
Blessed are the meek, for they will inherit the. . .
Blessed are those who hunger and thirst for righteousness,
*   for they will be. . .*
Blessed are the merciful, for they will be shown. . .
Blessed are the pure in heart, for they will see. . .
Blessed are the peacemakers, for they will be called sons of. . .
Blessed are those who are persecuted because of their righteousness,
*   for theirs is the kingdom of. . .*

Matthew 5:3–10

Answer Key

kingdom of heaven
comforted
earth
filled
mercy
God
God
heaven

mark

Here's the scoop. . .

Written: *around A.D. 60*

Written by: *John Mark*

Writing style: *a biographical narrative*

One-liner: *Hey, Romans, Jesus was a servant-king. Look what He did!*

LIGHTS, ACTION!

Mark was a writer who loved action verbs. He wrote about what Christ did, His miracles especially. Mark's Gospel is the shortest of all four Gospels. It is the most "to the point."

Mark represented Jesus as a servant. He displayed Jesus' miracles as acts of compassion. Almost half of the book of Mark covers the last eight days of Jesus' life, during which He gave Himself away for our salvation—His greatest act of servanthood.

Mark and Matthew wrote from different standpoints. Matthew focused on the Messiah-ship of Jesus. Mark focused on the servant-leadership of Jesus. Matthew spoke to a Jewish audience and built his case based on Jewish tradition. Mark spoke to a Roman audience and focused on Jesus' compassion for all humanity. Mark told three miracles of Jesus in the first chapter, where Matthew only recorded one miracle in the first seven chapters. Matthew opened with the birth of Christ, but Mark opened with Jesus as an adult.

MARK'S SOURCES

Though Mark was not a disciple of Jesus, he was connected to Jesus in several ways. The disciples met at his mother's home. He was very close to the disciple Peter. His cousin was Barnabas, a colleague of the apostle Paul. Mark even traveled with Paul and Barnabas for a time on one of their missionary journeys.

Since Mark was a "cut-to-the-chase" kind of guy, he wrote some bottom-line verses that put a lot of truth in a little space for us to digest:

Then [Jesus] called the crowd to him along with his disciples and said: "If anyone would come after me, he must deny himself and take up his cross and follow me. For whoever wants to save his life will lose it, but whoever loses his life for me and for the gospel will save it. What good is it for a man to gain the whole world, yet forfeit his soul?" (Mark 8:34–36).

"For even the Son of Man did not come to be served, but to serve, and to give his life as a ransom for many" (Mark 10:45).

Mark's Gospel was such an action-packed, bottom-line kind of description of Jesus' life and work that Matthew and Luke used Mark's work as a source for their own Gospels.

THE LAST WEEK OF JESUS' MINISTRY

Of the sixteen chapters in Mark, the last seven cover the last week of Christ's life. Chapter 11 opens with Jesus' entry into Jerusalem. This event was perhaps the most misunderstood event of Christ's adult ministry. The people were looking for a king, a political military leader who could rid them of their oppression. When they welcomed Jesus that day into the city, they thought they were welcoming that kind of leader.

But Jesus was coming to Jerusalem to die for the sins of the world, not to become a national leader for a small nation.

Mark recorded several significant events from that last week of Jesus' life to help his readers understand Jesus' mission. He recorded conversations that Jesus had with the religious leaders of the day, trying to clarify for them that He was the Son of God. But all they could ask Him were questions about taxes and trick questions in a feeble attempt to prove their superiority.

Mark also recorded the story you've probably heard about the widow who gave her small offering—two coins. Jesus used her offering to teach the disciples what true giving is about. The impoverished woman had given more than anyone else at the temple that day, because she had given all she had.

MARK'S CLOSING REMARKS

Mark closed his Gospel with the resurrection of Christ, the empty tomb, and the angel explaining to the women (and to the world through Mark) that Jesus was, indeed, dead but had come back to life and was still all about doing God's business. This is the very thing Mark had set out to reveal all along.

SCRIPTURE BITS

A Revolutionary View

So Jesus called [the disciples] together and said, "You know that in this world kings are tyrants, and officials lord it over the people beneath them. But among you it should be quite different. Whoever wants to be a leader among you must be your servant, and whoever wants to be first must be the slave of all. For even I, the Son of Man, came here not to be served but to serve others, and to give my life as a ransom for many."

Mark 10:42–45 NLT

questions q&a

Q. *What is God's good news? (Mark 1:14)*

A. *The good news God has for people is all wrapped up in the person, life, and teachings of Jesus Christ. When Jesus started His ministry, He declared that a new time in history had arrived—the God who created this world and all its people was now on the planet in a human body. It was good news to know that God was not far away or disconnected from this world.*

In Jesus we see that God hears our cries and prayers. He knows us and the situations of our lives. We know God loves us and cares for us. It's good news—we are not alone.

The best part of Jesus' good news is that we can have peace with God despite our sinful nature and behavior. Although it seems too good to be true, God sent Jesus into the world to pay for our sins when He was crucified on the cross. God promises that if we believe on Jesus, we will be given everlasting life (see John 3:16). What we cannot do for ourselves, God has done for us through Jesus. Now that's good news!

Luke

IN CONTEXT

Here's the scoop. . .

Written: *around* A.D. *60*

Written by: *Luke*

Writing style: *a biographical narrative*

One-liner: *Amazing news! Jesus is God and yet totally human. He understands our journey.*

THE GOOD DOCTOR

Matthew, the disciple and former tax collector, wrote to convince the Jewish people that Jesus was the promised Messiah. Mark, the missionary sidekick, wrote to convince the Romans that Jesus was a servant and a Savior. Luke, the doctor, wrote to convince his Greek friend Theophilus that Jesus was God but was also fully and completely human. In other words, since we couldn't reconcile with God on our own, He became one of us to accomplish the task.

> *Having carefully investigated all of these accounts from the beginning, I have decided to write a careful summary for you, to reassure you of the truth of all you were taught (Luke 1:3–4 NLT).*

There's a lot of joy in the opening of Luke. Zechariah, an old priest, was happy that his wife would finally bear a child. Mary, the mother of Jesus was happy that God had chosen to use her. Elizabeth, Zechariah's wife, was happy that she and Mary were pregnant with boys who would make a difference for God. Zechariah was even happier when he finally got his voice back after the birth of his son, John.

The angels were happy when they told the shepherds that Jesus was finally born. The shepherds were happy enough to travel into the city and greet this baby-king.

When Mary and Joseph took Jesus to the temple to dedicate their baby, they met two older people, Anna and Simeon, who recognized that Jesus wasn't just any baby, and they celebrated right then and there. A sacred party was going on.

LUKE'S STRATEGY

Because Luke was writing from the perspective of the wonder of Jesus' humanity, he included some interesting facts that the other Gospel writers didn't include. He gave insights into Christ's childhood. He documented Christ's compassion in dealing with the people around Him. Luke's Gospel makes the point that Jesus wasn't too high and mighty to get down and dirty when ministry demanded it. His priority was becoming a part of our journey and teaching us a better way.

Luke reveals to us Jesus' friendships. He mentions more women than any other Gospel. He reveals to us that Jesus really was God come to earth to walk many hard miles in our sandals. Luke reveals to us a Jesus who ultimately died so that we could find forgiveness.

THE LUKE EXCLUSIVE

Here are some stories that Luke included that none of the other Gospel writers included. These stories offer insight into Jesus' everyday life.

Jesus visited two friends, Mary and Martha, in their home. Martha was an organizer and was running around breathlessly. Mary was an admirer and spent her time sitting at Jesus' feet. When Martha complained, Jesus affirmed Mary's choice—to just be with Him (Luke 10:38–42).

IN CONTEXT

Matthew opened with a genealogy because that's what would matter to his audience. Mark opened with Jesus' adult ministry because that's what would matter to his audience. Luke opened with a whole lot of celebration. Maybe that's what Theophilus needed to hear. Maybe it's what we need to hear, as well.

SCRIPTURE BITS

if i've heard it once...

These verses have appeared everywhere from rural church Christmas pageants to Charlie Brown's Christmas special. All from Luke's commitment to making sure his friend Theophilus knew who Jesus was.

Now there were in the same country shepherds living out in the fields, keeping watch over their flock by night. And behold, an angel of the Lord stood before them, and the glory of the Lord shone around them, and they were greatly afraid. Then the angel said to them, "Do not be afraid, for behold, I bring you good tidings of great joy which will be to all people. For there is born to you this day in the city of David a Savior, who is Christ the Lord. And this will be the sign to you: You will find a Babe wrapped in swaddling cloths, lying in a manger." And suddenly there was with the angel a multitude of the heavenly host praising God and saying: "Glory to God in the highest, and on earth peace, goodwill toward men!" So it was, when the angels had gone away from them into heaven, that the shepherds said to one another, "Let us now go to Bethlehem and see this thing that has come to pass, which the Lord has made known to us." And they came with haste and found Mary and Joseph, and the Babe lying in a manger. Now when they had seen Him, they made widely known the saying which was told them concerning this Child. And all those who heard it marveled at those things which were told them by the shepherds. But Mary kept all these things and pondered them in her heart. Then the shepherds returned, glorifying and praising God for all the things that they had heard and seen, as it was told them.

Luke 2:8–20 NKJV

One day Jesus was teaching His disciples within earshot of the Pharisees, religious leaders who had (more often than not) made a business of their piety. These leaders loved money, and more than that they loved looking righteous. In their presence Jesus told a story about some workers who were given the responsibility to invest their boss's money while he was out of town. Some of the workers invested in the wrong kinds of things, or just didn't invest at all. Then when their boss came back, he held them accountable. They didn't have much to say for their lives (Luke 16:1–17:10). Jesus didn't win any points with the Pharisees that day.

Then there was the day that ten, count 'em, ten lepers came to Jesus to be healed. Jesus healed them and sent them to the priest to be proclaimed well. Out of the ten, only one came back to express his gratitude. Jesus asked him, with perhaps a twinkle in His eye, something like this: "Now weren't there ten of you? Where are your buddies?" (Luke 17:11–19).

Jesus told two parables about prayer that only Luke recorded. In the first, a widow came to a judge to ask for a judgment against her enemy. She was a woman and she was a widow, so she was not high on the power scale or the social ladder. Because of her perseverance, though, the judge finally granted her request. Jesus' message? Don't stop praying.

In the second parable, two men went to pray at the temple. One was proud and prayed to be seen by others. The other was humble and prayed to be forgiven by God. What was the point? The humble man was the one God heard (Luke 18:1–14).

questions q&a

Q. *What makes Luke's Gospel "inspired" while other Gospels (the Gospel of Barnabas, the Gospel of Thomas) are not included in the Bible? (Luke 1:1)*

A. Luke was a physician (Colossians 4:14) and a traveling companion to the apostle Paul, and he is the only Gentile author in the New Testament. He wrote the third Gospel and Acts.

Scholars regard Luke as a historian of the first rank. His account of the life of Christ and the birth and growth of the church is marked by careful research and rings with authenticity. Because he traveled with Paul, an eyewitness of the risen Christ, he was qualified to write an account of the life of Christ.

A book of ancient writing had to meet certain standards to be included in the canon. Various early church councils sorted through the many circulated writings to canonize those that bore the mark of being "inspired by God" (2 Timothy 3:16).

Luke's Gospel met these standards: (1) authority—it is backed by an apostle, Paul of Tarsus; (2) unity—it harmonizes with (rather than diverges from) the rest of the scriptural record; (3) uniqueness—internal evidence indicates its inspiration; and (4) acceptance—circulated soon after its writing, the Gospel of Luke was regarded by the churches as an inspired book.

Writings that failed to pass these tests were regarded as either apocryphal books or the so-called pseudepigrapha (the "false writings").

John

Here's the scoop. . .

Written: *around* A.D. *90*

Written by: *John, the disciple*

Writing style: *a biographical profile*

One-liner: *It really is true. Jesus Christ is God Himself.*

JOHN'S GOSPEL

John wrote his Gospel after Matthew, Mark, and Luke's were already written. The first three Gospels had a lot of similarities. The book of John added some variety.

Matthew opened with a genealogy. Mark opened with the beginning of Jesus' adult ministry. Luke opened with the celebration of Jesus' birth. John opened with a symbolic, almost poetic, definitely philosophic introduction of Jesus at the very creation of the world.

> *In the beginning was the Word, and the Word was with God, and the Word was God. He was with God in the beginning. Through him all things were made; without him nothing was made that has been made. In him was life, and that life was the light of men.*
>
> *The Word became flesh and made his dwelling among us. We have seen his glory, the glory of the One and Only, who came from the Father, full of grace and truth (John 1:1–4, 14).*

John established Jesus' deity by revealing that He created the very world in which we live.

THE INCARNATION

Jesus' act of becoming man and taking on a human body is called the "incarnation." (You've probably heard *reincarnation* more than just *incarnation*.) It was and still is a mystery. How can someone be fully God and fully person? It takes faith to believe.

If God wasn't fully human, His death for our sins wouldn't mean the same thing. He wouldn't have been one of us. If He wasn't fully God, His death for our sins wouldn't mean anything, either. One person can't just decide to take a punishment for the whole world. It takes God, the Creator of the universe, to decide that.

ONLY IN JOHN

Here are some stories from the life of Jesus that you can find only in the Gospel of John.

John is the only Gospel that records Jesus' first miracle at a wedding in Cana. They ran out of wine. At the request of His mother, and with a little negotiation between them, Jesus changed some plain old well water into wine so the host wouldn't be embarrassed (John 2:1–11).

From the beginning of His ministry, Jesus ferociously confronted the men who made the temple into a marketplace. He defended the temple as his own territory (John 2:12–25).

An enlightened Pharisee, Nicodemus, came to Jesus at night to find out if He was for real. It was during this conversation that Jesus firmly established the concept of being "born again." It's also where Jesus spoke the famous words we now know as John 3:16—"God so loved the world that He gave his one and only Son. . ." (John 3:1–21).

You may have heard the story that is often called the story of the woman at the well. Besides being a woman (in a culture that devalued women), this woman was a Samaritan (with whom the Jewish people had a major racial conflict). Her conversation with Jesus revealed His lack of concern for status and His love for humans in general (John 4:1–42).

IN CONTEXT

Matthew focused on Christ's Messiahship, which was a very Jewish issue. Mark focused on Jesus as a servant. Luke focused on Christ's humanity, even though He was deity. John focused on Jesus as the Son of God—on His deity—even though He was human.

In an amazing account, Jesus was confronted by the religious leaders with a woman who was caught in adultery (which at that time was punishable by death). Because of the absence of the man who had been caught with her, and because of the political climate, Jesus recognized this confrontation as a trap. Rather than condemn her, Jesus confronted the sin in the lives of the accusers (John 8:1–11).

Jesus also raised His friend Lazarus from the dead just by calling out his name (John 11:1–44).

SCRIPTURE BITS

john's Bottom Line

But although the world was made through him, the world didn't recognize him when he came. Even in his own land and among his own people, he was not accepted. But to all who believed him and accepted him, he gave the right to become children of God. They are reborn! This is not a physical birth resulting from human passion or plan—this rebirth comes from God. So the Word [Jesus] became human and lived here on earth among us. He was full of unfailing love and faithfulness. And we have seen his glory, the glory of the only Son of the Father.

John 1:10–14 NLT

questions & a

Q. *In what way was Jesus the "Word"? (John 1:1)*

A. *John's use of "Word" to describe Jesus was a startling new application of a popular expression. The term was used widely by theologians and philosophers, both Jews and Greeks. It described the agent of creation (Psalm 33:6); God's message to His people through the prophets (Hosea 1:2); and God's law, His standard of holiness (Psalm 119:11). In Greek philosophy, "the Word" was the principle of reason that governed the world. John's description shows clearly that he is speaking of Jesus (John 1:14)—a human being he knew and loved, yet at the same time the Creator of the universe, the revelation of God, the living picture of God's holiness.*

Use of the term held certain risks for John's Gospel. Jewish readers would hear blasphemy in calling any human person the Word of God. Learned Greek readers would consider "the Word became flesh" (John 1:14) unthinkable, incomprehensible. To John and to all Christians after him, this new understanding of the Word was gospel, the good news of Jesus Christ.

HISTORY BOOKS

After the life and ministry of Jesus Christ, the New Testament focuses on the church, the followers Jesus left behind to do His work. We often think of this period of history as archaic. After all, they didn't even have big buses to carry youth groups on mission trips! But if you'll look closely, they were pretty organized for a world that had just figured out they needed to use antiseptic on wounds.

ACTS

IN CONTEXT

Here's the scoop. . .

Written: *around* A.D. *65*

Written by: *Luke (the same Luke who wrote the Gospel)*

Writing style: *a chronological narrative*

One-liner: *A new church organizes: Jesus' sacrifice makes us right with God. Spread the news!*

WALKING ACROSS ACTS

The book of Acts is a sequel to the Gospel of Luke and is a bridge between the Gospels and the epistles (or letters) of the New Testament. The Gospels contain the story of Jesus' life and ministry. The epistles contain encouragement and training for the early church. The book of Acts records how the church got organized from a group of bewildered disciples into the "body of Christ" in the world.

PENTECOST

Just after Jesus returned to heaven (this was after His death and resurrection), the Jewish people were scheduled to celebrate an annual feast called Pentecost. As they gathered together, an unexpected and wonderful thing happened. The Holy Spirit came. This was a huge event.

Jesus had given the disciples a promise about this: "The Counselor, the Holy Spirit, whom the Father will send in my name, will teach you all things and will remind you of everything I have said to you" (John 14:26).

Closing your eyes and imagining what it would cost a special effects team to recreate this event puts it into a little better perspective.

On the day of Pentecost, seven weeks after Jesus' resurrection, the believers were meeting together in one place. Suddenly, there was a sound from heaven like the roaring of a mighty windstorm in the skies above them, and it filled the house where they were meeting. Then, what looked like flames or tongues of fire appeared and settled on each of them. And everyone present was filled with the Holy Spirit and began speaking in other languages, as the Holy Spirit gave them this ability.

> *Godly Jews from many nations were living in Jerusalem at that time. When they heard this sound, they came running to see what it was all about, and they were bewildered to hear their own languages being spoken by the believers.*
>
> *They were beside themselves with wonder. "How can this be?" they exclaimed. "These people are all from Galilee, and yet we hear them speaking the languages of the lands where we were born!" (Acts 2:1–8 NLT).*

Do you understand the significance of this event? In the Old Testament, people, even believers, related to God mostly in the temple. It wasn't that God was any different. He was everywhere and wherever He wanted to be. But He was revealed to humanity through a holy place or a pillar of fire or a burning bush. Then God came to humanity as Jesus, to accomplish His own sacrifice. But at Pentecost God came to humanity to make His home in each of us. It was a whole different way of experiencing God's presence and power.

This was the beginning of the early church. At this point those who believed in Jesus' resurrection began to get organized. They began to determine specific ministry roles. They began to share their money and possessions with those who didn't have any. They began to organize to go out and share the news of Jesus' forgiveness through His death. Everything was fresh and new. The rules had all changed. The church was changing with them.

THE EARLY CHURCH

The early believers did the only thing they knew to do: They loved each other and shared the news of Christ's sacrifice and God's forgiveness. And they got organized to accomplish the mission that Jesus left with them—to tell the world.

One of the main leaders of the early church was, surprisingly, the disciple Peter. He was the guy who, during Jesus' trial, denied he even knew Christ. Yet after Pentecost, Peter became a mainstay of early church leadership.

It's interesting to note that the same religious leaders who had opposed Jesus when He was on earth also opposed the early church. They persecuted the apostles. From the perspective of these leaders, they were trying to stamp out heresy. They didn't believe that Jesus was the Messiah. They also didn't want to lose the power and prestige they enjoyed in their community.

DID YOU KNOW?

A Mind-Blower

During the crucifixion of Christ, the Bible records a specific event that happened in the temple. It's almost easy to miss in Luke's Gospel nestled between all the intense events surrounding Jesus' death. Here it is:

> *By this time it was noon, and darkness fell across the whole land until three o'clock. The light from the sun was gone. And suddenly, the thick veil hanging in the Temple was torn apart. Then Jesus shouted, "Father, I entrust my spirit into your hands!" And with those words he breathed his last (Luke 23:44–46 NLT).*

The veil that tore in the temple was the curtain that separated the Holy of Holies (which was the place where God was supposed to dwell) from the place where the people came to sacrifice and worship. Do you get what that means? It's really the main event leading into the coming of the Holy Spirit in Acts.

One of the names Jesus was given was Emmanuel. That meant "God with us." When Jesus came, God was with humanity in a whole new and different way. He walked among us. He dealt with our same circumstances and feelings. But at Jesus' death, God came even closer. Do you get that? When the curtain tore and then the Holy Spirit came, it meant that God was in us and with us like never before.

It wasn't that God changed, but it was a whole new way of our understanding His presence and experiencing His life and knowing Him.

It was an atomic bomb of revelation. God with us. God in us. A whole new life of faith.

Wow. It gets me every time.

MISSION TRIPS

Once the church had their main base organized, it was time to spread out. Acts records several "missionary journeys" in which Paul and others spread the good news that Christ had risen from the dead and could forgive sin once and for all.

Missionary Journey #1

Paul and Barnabas made this journey together. Barnabas was one of the Christians who was brave enough to befriend Paul soon after his conversion. (Before his conversion, he persecuted and killed Christians.) Paul and Barnabas traveled together from Antioch to Cyprus and then Galatia. The New Testament book Galatians was written by Paul to the churches he had helped on this journey.

Missionary Journey #2

Paul took a team of missionaries with him on this second journey: Silas, Luke, and Timothy. They visited Philippi, Thessalonica, Berea, Corinth, and Athens. You may recognize several books of the Bible that were written back to these churches: Philippians, 1 and 2 Thessalonians, and 1 and 2 Corinthians.

Missionary Journey #3

Paul went to Ephesus for a lengthy stay (he later wrote a letter to the churches there: Ephesians), then traveled back through Greece and to Jerusalem.

REMEMBER THE CONTEXT

By the time the three missionary journeys were completed, Christianity was raising quite a ruckus. The message and life of Jesus Christ had upset everyone from the Jewish religious leaders to the Roman emperors (who saw themselves as gods to be worshiped).

After the third missionary journey, Paul was put in jail. What the government had in mind was to squelch Paul's influence. So what did the government do? They transported him to Rome, the center of all commerce and communication! They placed him under house arrest (which allowed him visitors), and he basically set up a base of operations right under their noses. He wrote many of the letters we know as the epistles of the New Testament and encouraged Christians everywhere.

IN CONTEXT

The Jew versus Gentile Revolution

If you remember anything about the Old Testament, you should remember that most of it is about the history of the Jewish nation. Their whole story came out of a promise God made to a man named Abraham. Their prophets constantly promised them a messiah, a deliverer.

With such a rich history, it isn't surprising that the Jewish people who accepted Christ's deity didn't really want to share Him with the non-Jewish world. He was their promised Messiah, after all. If anyone wanted to accept Christ's substitution for his sin, let him be circumcised and become a Jew!

During Acts, God was consistently breaking down these barriers. No one needed to become a Jew. Jesus had completed what the Jewish law required. Now it was time for everyone to have access to God just because of his or her faith in Christ. God's original promise to Abraham (father of the Jewish nation) was completed through Jesus' life and work. Faith in what Christ did, rather than nationality or ritual, was now the issue in being accepted by God. This was a *huge* concept for the people of that day to take in.

We take for granted this kind of thinking today: God's love for everyone. But at that time, it was a major shift in thought and probably a scary one for these people who had suffered so much to believe.

It truly was a revolution.

Eventually Paul was killed for his faith, but until then he didn't miss an opportunity to share the news that had really turned the world on its ear: Jesus Christ was the Son of God and gave Himself for our sins.

questions

Q. *What languages were spoken at Pentecost? (Acts 2:4)*

A. *The Jews gathered in Jerusalem for the feast of Pentecost were amazed that these men from Galilee who were not well educated were using the languages of their own lands and nations (see the list in Acts 2:9–11). As a result of this astounding gift of language, three thousand people became believers in Christ and joined the church. They had heard God's good news in their mother tongues. It had touched deep emotions with crystal clarity—and they believed.*

The Letters (or Epistles)

Talk about invasion of privacy. This section of the Bible is made up of somebody else's mail! As the early church was organizing, they had no access to e-mail or telephones, so the snail-est of mail (often carried by foot) was the best communication process they had. You can imagine the excitement when a town received a letter back from Paul after he had started a church there. They probably read it, reread it, passed it around, and almost wore it out (no copiers, either, remember).

The writers of these letters had a similar role with the early church that the prophets had with the Old Testament Hebrews. The prophets spoke out and said, "Since God is God and the Messiah is coming, we should live this way." The New Testament church leaders said, "Since God is God and Jesus came to provide a sacrifice, we should live this way." One was faith through foresight, and the other was faith through hindsight.

We know the first thirteen of these letters are from Paul. The first nine are to churches. The next four are to people. The second letter to Timothy is probably the last letter Paul wrote before his death. This is some pretty significant mail to get to sift through.

The Epistles

- Romans
- 1 and 2 Corinthians
- Galatians
- Ephesians
- Philippians
- Colossians
- 1 and 2 Thessalonians
- 1 and 2 Timothy
- Titus
- Philemon
- Hebrews
- James
- 1 and 2 Peter
- 1, 2, and 3 John
- Jude

Romans

IN CONTEXT

Here's the scoop. . .

Written: *around A.D. 60*

Written by: *Paul the apostle*

Writing style: *a letter of explanation*

One-liner: *Dear church: The only way we can be right with God is through faith.*

WHAT IT ALL MEANS

Paul wrote to the Romans in preparation for his trip there. He wanted them to know as much as possible up front. That way, when he arrived they could spend their time together digging deeper into their understanding of what Jesus Christ's life and death meant.

While the book of Romans isn't a stuffy book, it is a doctrinal book. It is a book that lays out the logic of Christianity:

- We all have a fatal human flaw: We sin and choose ourselves over God; we are spiritually dead (Romans 3:23).

- No matter how many good things we try to do to cover up this flaw, they do not make us clean before God. He wants us to be in relationship with Him. The good things we do don't make us spiritually alive (Romans 5:12).

- Jesus came as a sacrifice for all of our sin; He took our punishment. He died a physical death so we could have a spiritual rebirth (Romans 5:21).

- Because He did that, we can have an open and loving relationship with God—we can be spiritually alive—even though we are still flawed humans who struggle with our self-centeredness (Romans 6:5–7).

- Before we can be really alive spiritually, we have to believe that only through Christ's death and resurrection can we have this new life. It is an act of faith in this gift God offers (Romans 5:1–2).

- God gives us this new life only through this act of faith. We can't earn it. We can't buy it. We can't deserve it. We can't bring ourselves to life spiritually. Only God can do that for us—if we believe (Romans 11:6).

Pretty cool stuff.

THE REFORMATION

You might remember a period of history called the Reformation. This religious movement was begun by Martin Luther. (Not Martin Luther King Jr. That was a different period of history.) Martin Luther didn't mean to start the Reformation. He didn't wake up one day and say, "Well, today is a good day for a revolution." Actually, all he did was read the book of Romans.

During Martin Luther's day, people worked harder and harder to try to make themselves right before God. Many of the church leadership exploited this desire to "work your way to heaven." People were even buying what they thought was forgiveness—with mere money! When Martin Luther read the book of Romans, he realized, "It's not about being good enough or working hard enough. It's about God's grace. He gave us a gift in Christ's death, and He just asks that we believe that He did it."

Martin Luther started preaching that message and it started a revolution of thought that we now call the Reformation. It changed the way the world did church, and things have never been the same.

questions

Q. *What does it mean to be "justified by faith"? (Romans 3:22)*

A. *This is surely the biggest announcement in the history of news: Salvation through following God's law is impossible since it requires flawlessness, but God has established another way through an acquittal process similar to a court's pardon of a guilty person. Declared guilty under God's law, we face the full force of God's penalty. Yet God announces a pardon based on Jesus' payment for all sin. The sinner is set free—no penalty at all. "Grace" is the biblical term to describe the movement of God to acquit based on Christ's work alone; "faith" is the biblical term to describe the movement of the sinner to accept God's sovereign claim on his or her life.*

The term "justified by faith" has this legal setting in mind. God justifies because He loves us, His justice being satisfied through Jesus' death on the cross. We respond in faith to that love. The term expresses the thought of being "right in God's sight" (NLT) through the only way possible, even for Old Testament people—grace and faith.

SCRIPTURE BITS

A famous verse in Romans

And we know that God causes everything to work together for the good of those who love God and are called according to his purpose for them. For God knew his people in advance, and he chose them to become like his Son, so that his Son would be the firstborn, with many brothers and sisters. And having chosen them, he called them to come to him. And he gave them right standing with himself, and he promised them his glory.

Romans 8:28–30 NLT

1 corinthians

IN CONTEXT

Here's the scoop. . .

Written: *around* A.D. 55

Written by: *Paul the apostle*

Writing style: *a letter of instruction*

One-liner: *Dear church: Don't be like the world around you. Be who God made you to be, pure and effective.*

THE CORINTHIAN CHURCH

Paul had helped start the church at Corinth. The Corinthian church had a lot of challenges, because Corinth was one wicked city. In that day people used the phrase "to live like a Corinthian" to mean "to be immoral." In fact, if there was a character in a play who was known to be a Corinthian, he almost always walked onstage drunk.

Also, Corinth was an important trade center. It was located on a thin strip of land between two oceans. One of the unique things about Corinth was a track that led from one of these oceans to the other. If certain ships didn't want to have to sail around the land, they could load their ships onto this track and carry their boats and cargo to the other side. (Who said it was not a technological age, huh?)

Because of its immorality and because of its great location for spreading the gospel, Corinth really needed a church. The problem, though, was that it was difficult for the church there not to get sucked back into the evil and (dare I say it?) debauchery around them.

Evidently, when Paul wrote this letter, the church wasn't doing too well at the not-getting-sucked-back-in thing. Husbands and wives were not being faithful. People in the church were not getting along. Things were getting pretty messy. Because of this, the church wrote Paul. What we call the "book" of 1 Corinthians is actually Paul's letter in response.

THE ISSUES AT HAND

Several passages in 1 Corinthians have been so relevant to the church in every generation that if you hear enough sermons, you are going to hear something from these passages. They show us that the issues we face in church today are not much different than the issues the early church faced. Cultures change, but human nature is human nature.

1. DIVISION AND DISAGREEMENTS

What I mean is this: One of you says, "I follow Paul"; another, "I follow Apollos"; another, "I follow Cephas"; still another, "I follow Christ." Is Christ divided? Was Paul crucified for you? Were you baptized into the name of Paul? (1 Corinthians 1:12–13).

Instead of following Jesus, the Corinthians were doing what people still do today. They were stargazing. They were focusing on Christian celebrities. They were forming spiritual cliques. They were following men, usually the man who introduced them to the faith. Paul directed their faith back to the only place it belonged—Jesus Christ, God in the flesh.

2. RIGHT AND WRONG

The Corinthian church was surrounded by a culture much like our own in which sexual purity (abstinence outside of marriage) was not "in."

Your own members are aware that there is sexual sin going on among them. This kind of sin is not even heard of among unbelievers—a man is actually married to his father's wife (1 Corinthians 5:1 GW).

Stay away from sexual sins. Other sins that people commit don't affect their bodies the same way sexual sins do. People who sin sexually sin against their own bodies (1 Corinthians 6:18 GW).

It's easy for a church to be influenced by the culture around it. The Corinthian church lived in a land flowing over with "everybody's doing it." Paul reminded them to follow the teachings of Christ, even if it meant giving up destructive behaviors they enjoyed. (Anything relevant to contemporary culture there?)

3. SPIRITUAL GIFTS

In chapter 12 of 1 Corinthians, Paul explains the concept of spiritual gifts. He says that each person has a gift given through the Holy Spirit. The purpose of the gift is "for the common good." In other words, we all have something to offer, some ability that God can use to make the world a better place.

Paul had to remind the Corinthians that their gifts didn't do anyone any good if they were bickering and fighting over them. His words are telling us the same thing today.

SCRIPTURE BITS

what the world needs now is love. . .

1 Corinthians 13 gives us a description of true love.

> *Love is patient,*
> *love is kind.*
> *It does not envy,*
> *it does not boast,*
> *it is not proud.*
> *It is not rude,*
> *it is not self-seeking,*
> *it is not easily angered,*
> *it keeps no record of wrongs.*
> *Love does not delight in evil*
> *but rejoices with the truth.*
> *It always protects,*
> *always trusts,*
> *always hopes,*
> *always perseveres.*
> *Love never fails.*
>
> **1 Corinthians 13:4–8**

questions

Q. *Should a church discipline its members? (1 Corinthians 5:5–13)*

A. *Yes. Church discipline is that unpleasant but sometimes necessary final process in maintaining purity among the people of God. It is a radical kind of churchwide accountability that says, "We cannot and will not allow you to continue to live in sin," and "We will exert extreme pressure on you in order to get you to do what is right."*

While other Bible books and passages speak to this issue, 1 Corinthians reveals that church discipline is reserved for believers in Christ. As a final measure (Matthew 18:15–17), the sinning, unrepentant church member is to be expelled from the fellowship of the saints. The goal of such a drastic measure is to effect change in the guilty party and to preserve the purity of the congregation. For discipline to work, the church must be united in its disapproval. The disciplined member is to be shunned (2 Thessalonians 3:14–15) until he or she repents. At that point, forgiveness and comfort are required (2 Corinthians 2:5–7), and restoration can result.

Church discipline is one way God helps us face difficult choices. When the process works as it should, it helps us make the choices that get us back to God.

2 corinthians

IN CONTEXT

Here's the scoop. . .

Written: *around* A.D. 55

Written by: *Paul the apostle*

Writing style: *a personal letter*

One-liner: *Dear church: Here's who I am. Now let me tell you who you should be.*

THE SITUATION

Have you ever tried to work out a conflict long-distance? It's difficult, isn't it? All the he-saids, she-saids seem impossible to control through phone calls or e-mail or letters.

That's the kind of battle Paul was fighting when he wrote 2 Corinthians. He had helped start the church at Corinth on one of his missionary journeys. After leaving, though, he heard about some shaky situations there. That caused him to write 1 Corinthians. It was a firm and confrontational letter.

After that, things seemed to calm down. Then Paul started hearing that people in the church were criticizing him and actually trying to discredit him. He wrote them again. This time his letter was very personal and less confrontational. This time he let them know more of who he was than just what he thought. He opened his heart a bit and let them know of his love and his commitment to them.

STANDING UP FOR HIMSELF

Because people were discrediting him, Paul stood up for himself to the Corinthians. He traced his path in ministry. He established the experiences that had allowed him to be used by God. He walked that thin line between bragging and just telling it like it is.

Paul knew that in order to continue ministering to the church at Corinth, he needed to stand up to his detractors. That's exactly what he did in 2 Corinthians.

A GOOD LESSON

There's a good lesson for us in what happened between Paul's first and second letters to the Corinthians. Paul's first letter was a strong confrontational letter. The Corinthians could have become resentful. They could have gotten even worse than they were. They could have gotten defensive. But when you look at Paul's second letter, you see that he was praising them. They heard the truth and they changed according to it. That's to their credit. . .and a good lesson for us.

questions

Q. *Why was Paul beaten up so much? (2 Corinthians 4:8–12)*

A. *As the gospel confronts people with the weakness of their support systems, the futility of their wealth, and the wickedness of their hearts, it often fuels a vicious response. Paul faced such a response many times, but especially when he confronted the religious and the politically powerful. These two groups especially despised the notion that God had a better way. To shut Paul's mouth, they often resorted to physical violence in some form, only to discover that Paul would not be quiet for any reason, especially under duress.*

Had Paul been frightened by the violence, he would have been beaten less. Had he succumbed to the threats, adjusted his rhetoric, or given up his teaching, no doubt his body would have hurt less. But passion in the soul always meets pain with faith and hope. Paul did not seek the beatings and sometimes took precautionary steps to avoid them; however, he accepted pain as the price of his calling and used it to identify more fully with Jesus.

Q. *Never "team up" with unbelievers. How far should we take that advice? (2 Corinthians 6:14)*

A. *The warning alerts us to the difficulty of a Christian's sharing basic motivation with someone whose loyalty is to wealth or self-interest. Much can be shared with such a person, but the deeper the sharing, the more problematic the motivational disparity.*

Paul does not stipulate with precision: Never sign a contract with a nonbeliever; never start a business; never marry. But the principle is that the deeper your investment with someone as a team member, the more important your mutual loyalties. Thus, it is rare when the church would advise a Christian to marry outside the faith, but common cause across faiths on many matters of public interest is entirely warranted.

Separatist Christians spoil Paul's advice by using it as an excuse never to interact with people outside their comfort zone. Likewise, a Christian who rarely seeks the company of other believers for nurture and support will miss an important source of strength. The more intimate the relationship, the stronger the emotional linkage, the greater the impact on one's life. Friendship, like all of God's gifts, should assist in the process of spiritual growth, not detract from it.

GaLatians

IN CONTEXT

Here's the scoop. . .

Written: *around* A.D. *50*

Written by: *Paul the apostle*

Writing style: *a letter of instruction and explanation*

One-liner: *Dear church: You can't earn God's approval by obeying rules. It takes faith.*

FREEDOM VERSUS CHAINS

When Paul visited Galatia, he explained Christianity to people who were not Jewish. After he left, though, these new Christians were influenced by people called "Judaizers." The Judaizers believed that anyone who wanted to be a Christian should become a Jew, or at least observe Jewish customs and law, such as circumcision, keeping kosher, and yearly feasts.

The problem was not the Jewish customs so much as the attitude that a person couldn't be a Christian unless he or she observed these customs. If that were true, then salvation was about more than grace and faith—it was about earning your righteousness. Paul wrote,

I am astonished that you are so quickly deserting the one who called you by the grace of Christ and are turning to a different gospel—which is really no gospel at all (Galatians 1:6–7).

It was because of the influence of the Judaizers that Paul wrote the book of Galatians. He wrote to emphasize that the grace of God is free, absolutely free. There is nothing anyone can do to deserve it or earn it. If we think we can, then we lock ourselves up in chains of obedience to something that really doesn't matter.

GALATIANS, THE COUSIN TO ROMANS

In many ways Galatians has the same message as Romans. Galatians is shorter, though, and not so technical. In both letters Paul tries to make the point that God's grace, His love-no-matter-what-we've-done, is free for those who believe in Him. It doesn't do any good to try to earn it. "Earning it" is not what Christianity is about. Christianity is about "believing it."

SCRIPTURE BITS

TO Pay or NOT TO Pay

Sometimes it's easiest to feel that we can earn God's love and acceptance. After all, if He gives it to us for free, we don't feel we've paid our dues. No matter what feels good to us, though, we can never be good enough or perfect enough to really deserve God's approval. Getting it for free, out of His grace, is the only way we're ever going to get it.

Christ is useless to you if you are counting on clearing your debt to God by keeping those laws; you are lost from God's grace.
Galatians 5:4 TLB

questions q&a

Q. *What was God's plan for people who lived and died before Jesus came? (Galatians 3:5–7)*

A. God's plan for people who lived before Jesus involved salvation by faith just as it does for people who followed Jesus. Jesus' atonement for sin on the cross applies backward in history as well as forward. People like Abraham placed their faith in God's promise to do something about sin, while people in the Christian era place faith in God's fulfilled promise to take care of sin, Jesus Himself.

Old Testament faith was not blind belief. It simply had fewer details than we do. The real children of Abraham, as Paul put it, are not those linked by ethnicity or geography, but those who put their faith in God.

Ephesians

IN CONTEXT

Here's the scoop. . .

Written: *around* A.D. 60

Written by: *Paul the apostle (from prison!)*

Writing style: *a letter of encouragement*

One-liner: *Dear church: Receive God's amazing love for you. Then love each other well.*

JUST CHECKING IN

We know Paul was in prison in Rome when he wrote this letter. We know that he had Tychicus deliver it. (Tychicus also delivered Colossians and Philemon.) We just don't know exactly why Paul wrote to this church at this time. For all we know, he was just checking in, tending a garden that he had helped plant. It was a good thing for us that he did.

Ephesians is a beautiful letter full of profound and meaningful thoughts. If you are one of those people who keeps a pen with your Bible to underline the verses that really jump out at you, you'll underline a lot of Ephesians.

AN ENCOURAGING WORD

The first part of the book of Ephesians is a lesson in encouragement. It is a wonderful reminder of God's love and grace. Some verses remind us of the truths of some of Paul's other letters:

> *Because of his kindness you have been saved through trusting Christ. And even trusting is not of yourselves; it too is a gift from God (Ephesians 2:8 TLB).*

It's difficult to read Ephesians without feeling loved and fortunate to be a part of God's family.

> *Long ago, even before he made the world, God chose us to be his very own, through what Christ would do for us; he decided then to make us holy in his eyes, without a single fault—we who stand before him covered with his love. His unchanging plan has always been to adopt us into his own family by sending Jesus*

SCRIPTURE BITS

GOOD NEWS

When someone becomes a Christian he becomes a brand new person inside. He is not the same any more. A new life has begun!
2 Corinthians 5:17 TLB

Christ to die for us. And he did this because he wanted to! (Ephesians 1:4–5 TLB).

It's a big enough deal to realize that God offers us an opportunity to know Him and to be loved by Him. It's even bigger to realize that God really has had our adoption into His family planned from the beginning of the world. His intentions toward us have never changed, starting before Genesis and continuing on through today.

Basically, by telling the church all this, Paul was just loving on them, letting them know that God didn't love them sparingly. Instead, God lavished love on them. Who doesn't need to read that?

THE CHURCH

The last part of Ephesians focuses more specifically on how the people of the church love each other. Paul writes about the gifts that each person brings. He writes about basic decency: being truthful with each other, not stealing. He writes about who the church should be in the world—Christ's body, the physical manifestation of God. When you think about it, that's a mind-blower. Just as surely as God put on a human form as Christ so that we could see Him, now the church is that body so that the world can still see God.

If the church lived together the way that Paul describes in the book of Ephesians, what a great reflection of God we would be.

SCRIPTURE BITS

what the church is ALL about

Be humble and gentle. Be patient with each other, making allowance for each other's faults because of your love. Try always to be led along together by the Holy Spirit, and so be at peace with one another.

We are all parts of one body, we have the same Spirit, and we have all been called to the same glorious future. For us there is only one Lord, one faith, one baptism, and we all have the same God and Father who is over us all and in us all, and living through every part of us. However, Christ has given each of us special abilities— whatever he wants us to have out of his rich storehouse of gifts.

Ephesians 4:2–7 TLB

Stop being mean, bad-tempered and angry. Quarreling, harsh words, and dislike of others should have no place in your lives. Instead, be kind to each other, tenderhearted, forgiving one another, just as God has forgiven you because you belong to Christ.

Follow God's example in everything you do just as a much loved child imitates his father.

Ephesians 4:31–5:1 TLB

questions q&a

Q. *Why is the gospel sometimes called a "mystery"? (Ephesians 1:9)*

A. *Many of the pagan religions in Paul's day bragged about secret knowledge available only to their own members. Such claims made membership special. The same sense of mystery carries into our own day with secret or semi-secret societies and even within some Christian movements which initiates pledges "not to tell" what the teacher is teaching. Paul used the term "mystery" in a radically different way—to indicate that God's truth was now revealed in Christ for all the world to know.*

Until Christ came, died, and rose again, who could have imagined that God's plan for saving the world would involve the death of the Son of God? Now the mystery is out! And the news is good! And there's nothing secret about it.

Teachers today who offer secret knowledge are continuing an age-old marketing scheme that isn't worth the price of admission and may be dangerously misleading. Learn about your faith in the open air of genuine Christian teaching—mysteries revealed; Christ the Lord of all the earth!

philippians

IN CONTEXT

Here's the scoop. . .

Written: *around* A.D. *60*

Written by: *Paul the apostle (from prison!)*

Writing style: *a thank-you note*

One-liner: *Dear church: Knowing you brings me joy. Knowing God brings us all joy.*

OLD FRIENDS ARE THE BEST

Paul (with Silas, Timothy, and Luke) founded the church at Philippi on his second missionary journey. It was the first European church founded by Paul, and it was the push of the gospel into a predominantly Gentile culture. Philippi was located on a plain. It was a central location for all the roads in northern Greece. Because of this, it was a strategic location for the gospel to take hold.

The church at Philippi was an old friend of Paul's. They supported Paul in his ministry. In fact, Philippians is partly a thank-you note from Paul for their financial support.

BE JOYFUL

Philippians is a letter of joy. It is the kind of letter that has you smiling all the way back from the mailbox. Even though Paul wrote Philippians to thank them for their kindness, he took the opportunity to give a little lesson with his thank you.

Paul's lesson came first from his own life. He was chained to a Roman guard while he was writing, for goodness' sake! He was in jail, yet he was writing about joy. Here are some of his key points for the Philippians:

- Have integrity (Philippians 1:27).

- Be humble (Philippians 2:3–4).

- Be positive (Philippians 2:14).

- Remember what matters (Philippians 3:13–14).

- Be content (Philippians 4:11–12).

Paul's letter to the Philippians reads almost like a letter written to the folks back home. Paul tells them thanks and then tells them stuff that's important to him, just because it is.

SCRIPTURE BITS

Philippians is a book full of verses that make you go, "Hmm." Here's one:

I have learned to be content whatever the circumstances. I know what it is to be in need, and I know what it is to have plenty. I have learned the secret of being content in any and every situation, whether well fed or hungry, whether living in plenty or in want.

Philippians 4:11–12

I no longer count on my own goodness or my ability to obey God's law, but I trust Christ to save me. For God's way of making us right with himself depends on faith.

Philippians 3:9 NLT

questions q&a

Q. *Why was Paul in prison? (Philippians 1:12–13)*

A. *Under house arrest in Rome, Paul writes about the real reason for his imprisonment: It was for the sake of Christ. His extensive missionary activity ran afoul of religious and secular authorities, who arrested Paul on political and religious grounds. But finally, Paul understood his experience to be ordained by God and blessed by divine call. Secular authority might have claimed power over Paul's movement and career, but Paul served a higher power and in that service felt immense joy and freedom. Indeed, Paul's imprisonment had resulted in the opposite of its intention: Instead of being suppressed, the message was taking hold in the heart of the Roman Empire. Other believers, watching Paul's boldness and faith, were speaking out, as well. State authority could restrict his movement but could not arrest his message or still his purpose.*

coLossians

IN CONTEXT

Here's the scoop. . .

Written: *around* A.D. *60*

Written by: *Paul the apostle*

Writing style: *a letter of correction*

One-liner: *Dear church: Faith in Christ is enough. Don't add anything else to it.*

INFLUENCED BY MODERN CULTURE

The city of Colossae was a cultural and philosophical mixture, a melting pot. The Colossians claimed a variety of religions and variations within each. Paul had evidently heard that the church at Colossae was being influenced by the culture around them. Paul called these influences heresies. They included the following:

- Worshiping angels

- Believing rules and regulations could create righteousness

- Trusting personal goodness instead of God's goodness

- Trusting philosophical prowess and intellectual arrogance

Paul wrote this letter to simplify and clarify exactly what faith does and is. His message was simple: All of this "stuff" you're adding on has nothing to do with your faith. Knowing who Jesus is—that is the most important thing.

The Colossians were being tempted by the same thing that tempts the church today: They were trying to make their relationship with God more complicated. Life is hard enough without making it even more complicated! But somehow we humans find a way to do it. Maybe we feel we need more of a system than "God has made a way for you—believe, love, and obey him." Throughout history we have struggled with letting faith in God be enough. The church at Colossae was adding parts of their culture into their faith because it was fashionable. They were not the first church to struggle with this mix-and-match kind of faith, and they were definitely not the last.

SCRIPTURE BITS

The Gospel According to Colossians

Don't let others spoil your faith and joy with their philosophies, their wrong and shallow answers built on men's thoughts and ideas, instead of on what Christ has said. For in Christ there is all of God in a human body, so you have everything when you have Christ, and you are filled with God through your union with Christ. He is the highest Ruler, with authority over every other power.
Colossians 2:8–10 TLB

questions

Q. *How does the good news actually change a person's life?*
(Colossians 1:6)

A. *The good news is powerful and life changing. It's the true story of Jesus Christ's coming to earth as a human to give His life as a sacrifice and payment for our sins. Through Jesus we have an open door to God's forgiveness and eternal life. The good news is full of hope, and responding to Jesus is the start of a new life. God's Holy Spirit makes us a new creation (see 2 Corinthians 5:17). We're not just turning over a new leaf; we are starting a new life and putting Jesus in charge.*

The good news rebuilds our self-esteem when we realize that God not only created us but loves us so much that He sent Jesus so that we could be reconciled with Him. We learn that God is not far away or uninterested in us. We can pray and share our burdens with God because He cares for us.

Our behavior is dramatically changed as God's Holy Spirit reveals changes we need to make in our lifestyle. The Holy Spirit gives us power to break the bonds of self-destructive habits. Although we will struggle with sin as long as we live on this earth, God does not give up on us. He guides us each day like a loving father and cares for us even when we fail.

The old agenda of self-advancement and competition with others is discarded. There is no reason to fear others or live in guilt, because God accepts us as we are and continues to mold us into the image of Jesus. Life now has a clear purpose—to love God with all our heart, mind, and strength and to love others as we love ourselves. Success is redefined as obeying God and becoming like Jesus. Our life focus is no longer on serving ourselves but on serving God and pleasing Him.

Q. *How is Jesus Christ different from any other famous man who founded a religion? (Colossians 1:15)*

A. *Jesus Christ stands apart from all of the other founders of major religions. The claims of His deity are extensive. He has always existed as the second person of the eternal triune God with all power and knowledge and supremacy over all things that exist. He is Lord over all creation, and in Him all things hold together.*

The history of Christianity is that this deity came to earth and lived in a human body. He was God in the flesh. He was an exact reflection of the invisible God. He lived a sinless life while teaching and showing us what we need to know about God.

The ultimate purpose of Jesus' life on earth was revealed when He gave His life to be executed as a sacrifice for sin. Through His death, God made a way for all of us to obtain forgiveness and eternal life if we put our faith and trust in Jesus as Savior and Lord.

This wasn't spiritual talk and premature martyrdom by Jesus Christ. He did what no other religious leader ever did. Three days after He was crucified and buried, He rose from the dead—conquering death and sin. He was seen alive by more than five hundred eyewitnesses before He ascended back into heaven.

No other religious leader can make and substantiate claims equal to the life of Jesus Christ. He stands alone as Lord over our world.

1 Thessalonians

IN CONTEXT

Here's the scoop. . .

Written: *around* A.D. *50*

Written by: *Paul the apostle*

Writing style: *a letter of instruction and encouragement*

One-liner: *Dear church: Look forward to Christ's return!*

HARD TIMES

Being a Christian at the time this letter was written was not a lot of fun. Today Christians wear cool T-shirts with spiritual sayings, and they attend large conferences where they learn more and more about the life they should live. Not so in Paul's day. Being a Christian was unpopular and even outlawed in some places. When someone became a Christian, he often had to leave his family behind and live in hiding. Christians needed all the encouragement they could get to keep the faith.

That's much of the reason Paul wrote to the Christians at Thessalonica. He couldn't make their situation any easier, and he couldn't promise them it wouldn't get worse before it got better. So he promised them the only thing he could. He promised them that one day Jesus would return and make things okay. In fact, this book includes one of the most famous Bible passages about Jesus' return to the earth:

> *For the Lord himself will come down from heaven with a mighty shout and with the soul-stirring cry of the archangel and the great trumpet-call of God. And the believers who are dead will be the first to rise to meet the Lord. Then we who are still alive and remain on the earth will be caught up with them in the clouds to meet the Lord in the air and remain with him forever. So comfort and encourage each other with this news.*
>
> *When is all this going to happen? I really don't need to say anything about that, dear brothers, for you know perfectly well that no one knows. That day of the Lord will come unexpectedly like a thief in the night* (1 Thessalonians 4:16–5:2 TLB).

SECOND COMING?

When Jesus left the earth after His resurrection, He promised to come again. The people who heard Him make those promises believed that would happen during their lifetime. The Thessalonians lived in that generation. Almost every generation since then has thought the same thing. Because we are still waiting for that return, which many call the second coming, Paul's word of encouragement to them applies to us, as well.

questions

Q. *What does it mean to be chosen by God? Are some people not chosen? (1 Thessalonians 1:4)*

A. *This question has always frustrated the human mind and sometimes divided the church. How do people become part of God's family—through their own choice or through God's choosing them? Another way to put it: Given our spiritual deadness, what makes us able to choose faith? Is it choice itself, or is it God's enablement through a prior choice of us? Avoiding theological labels, let's characterize the two sides of the question:*

(1) God chooses strongly for some, in the context of His broad choice for all. Clearly God extends His invitation to all sinners, and Christ's death covers the penalty for everyone's sin. But spiritual deadness means that no one can accept God's offer of life until God, through the Holy Spirit, enables the person's faith. In this view, we cannot even take credit for believing. God gets all the credit all the way.

(2) God chooses broadly for everyone but preferentially for no one, since that would be unfair. The offer of eternal life is available to all who know about it, and it's the church's job to get the message out. Everyone can and should believe. Don't blame God if you fail to fulfill His conditions for eternal life. Everyone (within earshot of the gospel) has a chance.

As you read the Bible, try to understand how your choice of faith is crucial and how God's choice of you is essential. The relationship is not cooperative (as if God needs your help), but neither is your will irrelevant (as if God would force a choice on you). Don't hesitate a moment to believe, giving credit to God for your ability to do so.

Q. *How could Satan thwart the plans of a spiritual man like Paul? (1 Thessalonians 2:18)*

A. *We might imagine ourselves falling to a satanic scheme, but why the spiritual giant Paul? The question leads to an unexpected element of the spiritual battle between God and evil: The greater the life of faith, the stronger the opposition from the great opponent.*

Compare schoolyard basketball to the level of competition in a professional game. The better the players, the tougher the game. The same apparently holds true in spiritual life. Paul was devoted to Christ and hounded by the devil. Lesser saints may live the life of spiritual ease and comfort; the devil need not trouble them, for their faith will stir no waters and make little difference to anyone. But Paul. . .

Paul was frustrated by satanic opposition but not defeated by it. In his life was a strong sense of ultimate victory, for he knew God would see him through. He was playing in the big leagues, so to speak, and could expect trouble from the devil. But the game's outcome was never in doubt, and Paul put every effort toward playing hard until his substitute came in.

2 Thessalonians

Here's the scoop. . .

Written: *around* A.D. *50*

Written by: *Paul the apostle*

Writing style: *a letter of clarification*

One-liner: *Dear church: Look forward to Christ's return, but keep living full lives and working hard!*

OOPS! CHURCH OVERBOARD!

Now, it is true that when Christ returns it is going to be an amazing event, but when the bills come due, we need to be responsible to pay them. These Thessalonians were so consumed with that one event that they were letting go of their lives on earth. Paul needed to set them straight.

That was the first problem, but there was another related problem. Since the hanger-outers didn't have anything to do and were bored, they began to do what people do when they are hanging out and bored. They began to make trouble, gossip, become busybodies, and get into everyone else's business. They began to mooch off each other because they had no money to pay their own bills.

That is why Paul wrote his second letter to the Thessalonian church. He needed to pull them back to center, back to a balance.

Yet we hear that some of you are living idle lives, refusing to work and wasting time meddling in other people's business. In the name of the Lord Jesus Christ, we appeal to such people—no, we command them: Settle down and get to work. Earn your own living (2 Thessalonians 3:11–12 NLT).

questions

Q. *What signs tell us that God's plan is on schedule, even if we cannot know God's timetable? (2 Thessalonians 2:2)*

A. *Christians are called to live obediently in the light of two promises: (1) Jesus can and may return today—"You also must be ready all the time. For the Son of Man will come when least expected" (Matthew 24:44); (2) We cannot pinpoint a schedule—"No one knows the day or the hour when these things will happen, not even the angels in heaven or the Son himself. Only the Father knows" (Matthew 24:36).*

The Bible offers a number of "signs" that precede or accompany Christ's return (see Matthew 24; 2 Thessalonians 2; and Revelation 4–22). Some of these signs are natural (earthquakes and other natural disasters); others are political (wars, rumors of war, shifts in power leading to a world domination); many are spiritual (growing world religious movements that reject God, intense persecution of Christians); some are even positive (the spread of the gospel around the world, the renewal of the Jewish nation). History demonstrates that Christians have always been able to see in their immediate context enough possible fulfillments of these signs to conclude that Jesus might come soon.

These signs are to be an encouragement to faith. As long as they inspire our ongoing faithfulness, well and good. But if we use them to plot a chart of future events, we err. Paul warns here about the passion to know what no one can—the details of God's timetable for history.

Q. *What's wrong with idleness?*

A. *Paul warns against those who use the possibility of Christ's immediate return as an excuse for laziness. Apparently a group in Thessalonica had dropped out of daily life. They were teaching others to set aside responsibilities, quit work, and do no planning for the future.*

The idea that doing nothing is an effective way to anticipate Christ's return is a damaging deception. Jesus did not command believers to stop everything and wait. Instead, He instructed them to live in obedient anticipation (Matthew 5:13–16). Idle Christians are neither modeling a life of faith nor fulfilling Jesus' command to make disciples (Matthew 28:19–20). Idleness fails to respond to God's promises with gratitude and joy.

1 Timothy

IN CONTEXT

Here's the scoop. . .

Written: *around* A.D. *65*

Written by: *Paul the apostle*

Writing style: *a personal letter*

One-liner: *Dear Tim: You're doing well. Here are some things to remember about leading a church.*

LIKE A SON

Timothy was an up-and-comer in the early church. We don't know much about his dad except that he was Greek. Timothy's mom was Jewish. One of the most well-known things about Timothy is that his mom (Lois) and his grandmom (Eunice) were big influences on his faith. Paul even mentions them in his second letter to Timothy.

At the time when Paul wrote this letter, Timothy was in Ephesus helping lead the church. Timothy and Paul had traveled to Ephesus together. Paul left Timothy there to keep the church on track. Remember, at that point, churches didn't have big buildings and programs. The church was simply groups of people meeting at different places, often homes, around town. Timothy's greatest challenge in Ephesus was the mixture of philosophy and thoughts that continually pulled people away from the simple truth of the gospel. Because of that, Paul wrote much about how to stay away from heresy.

Paul wrote this letter to encourage Timothy and to train him a little. It is a straightforward letter that is chock-full of advice for a young Christian (or a Christian of any age, really) who wants to serve God in a meaningful way.

In this letter Paul covers some of the same ground that he touches on in other letters, such as the following:

- Worship

- False teachers

- Church leadership

Paul had invested so much in their relationship that Timothy was like a son to him. That's why in this first letter to Timothy, Paul talks about these issues in a more personal way than in some of the earlier letters from Paul in the New Testament. You can imagine how you would write to someone whom you had worked alongside and felt very parental toward. Paul also writes to Timothy with the urgency of an older man who wants to pour his years of experience into someone younger who can carry on the work.

IN CONTEXT

In his first letter to the Thessalonians, Paul reminded them that Jesus would come again to claim them and make a better world. Paul didn't know, though, that the church would take him so literally. Some of them actually quit their jobs so they could watch for Christ. Others just started hanging out, looking for Christ's return. Still others got scared that Jesus had already come and they had been left behind.

SCRIPTURE BITS

Now the overseer [church leader] must be above reproach, the husband of but one wife, temperate, self-controlled, respectable, hospitable, able to teach, not given to much wine, not violent but gentle, not quarrelsome, not a lover of money.

1 Timothy 3:2–3

But godliness with contentment is great gain. For we brought nothing into the world, and we can take nothing out of it. But if we have food and clothing, we will be content with that.

1 Timothy 6:6–8

questions

Q. *Must an elder or deacon be married? (1 Timothy 3:2, 12)*

A. *No, but if they are married, they must be sexually faithful. Promiscuity cannot be tolerated in church leadership. The direction of the charge here is toward faithful support in other ways, too. Married church leaders should witness to the church of God's love through their own growing and deepening relationship.*

Q. *Why does Paul urge the use of alcohol? (1 Timothy 5:23)*

A. *"A little wine" for the sake of settling a prolonged health condition is apparently no violation of biblical directives concerning drunkenness. Though many Christians have taken the position that all alcoholic drink is wrong and must be studiously avoided, Paul seemed to hold a more moderate view. Gluttony in any form is unhealthy and morally wrong because it spoils the body and weakens the individual. Moderate use of wine is no violation of Christian standards in Paul's eyes.*

2 Timothy

IN CONTEXT

Here's the scoop. . .

Written: *around* A.D. *65*

Written by: *Paul the apostle*

Writing style: *a personal letter*

One-liner: *Dear Tim: Come soon. I don't know how much longer I'll be here. Keep the faith!*

FINAL INSTRUCTIONS

Paul's second letter to Timothy is a poignant one. Paul knew that he was going to die soon. He was in prison. He had gone through several appeals. He knew that this was very possibly his last letter to Timothy, his last chance to tell him the things that matter.

It is a wonderful thing that this letter is a part of the Bible. We are made privy to the most significant thoughts of one of the most famous preachers in the history of the world.

What would you say to your son if you knew it was probably the last time you were going to be able to communicate with him? That's what the second letter from Paul to Timothy is all about.

Here are some of Paul's last words to Timothy, his friend and almost-son:

> But as for you, continue in what you have learned and have become convinced of, because you know those from whom you learned it, and how from infancy you have known the holy Scriptures, which are able to make you wise for salvation through faith in Christ Jesus. All Scripture is God-breathed and is useful for teaching, rebuking, correcting and training in righteousness, so that the man of God may be thoroughly equipped for every good work (2 Timothy 3:14–17).

> For I am already being poured out like a drink offering, and the time has come for my departure. I have fought the good fight, I have finished the race, I have kept the faith (2 Timothy 4:6–7).

questions

Q. *Paul cites Timothy's mother and grandmother as people of faith. Where was Timothy's father? (2 Timothy 1:5)*

A. *Acts 16:1 informs us that Timothy's father was a Greek. Since Luke (in Acts) makes a point of indicating that Timothy's Jewish mother was a Christian, we may infer that Timothy's father was not. With respect to spiritual parentage, Timothy experienced a son-father relationship with Paul. Several times in 2 Timothy, Paul calls Timothy "my dear son."*

Q. *What overcomes fear? (2 Timothy 1:7)*

A. *Likely, Timothy was a timid person, but Paul recognized in him the qualities of a leader. Instead of urging Timothy to become more courageous, Paul wants to plant in his heart three virtues: (1) power—the ability to act responsibly in the face of fear; (2) love—the first fruit of the Spirit (Galatians 5:22); and (3) self-discipline—the last fruit of the Spirit (Galatians 5:23). Paul is reminding the young leader that fears are no match for the resources God's Spirit brings to the life of a believer.*

Titus

IN CONTEXT

Here's the scoop...

Written: *around* A.D. *65*

Written by: *Paul the apostle*

Writing style: *a letter of instruction and training*

One-liner: *Dear Titus: Here are some helpful hints about leading your church.*

FOLLOW THE LEADER

Titus was a young pastor in a very difficult parish. He was a pastor in Crete, a small island south of Greece. The people of Crete were known for their lies, their laziness, and their cruelty. It was a place that needed a church, but was it a place in which you could find any leadership for the church?

This was the challenge in front of Titus. It was also one of the reasons Paul wrote so much to Titus about the qualities of a leader. Most churches still use Paul's criteria today when they are choosing their leaders (pastors, deacons, or elders).

Here's how Paul believed leaders should behave:

For the grace of God that brings salvation has appeared to all men. It teaches us to say "No" to ungodliness and worldly passions, and to live self-controlled, upright and godly lives in this present age (Titus 2:11–12).

But avoid foolish controversies and genealogies and arguments and quarrels about the law, because these are unprofitable and useless (Titus 3:9).

questions&a

Q. *What qualities make a good leader? (Titus 1:5–9)*

A. *The letters 1 Timothy, 2 Timothy, and Titus are also known as the Pastoral Epistles because they contain practical guidelines for training and choosing leaders in the church. Leadership qualities cited here include the following:*

- **A good reputation.** *Someone who has the respect of other people has already shown his or her ability to put others first.*
- **Marital faithfulness.** *Loyalty to the primary commitment of marriage usually foretells loyalty to the rest of one's commitments.*
- **Children who believe and act like it.** *Can a leader in the church hope to disciple others if those closest to him or her do not embrace the faith?*
- **Blameless living.** *This means not just abiding by rules but positively and consistently seeking God's way.*
- **No arrogance.** *People inflated with their self-importance leave little room for God to lead them.*
- **No quick temper.** *In a world of interpersonal violence, Christian leaders must be devoted to peace, goodwill, and self-control.*
- **No drunkenness.** *No leader can himself or herself be led by any substance.*
- **No violence.** *As violence breeds the spirit of revenge, the church needs the spirit of goodwill. The church is a community devoted to each other in God's service, not a fractured community at war.*
- **No greed.** *Leaders have access to money but cannot love it or make decisions based on the bottom line.*
- **Hospitality.** *This means active sharing of one's personal space, enlarging one's home to people not part of the immediate family.*
- **Pleasure in good.** *Most public pleasures operate at the periphery of civic standards. Christian leaders find their recreation at the center of moral goodness.*

- **Wise living and fair judgments.** *This involves making good decisions based on available facts and counsel.*
- **Devout and disciplined.** *The leader is able to corral the occasional temptation to spin out of control, to binge, to chuck. He or she is someone others can depend on.*
- **Clear, consistent beliefs and teaching.** *A growing person in mind and heart, the leader is a learner and a reasonably decent communicator.*

That's a long list, but leadership is a high privilege.

phiLemon

IN CONTEXT

Here's the scoop. . .

Written: *around* A.D. *60*

Written by: *Paul the apostle*

Writing style: *a letter of recommendation*

One-liner: *Dear Philemon: Forgive Onesimus not as a runaway, but as your brother in faith.*

WHO SAYS YOU CAN'T GO HOME AGAIN?

Paul's letter to Philemon is a unique letter in the New Testament. It is simply a cross-sectional slice of life in the first century. The basic story is this: Philemon was a friend of Paul's. Philemon's slave, Onesimus, ran away and took some of Philemon's money with him. While Onesimus was wandering, he became a Christian and came in contact with Paul. After that, Onesimus decided to right his wrong and return to Philemon. Paul sent him back with a letter, hoping to soften Philemon's reaction. This book is that letter.

Basically Paul was calling in a favor. He reminded Philemon that he had received from life and it was time for the tables to turn. Here is Paul's logic:

Although in Christ I could be bold and order you to do what you ought to do, yet I appeal to you on the basis of love (Philemon 8–9). [Paul appeals to Philemon's better self.]

So if you consider me a partner, welcome him as you would welcome me (Philemon 17). [Paul appeals to their friendship.]

I, Paul, am writing this with my own hand. . .not to mention that you owe me your very self (Philemon 19). [Paul is bordering on arm-twisting here!]

Confident of your obedience, I write to you, knowing that you will do even more than I ask (Philemon 21). [You always know you'd better come through when the person asking the favor thanks you ahead of time.]

questions

Q. *Why "appeal" when you could "demand"? (Philemon 8)*

A. *Military officers enjoy the privilege of "orders"—the word of the officer must be obeyed. But even military orders are disobeyed (and legally must be disobeyed) when they stray from military discipline and law.*

Paul knows that his spiritual authority includes the privilege of "orders"—requests enforced not by the state but rather by the conscience and ultimately by God. Yet he takes a much softer approach here.

Paul's purpose is to count Philemon as a mature Christian who needs no "orders" to understand his duty and requires no coercion to respond to that duty. By appealing to Philemon instead of commanding him, Paul sets the stage for Philemon to adopt a new posture toward slaves. Paul was willing to trust the work of the Holy Spirit in Philemon's heart.

As children grow, parents lose control—but not really. They must, however, change from commanding to appealing, to signal the growth of the child's own conscience. Leaders in the church must do the same. No church operates well when motivated by coercion or guilt. Churches grow as people take personal and corporate responsibility for their attitudes and actions. Leaders who want their vision enacted immediately, and command it be done, should be quickly dismissed as little tyrants wearing the wrong uniform. They have failed to grow, and all who follow them will be stunted and small-hearted.

Hebrews

IN CONTEXT

Here's the scoop. . .

Written: *around* A.D. *70*

Written by: *Paul the apostle*

Writing style: *a letter to the New Testament Jews*

One-liner: *To all Jewish Christians: Now that Christ has come, focus on Him rather than the rituals that pointed you to Him.*

WHEN IT ALL BEGAN. . .

Back when the Jewish nation was young, Moses wrote down the laws for the nation as God told them to him. (See Exodus and Leviticus if you need a refresher.) Some of these laws were *very* specific. As time passed and the Jewish people got more organized, some people made it their life's ambition to follow these laws. They concentrated so much on following the laws that sometimes they missed the point of having faith in God: loving God and loving others. They were too busy following rules and regulations to do that.

WHEN IT ALL CONTINUED. . .

Jesus spent much of His energies addressing this kind of issue. We still address it today. Some people say, "I don't consider myself religious, but I'm a Christian." This usually means that they believe they follow the heart of faith instead of the head of faith, that to them it's not just a bunch of do's and don'ts.

WHEN WILL IT ALL END?

Hebrews is addressing the same kind of thing. Some of the Jewish people were feeling that Jesus didn't make much of a difference, that they could just keep following their laws and customs and that would make them righteous. The writer of Hebrews is saying to them that Jesus *did* make a difference. He made all the difference. It's a whole different way of attaining righteousness—through faith in Christ, not in perfectly keeping the rules and making the sacrifices.

WHAT YOU FIND OUT ALONG THE WAY

Hebrews gives some interesting insights into Jesus' role in our lives as a priest:

> But Jesus the Son of God is our great High Priest who has gone to heaven itself to help us; therefore let us never stop trusting him. This High Priest of ours understands our weaknesses, since he had the same temptations we do, though he never once gave way to them and sinned. So let us come boldly to the very throne of God and stay there to receive his mercy and to find grace to help us in our times of need (Hebrews 4:14–16 TLB).

questions

Q. *What's the typical job description for angels? (Hebrews 1:14)*

A. *Angels apparently spend most of their career serving Christians, working as bodyguards or perhaps spirit guards, helping Christians remain faithful throughout life. It is interesting that this type of job would be noted in the book of the Bible that describes Christians as most vulnerable to defeat and loss. Surely Jesus is the captain of all the company of the saved, but angels are the rank-and-file "coast guardsmen," defending the spiritual perimeter against attack from the evil one.*

This job function does not prevent Christians from suffering disaster or defeat, as experience clearly attests. The effectiveness of the angels' work will be known only in heaven, but the hints we have concerning these guardsmen suggest that heavenly praise to God will be all the more joyous for the help we unknowingly received from these unseen agents.

Q. *Did Jesus need to suffer to become perfect? (Hebrews 2:10)*

A. *No other Bible book portrays the humanity of Jesus as dramatically as Hebrews. Jesus reflects God's glory and sustains the universe, yet He as man was also, for a time, a little lower than the angels. Then there is this quizzical note that suggests Jesus went through a developmental process in attaining a seat at the right hand of God.*

As to Jesus' divine nature, no developmental process is in view. Jesus did not grow into deity or sonship, as if God picked the man Jesus and made Him into the Christ. As to Jesus' human nature, there was development (see Luke 2:42), as there is for every person. Jesus experienced pain and, in that pain, grew to know—as a man—the protection and presence of God, His Father. The real pain Jesus endured made His death on the cross a real sacrifice for sin. Pain was the price for the fulfillment (perfection) of the mission begun in the incarnation and completed in the resurrection.

James

IN CONTEXT

Here's the scoop. . .

Written: *around* A.D. *50*

Written by: *James, probably the brother of Jesus*

Writing style: *a letter of instruction*

One-liner: *Yes, salvation is by faith, but faith without action is useless.*

WHERE THE RUBBER MEETS THE ROAD

If theology were a seesaw, you would put Paul's understanding of faith at one end and James's understanding of faith at the other. They were a good balance, but they came from different directions. Paul emphasized that we can't work or earn our way into God's good graces. We can only have faith and accept His grace. Paul wasn't saying that our faith is without responsibility. He was just saying that the responsibility comes out of having received the gift God offers. James came to it from the opposite direction. While he didn't contradict Paul, he pointed out that once we come to true faith, then our actions will be evidence of that faith. In fact, James gave that as a guideline or a proof of faith—that true faith results in good actions.

Because of all that, James is a very practical book. It is a book that says not just what faith is, but what faith *does*. It is a book that explains not just what to believe, but how to live the life of a believer.

Even though James was probably written before Hebrews, it is a great book to come after Hebrews in the Bible. Hebrews is about faith. James is about faith applied.

James reminded his readers that being tempted and being tested weren't the worst things that could happen to them. He reminded them that listening is not enough without action. He reminded them that how they treated other people would tell the most about what they believed. He reminded them that how they used their words mattered—a lot. He reminded them that the easy life wasn't always the most nurturing environment for faith.

In reminding them of all that, he reminds us, as well.

THINK ABOUT IT THIS WAY

Q. As a Christian, how should I communicate?

A. Everyone should be quick to listen, slow to speak and slow
   to become angry (James 1:19).

Q. What is the true test of our religion?

A. Anyone who says he is a Christian but doesn't control his
   sharp tongue is just fooling himself, and his religion isn't
   worth much (James 1:26 TLB).

questions

Q. *What gets a person into heaven, faith in God or good deeds?*
(James 2:14)

A. *"He was a good person," we often say about a departed friend, hoping*
that whatever heaven there is will be open to such a person, given the good
deeds, on balance, that characterized the better days of his or her life. Fair-
ness mixed with a little lenience should open heaven's gates, we hope.

But the "good person" theory is as faulty as the "faith in word only"
theory of those who profess to be Christian but continue living like pagans,
looking out for the self only. Both approaches to heaven fail.

Then what unlocks those pearly gates, after all?

Faith demonstrated to be genuine through a life of obedience to God.
Faith means that we trust in Christ alone for salvation, not in anything we
do or in any good works we perform. Obedience means that faith changes
our priorities. That is, the change of heart that faith enacts must also change
our habits and goals. The practical dimensions of faith are expressed in
virtues such as generosity, patience, trustworthiness, and love. No one who
claims to have faith should be absent these virtues.

If you are an old curmudgeon (or young one) who scorns these virtues
on your drive to church every Sunday, you had better examine the faith
you profess. It's probably just an empty shell, which does nobody any good,
including you.

1 peter

Here's the scoop. . .

Written: *around* A.D. *60*

Written by: *Peter the disciple*

Writing style: *a personal letter*

One-liner: *These are difficult times. Let your faith help you endure. Don't let go just because troubles come.*

FINDING JOY

Remember those movies where prehistoric TicketMaster sold tickets to Romans to go to the Colosseum and watch Christians face lions? The book of 1 Peter was written about that very time. Christianity had even been outlawed! Anyone who claimed to be a Christian could be tortured, imprisoned, or even killed simply because he believed in God and believed that Jesus was God's Son.

You might think that if Peter was writing at such a volatile time, he would have been depressed or at least scared. You might think he would have written in code or revealed secret entrances to catacombs. When you read 1 Peter, though, you hear hope in Peter's message, not discouragement. You hear confidence, and if you listen really closely, you even hear joy. . . .

Praise be to the God and Father of our Lord Jesus Christ! In his great mercy he has given us new birth into a living hope through the resurrection of Jesus Christ from the dead (1 Peter 1:3).

Therefore, prepare your minds for action; be self-controlled; set your hopefully on the grace to be given you when Jesus Christ is revealed (1 Peter 1:13).

But you are a chosen people, a royal priesthood, a holy nation, a people belonging to God, that you may declare the praises of him who called you out of darkness into his wonderful light. Once you were not a people, but now you are the people of God; once you had not received mercy, but now you have received mercy (1 Peter 2:9–10).

The end of all things is near. Therefore be clear minded and self-controlled so that you can pray (1 Peter 4:7–8).

THAT'S AN INTERESTING POINT

Peter's first letter raises two interesting issues for us to consider. First, civil disobedience. When do we stop obeying the laws of our culture in order to obey God? Peter reminds us over and over to give respect to our government in every way possible. He doesn't give us easy permission to ignore the laws of our land.

Second, the issue of persecution in the face of our innocence. The people to whom Peter was writing were not criminals. The thing they were being punished for was merely their faith. The sad truth of life is that we will face difficulties and mistreatment even when we don't deserve it. God's plan for us is not retribution. It is the ability to obey Him no matter what our circumstances. It is the ability to leave the "getting even" to God Himself.

questions q&a

Q. *Doesn't the Bible promise happiness to all who follow Christ?*
(1 Peter 1:6; 4:12)

A. *The Bible also promises trouble, as these verses testify. The hard reality of the Bible's message is that life breeds trouble, and Christians are not exempt. In fact, Christians should expect more trouble, as the adversary seeks to derail faith and upset biblical promises.*

It is not pessimistic (just realistic and biblical) to say that trouble is the standard, peace the exception, this side of heaven. God uses trouble to build our faith, redeeming us from all trouble through the power of the Overcomer, Jesus.

Q. *Do angels study? (1 Peter 1:12)*

A. *Apparently angels either study or have the appetite to study. The meaning of the verb here implies observing with intensity and effort. If angels study, they study God's ways to marvel more fully at His will and power. On this model, angels are like intelligent and gifted apprentices who never move up but nonetheless eagerly seek to understand the mind of the Master.*

Perhaps angels do not learn but show an appetite for it anyhow. On that model, angels would be the singular beings in all creation who cannot hope to realize their purpose or potential. Such a model, while possible, fails to cohere with one of the most obvious purposes expressed in God's creative plan: Intelligence that seeks understanding is equipped to find it.

2 Peter

IN CONTEXT

Here's the scoop. . .

Written: *around* A.D. *65*

Written by: *Peter the disciple*

Writing style: *a warning letter*

One-liner: *These are difficult times. Keep your faith and let it help you endure.*

SAME WRITER, DIFFERENT REASON

Peter's second letter was to the same audience as his first letter. That audience was still facing difficult times. In this second letter, though, Peter was not only helping them combat enemies outside of the church, he was also addressing enemies inside the church: false teachers.

Evidently Peter had heard that the false teachers were telling the church that Jesus wasn't *really* coming back again and that they wouldn't *really* be accountable for their actions. You can imagine the response. If I'm being persecuted for my faith and someone tells me that faith isn't really important, then what's the use? These false teachers were exploiting their listeners and misleading many, many people.

DIFFERENT REASON, NEW BENEFITS

Because Peter was trying to "set the record straight" in light of false teaching, this short book has some of the New Testament's most bottom-line spiritual truths. It just works that way sometimes; you speak the most clearly when you are addressing a particular cause.

The Word of God: "Above all, you must understand that no prophecy of Scripture came about by the prophet's own interpretation. For prophecy never had its origin in the will of man, but men spoke from God as they were carried along by the Holy Spirit" (2 Peter 1:20–21).

God's nature: "The Lord is not slow in keeping his promise, as some understand slowness. He is patient with you, not wanting anyone to perish, but everyone to come to repentance" (2 Peter 3:9).

The second coming of Christ: "But the day of the Lord will come like a thief. The heavens will disappear with a roar; the elements will be destroyed by fire, and the earth and everything in it will be laid bare" (2 Peter 3:10).

The Christian life: "For this very reason, make every effort to add to your faith goodness; and to goodness, knowledge; and to knowledge, self-control; and to self-control, perseverance; and to perseverance, godliness; and to godliness, brotherly kindness; and to brotherly kindness, love. For if you possess these qualities in increasing measure, they will keep you from being ineffective and unproductive in your knowledge of our Lord Jesus Christ" (2 Peter 1:5–8).

THINK ABOUT IT THIS WAY

The truth is that Christianity has historically grown the most during times of persecution. Why? Partly because it is during those times that people face the truth rather than all the accessories that we apply to the truth. It's easy to give up a Family Life Center or a church softball league if you're going to face a firing squad. It's not so easy to give up the one hope you have that life is more than what we see in this world.

questions

Q. *If my sins are forgiven and my eternal salvation is based on what Jesus has done for me, not on what I do, then why can't I relax and enjoy life instead of pushing and fighting to change old sinful habits and lifestyles? (2 Peter 1:5–9)*

A. Christian living is not fire insurance but a growing relationship with the holy God. This is the Christian's destiny. Imagine that God has promised you will become a virtuoso pianist some day, though you can't even tell a piano from a tuba. If you believe God's promise, what is your plan? Do you spend the day watching videos and cracking your knuckles or practicing the keyboard with the promise that your destiny is being fulfilled as you pursue it?

Being a Christian means knowing Christ better each day. God wants to produce Jesus' character in us. Peter writes that learning unselfish love for others can be done only through the disciplines of trust, obedience, and self-control.

Q. *How can we be sure that the stories about Jesus are true? (2 Peter 1:16)*

A. Eyewitnesses, Peter among them, verified what really happened. We see Jesus through the eyes of Peter and other disciples who testify to the truth through stories such as that of the transfiguration, where God declared Jesus to be His true Son.

Peter spent three years with Jesus, observing His miracles and ingesting His teaching. When Jesus asked, "Who do you say that I am?" Peter confessed that Jesus was the Christ, the Son of the living God.

Peter was in the center of the action in the days just before Jesus' arrest and death. Peter's denial was the low point of his life, yet Jesus forgave him and chose him to be a missionary of the good news. God used this flawed man, Peter, to establish the credibility of Jesus for future generations. Peter gives specific and clear testimony about Jesus' life and teachings. Add Peter to other Bible writers, and we have detailed eyewitness accounts that serve as the foundation of our faith.

Q. *Does it really matter that much if Jesus ever comes back to earth? (2 Peter 3:3)*

A. When Jesus makes a promise, He keeps it.

It has been a long wait. Previous generations thought they would see Jesus but did not. Through this long wait, God has been faithful to His people. The church has grown. God's family is getting larger.

No one knows the time schedule of Jesus' return, so we continue to wait, just as did believers in the early church. True believers refuse to turn to idols (immediate, though false, images of divine power) and enjoy a ready expectation of that day when Jesus will surely return (1 Thessalonians 1:10).

1 John

IN CONTEXT

Here's the scoop. . .

Written: *around* A.D. *90*

Written by: *John the disciple*

Writing style: *a letter of encouragement and instruction*

One-liner: *Ignore false teaching. Live righteously. Love each other. Know that Jesus was God in the flesh.*

SETTING THE RECORD STRAIGHT

In some ways, John wrote this first letter (which we call 1 John) to set the record straight. No sooner had the early church begun to organize itself than theological disagreements began.

"Maybe Christ wasn't really human," said one group.

"Maybe since Christ died for our sin, we don't have to try not to sin anymore," said another one.

John wrote to respond to these kinds of ideas. "Yes," he said, "Jesus was fully human and fully God. And yes, we must fight our sinful natures with everything we have, but when we fall, there is forgiveness."

John wrote to warn the people against heresies like these as well as the false teachers who spread their very unholy curricula. He also wrote to instruct Christians in the way of love. John reminded his readers that the very evidence of God's presence in us and with us is our love for each other. Some of the most famous verses about love in the Bible are found in 1 John.

This letter isn't a theological treatise, though. It's just thought after thought. It's sort of hard to outline, but it's a lot of truth in one place.

Dear children, let us stop just saying we love each other; let us really show it by our actions. It is by our actions that we know we are living in the truth, so we will be confident when we stand before the Lord, even if our hearts condemn us. For God is greater than our hearts, and he knows everything (1 John 3:18–20 NLT).

Dear friends, since God loved us that much, we surely ought to love each other. No one has ever seen God. But if we love each other, God lives in us, and his love has been brought to full expression through us (1 John 4:11–12 NLT).

questions

Q. *Which John wrote the New Testament letters that bear that name?*

A. *Tradition has identified the writer of these letters as John the son of Zebedee (Mark 1:19–20), the author of the Gospel of John and Revelation. He was the disciple whom Jesus loved (John 13:23). The epistles bear a striking resemblance in style and vocabulary to the Gospel of John. The early church fathers (Irenaeus, Clement of Alexandria, Origen, and Tertullian) all pointed to the apostle John as the writer of 1, 2, and 3 John.*

John was well qualified to write. In 1 John 1:1–4, John states his credentials as an eyewitness to the words and works of Jesus. Twice in the letters he mentions that he heard Christ himself (1:1, 3). Six times he makes reference to seeing Christ. Once (1:1) he speaks of touching Jesus with his hands. Clearly John was not relating secondhand stories. He spoke with apostolic authority.

IN CONTEXT

John wrote one of the most well-known verses about the love of God in his Gospel. Usually if people only know one verse in the Bible, they know John 3:16: "For God so loved the world that he gave his one and only Son, that whoever believes in him shall not perish but have eternal life." Much of the book of I John is an expanded form of this idea. In fact, John almost restates John 3:16 in I John 4:9: "This is how God showed his love among us: He sent his one and only Son into the world that we might live through him."

John was a man who had laughed and talked and traveled with Jesus. He was one of Jesus' best friends. He should know, better than just about anyone, how to explain God's love to us.

2 John

IN CONTEXT

Here's the scoop. . .

Written: *around* A.D. *90*

Written by: *John the disciple*

Writing style: *a letter*

One-liner: *Keep your chin up and your hearts open, but keep a close watch on your faith.*

HANG IN THERE!

The Bible isn't a book like an encyclopedia. It isn't just full of facts. It is the record of God's actions and people's reactions. Second John is a good example of the slice-of-life style of the Bible. It is a letter that John wrote either to an actual woman or to the church (using "lady" as a metaphor). It contains about the amount of words that would fit on one papyrus sheet of paper. It is a very personal letter like one you might write to a friend going through a difficult time. What would you tell him? You would tell him to concentrate on what matters. You would tell him to keep his chin up. You would tell him to listen to the right people. That's what John did.

Concentrate on what matters: "His command is that you walk in love" (2 John 6).

Listen to the right people: "Anyone who runs ahead and does not continue in the teaching of Christ does not have God" (2 John 9).

questions q&a

Q. *Who were the Gnostics?*

A. *The readers of John's letters were confronted with an attractive yet dangerous challenge to the truth, a religious system called Gnosticism. This term comes from the Greek word for "knowledge." The goal of this movement was to acquire secret spiritual insight and special knowledge and thereby achieve a state of existence higher than the norm: enlightenment.*

The Gnostics believed in two spheres of reality. The physical world was evil and inferior, while the spirit-mind world was good and worthy. One of Gnosticism's ideas, therefore, was that Christ could not have had an actual body. To be truly good, the real Jesus was necessarily a phantom or spirit.

Gnosticism produced two kinds of followers: those who pursued an ascetic life, shunning the evil physical world with its false sensual pleasures; and others who indulged in the physical world precisely because it was inferior. For this group, physical pleasure was okay because it was irrelevant to the real world, namely the spiritual.

Both versions of Gnosticism perverted biblical teaching about the value of material creation, the relevance of stewardship over the earth (including our bodies), and the importance of moral care. To imagine that Jesus was mere spirit was extremely dangerous to the Bible's consistent teaching that God became a man. To seek enlightenment in abstract ideas was to direct the soul away from the personal God of love. John directed early believers to avoid this heresy, as we should today. Learn the faith from biblical Christians, not from followers of strange aberrations like this.

3 John

IN CONTEXT

Here's the scoop. . .

Written: *around* A.D. *90*

Written by: *John the disciple*

Writing style: *a personal letter*

One-liner: *Keep up the good work! I'll be there soon to deal with the power struggle.*

ON PROBLEMS IN THE CHURCH. . .

John's third letter, like his second, could fit on one sheet of papyrus paper. This third letter was even more personal, though. It was addressed to Gaius.

This is what we know about Gaius—not much. The name Gaius is mentioned four times in the New Testament in association with the church, but we have no idea whether these are all the same man or not. We know from this letter, though, that *this* Gaius was much loved and valued by John. We know that he was hospitable to traveling preachers such as John and the apostle Paul. We know that Gaius was helpful. We can pretty easily assume that Gaius was a good person who was committed to following God and doing good things. He was the kind of person we would like to be.

John wrote to Gaius because of a power struggle that had risen in Gaius's church. (Already? In the first century there was a power struggle in the church!) Evidently Diotrephes had been placed (maybe by John) in charge of the church. Later, though, when John sent people back to check on the church, Diotrephes wouldn't allow them to visit. John promised Gaius that he would come and deal with the situation soon.

It must have been as difficult to deal with church problems from a distance as it is to deal with them face-to-face today.

SCRIPTURE BITS

I could have no greater joy than to hear that my children live in the truth.
3 John 4 NLT

questions

Q. Why is God said to be "light"? (1 John 1:5)

A. In the Bible, light indicates what is good, pure, and holy. Darkness is synonymous with sin and evil. To say that God is light is to assert that God is perfectly pure and holy. Only God is without sin. He is the standard of perfection and truth by which everything is measured.

Light reveals. Light shows the true nature of things. When confronted by God, people become painfully aware of their own failures and sin. God's "light" brings this painful crisis, then liberates us into true freedom and joy.

Like a brilliant spotlight, God guides His creatures out of the dangerous darkness of their sinful lives into a place of safety and peace. Darkness and light cannot coexist (1 John 1:5–6). To know God, we must put aside sin.

Q. Why did John emphasize love so much? (2 John)

A. For the Christian, love is not an option; it is the motivating heart of all God calls us to do and become. When we love, we reveal the reality of our God, and we demonstrate our true identity as God's children. Love is a believer's calling card. It is the mark of God on us. People who do not know God sit up and take notice at this unusual freedom from fear and selfishness.

One of the great hallmarks of the early Christians was their affection for each other, prompting even their enemies to marvel. Christians have failed to love many times, as history clearly shows. The record of the church is very spotty on this lofty calling to love each other. But the obligation and joy are still our primary task—to show the character of God by freely sharing and caring and by building others up in God's grace. No matter what your job or how big or small your family, love is your first priority, your highest privilege and responsibility.

Q. *Is everyone who does good a Christian? (3 John 11)*

A. *God's laws define the good, and many people who profess no Christian faith follow those laws. For example, the commandments to honor parents (Exodus 20:12) and refrain from murder (20:13) are respected and observed by every human culture. In that sense, a person may be loyal to God's laws while being unaware of the God who authored them.*

Other people who live in what we loosely call Christian cultures tend to observe God's laws because they are reflected in a country's civil laws and a people's social habits. Stealing and lying are wrong, first because God condemns them, and secondarily because governments punish the former and discourage the latter. Non-Christians who "fit in" with a Christian culture have the benefits of compliance with God's law. However, compliance with law is no substitute for faith in Jesus Christ, who alone has paid the debt for our outrageous failure to obey God.

The flip side to our question is the sad fact that a lot of Christians fail to do good. God's people both succeed and fail to obey Him, and people without faith do the same. But God has promised to judge everyone according to Jesus' payment for sins on the cross, not compliance with the law. Our trust in Christ alone saves us, and no one can "do" enough to make up for refusing to ask God, in humble faith, for the mercy Jesus provides.

Jude

IN CONTEXT

Here's the scoop. . .

Written: *around A.D. 90*

Written by: *Jude, probably one of Jesus' brothers*

Writing style: *a letter of warning*

One-liner: *Watch out for people who use God's grace as an excuse for irresponsibility!*

I WON'T STAND FOR IT!

If you had to describe the tone of the book of Jude and if your only choices were (1) a party-type tone, (2) a business-type tone, or (3) an intense, big brother–type tone. . .you would definitely choose #3: an intense, big brother–type tone. Jude had something to say, and he expected everyone to listen and to take it as seriously as he did.

Truthfully, what Jude said *was* serious. He had spotted people who were destroying what God had created in the early church. He wrote this book as if to say, "Not on my watch." Not only did these people teach false doctrine, but they destroyed fellowship, deceived others, and used people for their own means. They basically said that now that God had paid the price for sins, it didn't matter what anyone did. They threw morals to the wind and encouraged everyone else to do the same.

It seems that almost every heresy is a distortion of the truth. If they were out and out lies, they would be much easier to spot. This heresy took a good thing, God's grace, and made it into a bad thing, a lack of responsibility to keep sin out of our lives. Jude wouldn't stand for it. Obviously.

SCRIPTURE BITS

Jude in a Nutshell

Live in such a way that God's love can bless you as you wait for the eternal life that our Lord Jesus Christ in his mercy is going to give you. Show mercy to those whose faith is wavering.

Jude 21–22 NLT

questions

Q. *How can a person identify a false teacher? (Jude 8)*

A. *False teachers add or subtract from the Bible. They often have a revelation that allegedly supplies new data about divine matters—data that the Bible fails to reveal, so to speak.*

False teachers devalue the work of Jesus Christ by making Him less than God incarnate. They twist the truth about the meaning of His death or reject the truth of His resurrection.

False teachers build small empires around the three tilting towers of phony ministry—money, sex, and power. They scheme to defraud followers of money. They practice immorality and then justify sin from twisted biblical teaching. They manipulate people for selfish ends, proving again the gullibility of the human species.

False teachers cater to popular trends, designing new formulas for happiness and salvation. These formulas often promise prosperity in exchange for financial support, a contract as bogus as buying real estate in the lost city of Atlantis. Yet people still sign on.

False teachers often say things that sound close to Christian teaching, but their mixture of truth and falsehood is hurtful, sometimes deadly. The Christian who wishes to avoid losses is advised to study the scriptures, know the history of the faith, support a sound church, and develop a network of friends whose progress in faith is trustworthy and true.

PROPHETIC BOOKS

Revelation is the only book of prophecy in the New Testament. Most of it is a vision that John (the disciple) had while he was in exile on an island called Patmos. A lot of people consider Revelation a difficult book to understand. You can see why when you consider this: It's a description of heaven recorded by someone living in a world that has never even seen a video and hardly any special effects. Trying to describe another dimension with only the first-century world as a comparison? It's a stretch. But stretching is what John did, and in this book we have a picture of some pretty amazing stuff.

revelation

Here's the scoop. . .

Written: *around* A.D. *95*

Written by: *John the disciple*

Writing style: *a prophetic vision*

One-liner: *Here's the last page of world history—the end of the world as we know it.*

THE END OF THE WORLD AS WE KNOW IT

The bulk of the book of Revelation is about the end of the world, the apocalypse. In case you haven't noticed, a lot of people have spent a lot of energy preparing for, talking about, studying about, and just generally trying to figure out the details of the end of the world. One of the reasons it is so intriguing is that when the Bible talks about it, it is always in figurative language. It almost feels like a puzzle sometimes. While the Bible tells us Jesus will return like a thief when no one expects it, somehow we can't keep from trying to figure out just exactly when He'll return.

We have to remember, though, that the important thing about the "second coming of Christ" and the end of the world as we know it is the reminder to live each day honorably and connected with God, so should this be our last day, it is a good one.

THE SEVEN CHURCHES

Before John's Revelation went into its wilder end-times images, Jesus gave simple messages to seven churches through John. For most of the messages, Jesus gave both an affirmation and a warning. Here's a quick review of those messages:

The Church at Ephesus:

You do the right things: you hate evil, you work hard, you persevere. But you've lost your first love. Put some heart back into your obedience (Revelation 2:1–7).

The Church at Smyrna:

These are hard times for you, and they are going to get harder. Be faithful and remember that your suffering won't last forever (Revelation 2:8–11).

The Church at Pergamum:

You've remained true to God in an evil place, but you have not rid yourself of your evil influences. In this way you leave yourself at risk (Revelation 2:12–17).

The Church at Thyatira:

You do many good things, but you let the people who teach lies continue to teach. How can you stand by and do nothing? (Revelation 2:18–29).

The Church at Sardis:

Wake up! You are so lifeless. You have a few people who are true to Me, but you are a zombie as a church. I need you to pay attention (Revelation 3:1–6).

The Church at Philadelphia:

You have been faithful. Keep persevering and I will protect you (Revelation 3:7–13).

The Church at Laodicea:

You are complacent. You are hanging there in the middle. I'd rather you be hot or cold than just lukewarm like you are (Revelation 3:14–22).

SPECIAL FX

After Jesus gives His charges to the churches, the rest of Revelation reads like a special effects display (or a sci-fi thriller, though this is certainly not fiction). John is in the midst of a vision of a whole different dimension than the one in which we live. He uses earthly images and language to give us as close a description as is possible. But how possible is it, really, to describe heaven in the language of earth? This is one of the main reasons that

Revelation is so intriguing and yet so difficult to understand.

Basically, the end of the world will be a time when evil makes a last bid for people's allegiance through world leadership. There will be attempts to control our food, our loyalty, and our very survival, and it all will be somehow connected to where we place our faith. This is a big reason people of faith get so uptight when the government tries to control their behavior in terms of their religious beliefs.

A REVELATION GLOSSARY OF TERMS

There are many different opinions about the order of the last events of our world. But most agree that there will be these common elements: An evil power will rise who will eventually demand that the world worship him. Jesus will take believers from the earth. Some kind of brand or mark will be required for people to buy or sell. There will be a great battle between Jesus and the evil world leader. Jesus will win and Satan will be defeated permanently. Then we will all give account for our lives.

Here are some terms you might have heard along the way:

666: We don't know exactly how this number will be used, but Revelation 13:18 does say that the number of the "beast" (part of the evil powerhead) will be 666. While no one is sure how the number will be used, everybody from movie producers to survivalists seem to know it's a number to stay away from.

Antichrist: The New Testament uses this term sometimes to mean any false teachers who try to influence people away from Christ, but in Revelation this term applies to a certain very powerful leader, probably with a political platform, who will be in power for three and a half years. He will eventually require the world to worship him and then will be defeated by Christ Himself.

Armageddon: The place of the final battle between Christ and the Antichrist, between good and evil.

Heaven: Revelation promises a new heaven and a new earth. Heaven will be our home when the world as we know it is over and gone.

Last judgment: This is when we will face God and give account for our lives. At this point it will matter most whether we have trusted Christ's death to cleanse us from sin or whether we have mistakenly (and foolishly) trusted our own goodness to do that.

Millennium: A millennium is a thousand years. *The* millennium in Revelation is the thousand years that Jesus will reign in peace. There are differing opinions as to *when* this millennium will happen in the order of "end-times" events.

Rapture: This is the one-time event when Jesus will immediately call all Christians home to heaven. Sometimes this term is used interchangeably with "second coming of Christ."

Tribulation: This term refers to a time of terror and trouble for believers on earth. Some people believe this seven-year period will happen before Christ returns and the rapture occurs. Others believe it will happen after that.

THINK ABOUT IT THIS WAY

If you like to read the last page of a book first, then Revelation is for you. In the great war between God and evil, God wins. That makes every day look a lot better.

questions

Q. *Is Revelation to be understood literally? (Revelation 1:1)*

A. *Revelation uses three types of literature. First, it is a letter written by the apostle John to seven churches in Asia. Second, it is prophecy, speaking God's judgment and truth. Finally, it is apocalyptic writing, a common form of Jewish literature.*

Apocalyptic literature is written to people undergoing persecution. It contains symbolic imagery and visions and looks to God's triumph at the end of time to convey hope for the faithful. Apocalyptic literature is written not in chronological order but according to literary priorities. In addition, some visions or dreams contain symbols that are imaginative and powerful and read like fantasy—a beast with seven heads and ten horns (Revelation 13:1) or locusts with scorpions' tails and human heads (Revelation 9:10).

The reader of Revelation must decide whether a passage is epistolary, prophetic, or apocalyptic, then whether its intention is literal or figurative. The details of this important interpretive process will require your further study through Bible commentaries, original language, and theological reflection.

Q. *What are the "seven churches"? (Revelation 2–3)*

A. *John is writing to seven churches in Asia that are under growing persecution from Rome. As these churches cope with the pressure and temptations of living in a pagan culture, there remains a question whether they will faithfully serve the Lord until the end. John writes to affirm God's sovereignty and faithfulness and to encourage the churches to stand firm.*

The letters contain greetings to each church, an assessment of how the church is doing, a commendation or warning, a command to persevere, and a promise. The seven letters together describe what weakens the faith of churches and individuals: losing initial passion for Jesus, losing hope, becoming tolerant of sin, compromising moral behavior, and having inactive or lukewarm faith.

Given the deficits of these seven churches, they are still to be "lampstands"—light illuminating the gospel of Christ to the world. They are models for present-day churches of the difficulty and responsibility of keeping faith strong under adversity.

Q. *What is the great tribulation? (Revelation 7:14)*

A. *The meaning of this term must be integrated with other terms: the rapture, the millennium, and the identity of the 144,000 chosen people.*

Dispensational theology identifies the great tribulation as a seven-year future period of havoc and pain, Satan's last and greatest opportunity for evil before the second coming of Christ inaugurates God's heavenly kingdom. This view gained wide popularity through the Scofield Reference Bible and, in the 1960s, through the writings of Hal Lindsey. In this theology, the rapture occurs before the tribulation (although some allow for a rapture in the middle of the tribulation) or following it.

A more symbolic interpretation identifies the term as the period of spiritual warfare that the Christian church endures throughout its history. In great conflict with Satan, the gospel message is nevertheless carried to all the nations—God's good news told by those who love God more than life.

Q. *What does the number 666 mean? (Revelation 13:18)*

A. *The name is either a cryptic way of identifying an actual person (equal to the sum of the numeric equivalents of the letters in a name) or a symbol of evil.*

The latter interpretation derives from the idea of perfection associated with the number seven (seven days of creation, seven lampstands, etc.) and the idea of completion associated with the number three (the three persons of the Trinity). By these terms, the number six repeated three times would indicate complete imperfection, that is, evil. This fits the profile of the beast described here.

Some early commentators thought that Nero, emperor of Rome (A.D. 54–68) and persecutor of Christians, was identified in this text. The numerical value of his name in Hebrew equals 666.

Q. *What will the new heaven and the new earth be like? (Revelation 21:1)*

A. *We can hardly know. Surely they will be beyond anything we can imagine. The imagery of the Bible suggests an environment of superlative quality with no sense of diminishing resources. Competition is also eliminated, leaving no possible incentive for selfishness, hoarding, or private property (were those things even possible in the spiritual afterlife). The central focus of happiness in the biblical account, however, is not the richness of the environment but always the immediate presence of believers with the triune God.*

After the final defeat of Satan and the end of death and evil, all who have believed on the Lord Jesus Christ will be forever in the presence of God. No matter how hard, hurtful, or despairing life on earth has been, those who trust in Jesus will be united with Christ for eternity.

6. HOW DO I USE THE BIBLE?

The Bible's not just for sitting on a shelf or carrying to church. It's for reading and understanding. It's for changing our hearts, our habits, and our lives. Here are some tips.

How do I use it?

do you have any of those towels in your bathroom that are the "nice" towels that no one uses? They hang there and look pretty. They match the colors in the bathroom. They are cosmetic, aesthetic. Their purpose is not to clean or to dry, but to look good (and to provoke consternation when some oaf actually uses them to dry his hands).

Sometimes the Bible gets treated like a guest towel. Because it is a sacred and powerful book, we can sometimes hold it so separate from us that it doesn't do what it's meant to do in our lives. It doesn't get the chance to change us, to grow us, to let God whisper in our ear or call into our hearts.

When the books of the Bible were originally written, they were written as practical documents. They were written in everyday language. Even though some books were written as sermons, some were written as songs, and so on, they were still written to help people face everyday life, not just the big moments. They were often written with urgency.

Our challenge is to use those books in the same way they were written— every day, facing life squarely, sometimes urgently. The Bible is not a fancy guest towel. Don't leave it on the rack.

An overview

Using the Bible includes knowing what it says, understanding what it means, applying it to our lives, and letting it make us better people. Here's one way to break it down:

As a companion. We need to know what the Bible says. We need to interact with the truths of the Bible regularly. It's easy to think, "Oh, I need to really study the Bible, but I don't have time to really give it its due." Then weeks and even years pass and we never do anything at all with the Bible because we don't think we have the time to engage it the way we think we should. The good news is that there is a middle ground. You might never have time to do an in-depth word study. Nevertheless, just reading the Bible a little at a time is an important element of allowing God to use His truth to affect your life. A lot of people call this practice "having a quiet time."

As a guide. We need to understand what the Bible means. Sometimes it's not enough just to read the Bible. Sometimes we need to study it. We need to be able to dig a little deeper into a portion of the Bible and understand it through and through. We need to put pencil and paper to it. We can use the Bible as an instruction guide to help us figure out life.

As a tool. We need to apply the truth of the Bible to our lives. Studying the Bible is not just about knowing facts. It's about knowing God. It's about interacting with truth that changes us. We can use the Bible as a tool that will chisel away at us until we are better reflections of God's image in the world.

As a source of wisdom. We need to become better people because of the work God will do in us through the truths of Scripture. Once we know what's there, we need to meditate on it, to soak in it, to let it soften us and mold us. We can use the Bible to change not only our habits and our actions, but our perspective and our very caliber of being.

That's a lot to expect from one book, isn't it? That's what makes the Bible the Bible.

The Bible as a companion: on the QT

A lot of people have read the Bible every day for years and years. They set aside time somewhere in their day to sit down and read. You may hear them talk about their quiet time (QT). They make it a habit, like working out or eating breakfast.

In this fast-paced world, having a regular quiet time has advantages at every level of our lives. It centers us. It quiets us. It puts that pesky horse back in front of the cart. It makes the Bible a welcome friend that we check in with every day. It gives God the opportunity to align our agenda with His.

A quiet time usually consists of these things:

- *Stillness.* Stillness puts the "Q" in QT. Stillness is something that you may not get all day if you don't deliberately make it happen. Stillness is practically a prerequisite to hearing God speak even though stillness is almost extinct in our culture. Being still prepares us to hear from God and to learn from what we read.

- *Bible reading:* There is something about reading the Bible that connects us to good things. Many people follow a reading plan similar to the one included in this section. That way they know what to read each day. Others just pick a place and start reading. Either way, it's a good thing to open up the Bible and let God speak to you.

- *Prayer:* Prayer is listening and speaking. When we are quiet and still and we open ourselves up to God, that is prayer. When we verbalize our worship, that is prayer. When we ask God to help us or someone we know, that is prayer. Prayer is actually a simple act of faith. When we pray, we are acting out our faith that Someone is listening. However tenuous that faith, it is what God asks of us.

If we do these things, even for just a short amount of time, then we face life with more resilience. We have a little more fuel to keep us going, a little more ammunition to shoot down the crazies when life overwhelms us, a little more opportunity to let God do His thing in our lives rather than living our lives apart from Him. Reading the Bible is important.

If you grew up in the church, then you might have heard a lot about having a quiet time. Because reading the Bible is a good basic starting point for a life of faith, it's often the first thing people do when they search for God. A problem sometimes arises, though, when a person stops with just having a quick quiet time. Often you'll hear something like "Sometimes I feel like I'm going through the motions. I wonder if it's a good thing to read my

what's for Dinner?

Reading your Bible is like feeding yourself spiritually. Guess what? When it comes to how to read your Bible, the answer is a smorgasbord of choices. Different people gravitate toward different Bible study plans. Choose one that suits who you are.

An Appetizer—If you're just beginning to study the Bible, start with something that's really easy to digest. Begin with easy-to-read, well-known passages. Here are a few:

- John 14
- Romans 8
- Psalm 23
- Psalm 150

- 1 John 1
- John 10
- 1 Corinthians 15
- Hebrews 11

- Luke 24
- Matthew 5–7
- Psalm 1

After you've whet your appetite, try a whole book, such as John, Acts, 1 John, Romans, or Ephesians. Some good beginner books in the Old Testament include Psalms, Proverbs, and Ruth. Hey, you've got to start somewhere.

A Sampler Platter—A lot of Bibles include plans to read the whole Bible through in a year. Some Bibles are even divided into 365 daily readings combining selections from the Old and New Testaments, Psalms, and Proverbs for every day. Most of these plans will probably take at least fifteen to twenty minutes each day but will give you a variety. They can also be adjusted to stretch out over two or three years if that's where life takes you.

Meat and Potatoes—Start at page one and read through the whole Bible (not all in one sitting, of course). Many people follow this simplest of plans even though so many Bible study helps and plans are available at Christian bookstores. What makes this sometimes difficult is that the beginning of the Bible includes some record keeping that can make for a long read. Be careful not to get bogged down in that.

The Daily Special—Follow a Bible study guide, either one that studies a topic of interest to you or one focused on one of the books of the Bible. You can also join a small group Bible study and study with someone.

Bible just for the sake of being consistent." The next thing you'll hear is "I'm going to take a break until it feels like my heart's in it again."

Here's something important to remember. Just about everything in life is a balance. Sharing a few moments with the Bible (and thus with God) consistently (which means often enough that you miss it if you don't) is a mainstay of a life of faith. But the shape of that quiet time can take a lot of different forms. Some people read through the Bible from beginning to end. Others follow devotional guides that include a scripture passage. Still others read books about scripture.

Our journey with the Bible should be like a strand in a tapestry. Sometimes it may be very prominent; sometimes it may be really deep. Other times it might ride the surface—but it always needs to be there.

If you feel like you're just going through the motions, maybe the answer is not to stop the motion, but to find a new way to do it. The balance between the new discoveries and the same old routine is often the glue that holds a person together for the long term. Keep plugging away.

The Bible as a Guide: studying the Truth

Studying the Bible is a step further than reading the Bible. Studying the Bible is reading with a pencil and paper close at hand to take notes and to dig a little deeper into what you're reading.

> *But you have received the Holy Spirit, and he lives within you, so you don't need anyone to teach you what is true. For the Spirit teaches you all things (1 John 2:27 NLT).*

In other words, studying the Bible is inviting God to tutor you. That's sort of a mind-blower. You can take a night class from God Himself.

Yes, at times, it can be a little intimidating to think about studying the Bible. If you've hung around scholars at all, you've heard them talk about "hermeneutics" and "exegeses" and Greek words that sound something like "gargoyle oxymoron." But remember this: Sudying the Bible is not an esoteric practice reserved for preachers and monks. The whole point of having a Bible in your own language and shelves of study helps is that anyone can study.

THINK ABOUT IT THIS WAY

Here's a final warning about having a quiet time. More than any other spiritual discipline, this one seems to be thrown all the responsibility for marking our level of spirituality. If we are being pretty consistent with it, we feel pretty good about things. If we aren't, we often feel like a failure. Frankly, we need to get over that.

Think about it this way. What if a husband and wife agreed that they would spend an hour talking every night? Then they let that become the only barometer of their relationship. It would be a great thing if they kept up their commitment, but it wouldn't be enough to base the whole relationship on. What about whether they were serving each other, supporting each other, taking care of their kids and home? They would be foolish to define their relationship *only* by whether they kept their conversation appointment. They would be just as foolish to never even try to keep it.

Obviously from the way God talked to the Hebrews in the Old Testament, He wanted His relationship with them to be a priority. He wants the same with us. Spending time reading the Bible is one of those ways. But our relationship with God is even bigger than that. It's not just about our own efforts. Keep it all in balance.

Q. *When is the best time to read my Bible?*

A. Early morning is a great choice, but depending on your schedule, that may not be possible. The important thing is to pick a time you can stick with, whenever that is for you.

Where do you start? Start with your own curiosity. What do you want to know about? Is there a passage that you particularly like? A book of the Bible that you really respond to when you read it? Start there! Here are some tips.

Start with the study helps in your own Bible. Many Bibles have notes at the bottom of the page or scattered throughout the text. These notes are not inspired by God. They are written by regular everyday people—who have studied that scripture passage. Read the notes. Look up the other Bible verses that the notes refer you to. See what else the Bible has to say about the verses you are reading.

Here are some categories or methods of Bible study:

WORD STUDIES

You can learn a lot by researching a certain word. For instance, let's suppose you are reading along in Colossians and you read. . .

> *Since God chose you to be the holy people whom he loves, you must clothe yourselves with tenderhearted mercy, kindness, humility, gentleness, and patience (Colossians 3:12 NLT).*

You think, *Hmm, "mercy." Do I have enough mercy? I think I'd like to explore that a little.*

That means that you are going to do a word study on "mercy." So you grab your pencil and paper and write "Mercy" at the top; then under it you write "Col. 3:12." That's your starting point. Beside "Col. 3:12," you write what you know about mercy from that verse. "I need to show mercy by the way I live."

Next you look at any study notes that your Bible lists for Colossians. 3:12 to see if there is any information there about mercy.

If not, then you go to the concordance in the back of your Bible, if there is one. A concordance is like an index. For every word in it, it gives you a list of verses that include that word. Keep in mind that the concordance you find in the back of your Bible is more than likely not an "exhaustive" concordance. That means it doesn't list every single verse that includes the word "mercy."

But write down the verses that it does list and look them up. Make notes by each one that tells you one more thing about mercy and how to incorporate it into your life.

If you want to go a step further in this word study, then go to an exhaustive concordance. This is a separate book that is a big index to the Bible. You can check one out at the library (or, if it's a reference book, just use it there). You can find concordances at church libraries or at bookstores. You can also go to your favorite Internet book shopping site and do a search for "concordances." Wherever you go, you'll almost always find a concordance with the name "Strong" in it. That is a traditional concordance that has become a standard. You'll find some others, as well. Before you buy one, check to see what translations it lists. The original *Strong's Concordance* is based on the King James Bible, but now there are new editions for other Bible versions.

When you look up "mercy" in an exhaustive concordance, you have even more verses to look up and compare. Jot down what you find out about mercy from each verse. Mark through the verses that use your search word in a completely different way and so don't help with your particular study.

When you have seen the way "mercy" is used throughout the Bible, go back and read your original verse again. At the bottom of your paper, write your definition of "mercy" and what it means in your life based on all that you have read.

This is a simplified example of a word study.

DID YOU KNOW?

Another option for concordances is to buy a computer concordance. This way you can type in a search word and see it on the screen. Only you know your relationship with your computer well enough to know if this would be a help or a hindrance for you. If you'll end up throwing your computer and your Bible out the window, don't try it.

word study worksheet

THE WORD I'M STUDYING: _____

Verse   *What does this verse tell me about the word I'm studying?*

_____   _____

_____   _____

_____   _____

_____   _____

_____   _____

_____   _____

_____   _____

_____   _____

SO. . .WHAT DO I KNOW ABOUT _____ FROM ALL OF THIS?

_____

_____

_____

_____

VERSE-BY-VERSE STUDIES

Where a word study skips around in the Bible according to the word that you're looking up, a verse-by-verse study plods through a section of the Bible. For instance, if you read Colossians 3:12 in the process of reading through Colossians as a verse-by-verse study, you might ask yourself questions like these:

Since God chose you. . .

What does it mean that God chose me? How is that different than if I chose Him?

. . .to be the holy people whom he loves. . .

How do I know if I'm holy? What kind of holiness does God want from me? How does God's love affect my holiness? Perhaps you'd do a word study on holiness or simply look up the definition or find a character in the Bible who was considered holy. Then back to the verse.

. . .you must clothe yourselves with tenderhearted mercy, kindness, humility, gentleness, and patience.

How can I "clothe" myself with these attitudes? Can I make myself merciful? Humble? Gentle? Patient? What does each of these mean, and how can I "put them on"?

After you have lined out your questions, you might use a regular old dictionary to answer some of them. You might look up "holy" just to see what it means. Your Bible study notes might tell you to study election in order to know how God "chose" you.

You also might do some word studies. For instance, you might do a word study for each of the traits listed. On the other hand, you might sit before God and ask Him to teach you more of what a verse means. For instance, being "the holy people whom he loves." You might ask God to show you the ways He loves you so that you'll understand more of the kind of person He wants you to be.

DID YOU KNOW?

As you study the Bible, you'll probably purchase a few books to help, such as a concordance, which we've already mentioned, and a Bible dictionary. A dictionary gives more information about a topic than just the verses in which that topic is mentioned.

Another Bible study help that you might refer to is called a "commentary." A commentary is someone else's comments about sections of the Bible. If you know you are going to be studying a certain book, you might buy or check out a commentary on that book to see what someone else's studies turned up. That's a simple example of a verse-by-verse study.

TOPICAL STUDIES

This is all self-explanatory when you get down to it. A word study starts with a word in the Bible. A verse study starts with a verse. A topical study (not tropical) starts with a topic. Let's say for the last week you've been chewing out everyone around your house and job, so you decide to do a topical study on mercy.

First, you would look up what mercy means, including other words that mean about the same thing as mercy. You would then look those words up in a concordance and start tracking them down.

As you looked at the verses, you would notice if there are any particular people whom the Bible associates with mercy. (You'd probably discover that David showed mercy to King Saul back in the Old Testament.) Once you found examples of merciful people, you'd read about them. How did mercy show itself in their lives?

You might also check the library or the bookstore for books on mercy and read those books as part of your study. This is a simplified example of a topical study.

GROUP BIBLE STUDIES

You don't usually have to look too far to find a group Bible study. The closest place to find one is usually the Sunday school (morning program) of a church somewhere close by. Traditionally, churches are made up of a lot of groups of people studying the Bible. Churches often host many different kinds of Bible studies. If the church is big enough to publish a bulletin for its services, grab one and look through it. Often you'll find a list of Bible studies that are held during the week either at the church or in people's homes.

You might want to call the church office and ask the church secretary (who usually knows more than anybody about what is going on) about the Bible studies. Make sure the group is a study group, and if you can, find out what they are studying. Usually you'll be given the number for the leader of that group. Ask the leader what's going on. Ask when the next study starts or whether the one they are in would be easy for you to jump into.

Q. *I'm having trouble making the time. Any suggestions?*

A. You might consider making a pact with a friend who is also trying to read the Bible every day. Also, you might want to evaluate the time you've set aside to get this done. Life is hard enough by itself. Is there a more convenient time or a time that lends itself more to your discretion?

If you can't find a group Bible study to be a part of, you can always start one. How? Well, you can gather a few people and buy a group study book to follow (there are loads at Christian bookstores) or just read through a Bible book and ask your group the same questions you would ask yourself:

- What did this verse mean to the people it was written to?

- What does it mean for us today?

This is a simple description of a group Bible study. And on page 347, you'll find a sheet you can reproduce to lead a group Bible study or a personal Bible study of your own.

However you choose to study the Bible, it's a process that goes one step further than just reading the words. Studying the Bible means reading the words and then understanding what they mean. Studying the Bible means sifting through some other people's ideas and sitting in God's presence as you come up with ideas of your own. It's asking Him to teach you as you go along and trusting Him to do that. Studying the Bible is being brave enough to say, "At this point in my life, as best as I can tell with God's guidance, this truth means this to my life."

If you want to do more Bible study on your own, use the list of sources in the back of this book as a birthday wish list and dig in. It will be worth your while.

DID YOU KNOW?

The good thing about group studies is that you hear a lot of ideas. The bad thing about group studies is that you hear a lot of ideas. Hmm. Two sides of the same coin. Remember that people all have their own idea about what a phrase or word in the Bible means. What's important, though, in any study is that you discover God's intent for the Bible passage and how your lives should be affected by the truth there.

THINK ABOUT IT THIS WAY

Different opinions are sometimes difficult to work through no matter what the opinions are about. When you are discussing the Bible, differing opinions can be even more difficult. That's why, historically, wars and revolutions have broken out over biblical interpretations. Here are some tips to help you through those tight spots.

- Recognize the differences that are there rather than trying to resolve them or ignore them. It's okay to have different opinions. You can agree to disagree.
- Don't be discouraged by disagreements. We are all on a journey. We don't learn at the same pace or at the same time.
- Not all issues are right/wrong issues. Leave a little room to consider that each of you may bend a little bit as you grow and gain more information.

Bible study sheet

PASSAGE: _____

To whom was this verse written? _____

1. As far as I know, why was it written?

2. If I had to pick the theme of this passage, what would it be?

3. What was the significance of this passage to the first people who read it?

4. What is the significance of this passage to me today?

5. How should the truth of this passage affect my actions?

6. If I had to rewrite this passage in capsule form (one or two sentences), how would I word it?

The Bible as a tool: Applying the Truth

The Bible isn't an encyclopedia or a novel. It's not just a bound set of facts and figures, plotlines and poems. God gave us the Bible to communicate Himself to us and to change our lives through that knowledge of Him. Bible writers had a lot to say about applying the Bible to our lives. Here are just two examples:

Dear brothers and sisters, what's the use of saying you have faith if you don't prove it by your actions? That kind of faith can't save anyone (James 2:14 NLT).

Dear children, let us stop just saying we love each other; let us really show it by our actions. It is by our actions that we know we are living in the truth, so we will be confident when we stand before the Lord (1 John 3:18–19 NLT).

BANDAGES AND BIBLE VERSES

It's like this: If you cut your hand, it needs a bandage. If that bandage is sitting there on the counter in its wrapper, it's not doing any good. The bandage only helps when you apply it to the wound.

We are all wounded—we don't always do what's right even when we

Q. *What kind of Bible should I use?*

A. That's up to you. Check out the chapter in this book on different translations. Some Bibles are more formal than others. Pick the translation that you will enjoy reading the most. That will encourage you to read more often.

THINK ABOUT IT
THIS WAY

The Truth is a Chisel

Think of yourself as a block of marble. Think of the truth of the Bible as a chisel. Think of God as a master sculptor. Maybe the marble doesn't always want to get beaten and chipped away, but that's what it takes to be sculpted. The marble that faces its finest destiny is the marble that stays within reach of the chisel until the job is done.

Spend time courageously facing the truth and allowing God to change you in light of that truth. When you do, you are the marble wanting to be made into your destiny: God's image.

---

really, really want to. God has given us a bandage with a built-in antibiotic called the truth. It's up to us to apply that bandage and find the healing that is there.

So what does it mean to apply the Bible? It means to take it personally. If the Bible says that God desires our obedience, it's up to us to say, "Then how should I obey?" If the Bible tells a story about a man who is unmerciful and lives to regret it, it's up to us to say, "How do I measure up in the 'merciful' category?" If a Bible passage commends God's very nature and lavishes compliments on Him, then it's up to us to say, "Do I worship God this way? Am I this caught up in His power and majesty?"

The first step to applying a verse or a passage of the Bible is to ask yourself what kind of passage it is.

- Is it a story? (If so, you'll learn from someone's example or a conversation.)

- Is it a teaching passage, like a sermon or a letter? (If so, you'll probably need to respond to a direct command or lesson.)

- Is it an artistic passage, like a song or a poem? (If so, you'll probably be inspired by the thoughts of someone else to feel or think differently about God.)

You'll have to ask yourself, "Does this passage mean I should do exactly what the person in this story or passage is doing?" Sometimes that's easy; for instance, "Accept each other just as Christ has accepted you; then God will be glorified" (Romans 15:7 NLT). This verse is from a teaching passage, a letter from Paul to a church. It is easy to see the truth we should apply. Give people a break because God gave you a break. Accept them like they are.

Other times it's a little more complex. Let's say you read the story in which God told Abraham to sacrifice his only son. God stopped Abraham before he did it and commended his willingness to give up what was most important to him (Genesis 22). Now, watch closely: When you apply this passage, it has nothing to do with how you treat your children. It has to do with how you prioritize your life. Are there things so important you couldn't give them up even if God asked you to?

See? Ask yourself what the bottom line is. Then ask, how should my life be different in light of this? Then make the change. That's how you apply the Bible.

Are All Passages Equal?

When it comes to application, no, they aren't. When you compare the genealogies of Numbers to the teaching passages in Romans, Romans will be a lot easier to apply to your life. Admitting that is true doesn't mean that you are dishonoring part of the Bible. Those genealogies are essential to the whole story of the Bible. They have their place. They are just as inspired and authoritative as any other part of the Bible. But it's okay to admit that when you need encouragement, they're probably not the first passages you turn to.

The Bible as a source of wisdom: Meditating on the Truth

Wisdom is knowing how to do life. It's what we all wish we had. It's what we often wonder how to get. It's what God promises to the person who gets to know the Bible and, thus, to know Him. Check these verses out.

How can men be wise? The only way to begin is by reverence for God. For growth in wisdom comes from obeying his laws (Psalm 111:10 TLB).

How does a man become wise? The first step is to trust and reverence the Lord! (Proverbs 1:7 TLB).

For the Lord grants wisdom! His every word is a treasure of knowledge and understanding. He grants good sense to the godly—his saints. He is their shield, protecting them and guarding their pathway. He shows how to distinguish right from wrong, how to find the right decision every time. For wisdom and truth will enter the very center of your being, filling your life with joy (Proverbs 2:6–10 TLB).

For the reverence and fear of God are basic to all wisdom. Knowing God results in every other kind of understanding (Proverbs 9:10 TLB).

It makes sense that knowing God, the creator of life, is the best way to understand life. It also makes sense that the best path to knowing God is to read His thoughts and words—the Bible.

It's a great thing to read a bit of the Bible every day. It's also a great thing to study passages of the Bible deeply, to understand it more than to read it. Beyond that, it's absolutely essential that we apply the truths of the Bible to our lives. If we don't, then what is the knowledge for? The final step is literally giving ourselves over to the truths of the Bible, deliberately and passionately allowing God the time and space to carve those truths into us. As we read and study, we come to know the truth. As we carry that truth with us through the years, applying it to everyday life, soaking in it, meditating on it, then we are giving God time to change us, to grow us up, to make us wise, to make us like Him.

That is what using the Bible is ultimately all about.

THINK ABOUT IT THIS WAY

HOW NOT to use the Bible

The Bible could possibly be used in these ways, but it really wasn't intended to be.

10. As a booster seat for your child at the dinner table.

9. As a way to prove you are right and someone else is wrong, so you can say, "I told you so."

8. As a doorstop.

7. As a way to win a fight with your spouse.

6. As a way to justify something wrong you've done.

5. As only a coffee-table book.

4. As a source of mere intellectual knowledge.

3. As a quote to yell at your kid.

2. Like a magic eight ball by closing your eyes and pointing to a passage to find an arbitrary answer to some question you have.

1. As a reason to reject or mistreat somebody (yes, even if they're ugly or dirty or unkempt or have ten pierced body parts).

Q. How should I pray?

A. You should listen and you should speak. Think of God as an ideal father figure, in other words, a good dad. He wants to hear about what's important to you, and He wants to tell you things. Give yourself and Him the opportunity to do both.

Q. *How much time should I be spending in prayer and Bible Reading?*

A. That is ultimately going to be up to you. Use this rule of thumb, though. Spend enough time to relax, maybe at least ten minutes. But remember this. Don't set your goals so high that you never sit down to be with God. It's easy to let days slip by because you never had enough time to sit down. Sitting down for ten minutes every day for a week to read a few verses and connect with God is better than waiting a week looking for thirty available minutes.

Q. *Should I do anything else besides read my Bible and pray?*

A. We think of worship as something that happens in church, but worship is actually something that should happen every day. Acknowledging to God that He is worth your time and effort is worship. Singing softly is worship. Anytime we honor God, that is worship. Worship should go hand in hand with reading the Bible.

reading the bible in 365 days

Here's a plan for reading through the Bible in a year. You can find a lot of different plans for doing this. You can even buy Bibles that are literally divided into daily readings. The following plan is a good one to start with.

Here are the specifics. Following this plan, you will read the Old Testament first (while some plans give you a reading from both the Old and New Testaments each day). You'll find that some passages listed here are quite long, while others are short. We call these long passages "skimmable." Some of them are passages that are list or genealogy intensive. We could have divided them into a few days, but then you'd struggle through a difficult read for a few days rather than one day. Other passages are short because there is so much in them to digest. Feel free to customize this plan to fit your life.

Happy reading.

Day	*Date*	*Reference*
Day 1	January 1	Genesis 1:1–3:24
Day 2	January 2	Genesis 4:1–5:32
Day 3	January 3	Genesis 6:1–8:22
Day 4	January 4	Genesis 9:1–11:32
Day 5	January 5	Genesis 12:1–14:24
Day 6	January 6	Genesis 15:1–17:27
Day 7	January 7	Genesis 18:1–20:18
Day 8	January 8	Genesis 21:1–23:20
Day 9	January 9	Genesis 24:1–28:9
Day 10	January 10	Genesis 28:10–30:43
Day 11	January 11	Genesis 31:1–36:43

Day 12	January 12	Genesis 37:1–41:57
Day 13	January 13	Genesis 42:1–45:28
Day 14	January 14	Genesis 46:1–50:26
Day 15	January 15	Exodus 1:1–4:31
Day 16	January 16	Exodus 5:1–7:13
Day 17	January 17	Exodus 7:14–12:30
Day 18	January 18	Exodus 12:31–18:27
Day 19	January 19	Exodus 19:1–24:18
Day 20	January 20	Exodus 25:1–31:18
Day 21	January 21	Exodus 32:1–34:35
Day 22	January 22	Exodus 35:1–40:38
Day 23	January 23	Leviticus 1:1–7:38
Day 24	January 24	Leviticus 8:1–10:20
Day 25	January 25	Leviticus 11:1–17:16
Day 26	January 26	Leviticus 18:1–22:33
Day 27	January 27	Leviticus 23:1–25:55
Day 28	January 28	Leviticus 26:1–27:34
Day 29	January 29	Numbers 1:1–4:49
Day 30	January 30	Numbers 5:1–10:10
Day 31	January 31	Numbers 10:11–14:45

Day 32	February 1	Numbers 15:1–21:35
Day 33	February 2	Numbers 22:1–25:18
Day 34	February 3	Numbers 26:1–31:54
Day 35	February 4	Numbers 32:1–34:29
Day 36	February 5	Numbers 35:1–36:13
Day 37	February 6	Deuteronomy 1:1–5:33
Day 38	February 7	Deuteronomy 6:1–11:32
Day 39	February 8	Deuteronomy 12:1–15:23
Day 40	February 9	Deuteronomy 16:18–20:20
Day 41	February 10	Deuteronomy 21:1–26:19
Day 42	February 11	Deuteronomy 27:1–30:20
Day 43	February 12	Deuteronomy 31:1–34:12
Day 44	February 13	Joshua 1:1–5:12
Day 45	February 14	Joshua 5:13–8:35
Day 46	February 15	Joshua 9:1–12:24
Day 47	February 16	Joshua 13:1–19:51
Day 48	February 17	Joshua 20:1–24:33
Day 49	February 18	Judges 1:1–3:6
Day 50	February 19	Judges 3:7–8:35
Day 51	February 20	Judges 9:1–12:15

Day 52	February 21	Judges 13:1–16:31
Day 53	February 22	Judges 17:1–21:25
Day 54	February 23	Ruth 1:1–4:22
Day 55	February 24	1 Samuel 1:1–3:21
Day 56	February 25	1 Samuel 4:1–7:17
Day 57	February 26	1 Samuel 8:1–12:25
Day 58	February 27	1 Samuel 13:1–15:35
Day 59	February 28	1 Samuel 16:1–17:58
Day 60	March 1	1 Samuel 18:1–20:42
Day 61	March 2	1 Samuel 21:1–26:25
Day 62	March 3	1 Samuel 27:1–31:13
Day 63	March 4	2 Samuel 1:1–4:12
Day 64	March 5	2 Samuel 5:1–7:29
Day 65	March 6	2 Samuel 8:1–10:19
Day 66	March 7	2 Samuel 11:1–12:31
Day 67	March 8	2 Samuel 13:1–14:33
Day 68	March 9	2 Samuel 15:1–20:26
Day 69	March 10	2 Samuel 21:1–24:25
Day 70	March 11	1 Kings 1:1–4:34
Day 71	March 12	1 Kings 5:1–8:66

Day 72	March 13	1 Kings 9:1–11:43
Day 73	March 14	1 Kings 12:1–16:34
Day 74	March 15	1 Kings 17:1–19:21
Day 75	March 16	1 Kings 20:1–22:53
Day 76	March 17	2 Kings 1:1–8:15
Day 77	March 18	2 Kings 8:16–10:36
Day 78	March 19	2 Kings 11:1–13:25
Day 79	March 20	2 Kings 14:1–17:41
Day 80	March 21	2 Kings 18:1–21:26
Day 81	March 22	2 Kings 22:1–25:30
Day 82	March 23	1 Chronicles 1:1–9:44
Day 83	March 24	1 Chronicles 10:1–12:40
Day 84	March 25	1 Chronicles 13:1–17:27
Day 85	March 26	1 Chronicles 18:1–22:1
Day 86	March 27	1 Chronicles 22:2–27:34
Day 87	March 28	1 Chronicles 28:1–29:30
Day 88	March 29	2 Chronicles 1:1–5:1
Day 89	March 30	2 Chronicles 5:2–9:31
Day 90	March 31	2 Chronicles 10:1–14:1
Day 91	April 1	2 Chronicles 14:2–16:14

Day 92	April 2	2 Chronicles 17:1–21:3
Day 93	April 3	2 Chronicles 21:4–24:27
Day 94	April 4	2 Chronicles 25:1–28:27
Day 95	April 5	2 Chronicles 29:1–32:33
Day 96	April 6	2 Chronicles 33:1–36:1
Day 97	April 7	2 Chronicles 36:2–23
Day 98	April 8	Ezra 1:1–2:70
Day 99	April 9	Ezra 3:1–6:22
Day 100	April 10	Ezra 7:1–8:36
Day 101	April 11	Ezra 9:1–10:44
Day 102	April 12	Nehemiah 1:1–2:10
Day 103	April 13	Nehemiah 2:11–3:32
Day 104	April 14	Nehemiah 4:1–7:73
Day 105	April 15	Nehemiah 8:1–10:39
Day 106	April 16	Nehemiah 11:1–13:31
Day 107	April 17	Esther 1:1–2:23
Day 108	April 18	Esther 3:1–4:17
Day 109	April 19	Esther 5:1–10:3
Day 110	April 20	Job 1:1–2:13
Day 111	April 21	Job 3:1–14:22

Day 112	April 22	Job 15:1–21:34
Day 113	April 23	Job 22:1–31:40
Day 114	April 24	Job 32:1–37:24
Day 115	April 25	Job 38:1–41:34
Day 116	April 26	Job 42:1–17
Day 117	April 27	Psalms 1:1–4:8
Day 118	April 28	Psalms 5:1–8:9
Day 119	April 29	Psalms 9:1–12:8
Day 120	April 30	Psalms 13:1–16:11
Day 121	May 1	Psalms 17:1–20:9
Day 122	May 2	Psalms 21:1–24:10
Day 123	May 3	Psalms 25:1–28:9
Day 124	May 4	Psalms 29:1–32:11
Day 125	May 5	Psalms 33:1–36:12
Day 126	May 6	Psalms 37:1–41:13
Day 127	May 7	Psalms 42:1–45:17
Day 128	May 8	Psalms 46:1–49:20
Day 129	May 9	Psalms 50:1–53:6
Day 130	May 10	Psalms 54:1–56:13
Day 131	May 11	Psalms 57:1–59:17

Day 132	May 12	Psalms 60:1–62:12
Day 133	May 13	Psalms 63:1–65:13
Day 134	May 14	Psalms 66:1–68:35
Day 135	May 15	Psalms 69:1–72:20
Day 136	May 16	Psalms 73:1–75:10
Day 137	May 17	Psalms 76:1–78:72
Day 138	May 18	Psalms 79:1–81:16
Day 139	May 19	Psalms 82:1–84:12
Day 140	May 20	Psalms 85:1–89:52
Day 141	May 21	Psalms 90:1–92:15
Day 142	May 22	Psalms 93:1–95:11
Day 143	May 23	Psalms 96:1–98:9
Day 144	May 24	Psalms 99:1–101:8
Day 145	May 25	Psalms 102:1–104:35
Day 146	May 26	Psalms 105:1–106:48
Day 147	May 27	Psalms 107:1–109:31
Day 148	May 28	Psalms 110:1–112:10
Day 149	May 29	Psalms 113:1–115:18
Day 150	May 30	Psalms 116:1–118:29
Day 151	May 31	Psalm 119:1–176

Day 152	June 1	Psalms 120:1–124:8
Day 153	June 2	Psalms 125:1–129:8
Day 154	June 3	Psalms 130:1–134:3
Day 155	June 4	Psalms 135:1–137:9
Day 156	June 5	Psalms 138:1–140:13
Day 157	June 6	Psalms 141:1–144:15
Day 158	June 7	Psalms 145:1–150:6
Day 159	June 8	Proverbs 1:1–33
Day 160	June 9	Proverbs 2:1–22
Day 161	June 10	Proverbs 3:1–35
Day 162	June 11	Proverbs 4:1–27
Day 163	June 12	Proverbs 5:1–23
Day 164	June 13	Proverbs 6:1–35
Day 165	June 14	Proverbs 7:1–27
Day 166	June 15	Proverbs 8:1–36
Day 167	June 16	Proverbs 9:1–18
Day 168	June 17	Proverbs 10:1–32
Day 169	June 18	Proverbs 11:1–31
Day 170	June 19	Proverbs 12:1–28
Day 171	June 20	Proverbs 13:1–25

Day 172	June 21	Proverbs 14:1–35
Day 173	June 22	Proverbs 15:1–33
Day 174	June 23	Proverbs 16:1–33
Day 175	June 24	Proverbs 17:1–28
Day 176	June 25	Proverbs 18:1–24
Day 177	June 26	Proverbs 19:1–29
Day 178	June 27	Proverbs 20:1–30
Day 179	June 28	Proverbs 21:1–31
Day 180	June 29	Proverbs 22:1–29
Day 181	June 30	Proverbs 23:1–35
Day 182	July 1	Proverbs 24:1–34
Day 183	July 2	Proverbs 25:1–28
Day 184	July 3	Proverbs 26:1–28
Day 185	July 4	Proverbs 27:1–27
Day 186	July 5	Proverbs 28:1–28
Day 187	July 6	Proverbs 29:1–27
Day 188	July 7	Proverbs 30:1–33
Day 189	July 8	Proverbs 31:1–31
Day 190	July 9	Ecclesiastes 1:1–2:26
Day 191	July 10	Ecclesiastes 3:1–5:20

Day 192	July 11	Ecclesiastes 6:1–8:17
Day 193	July 12	Ecclesiastes 9:1–12:14
Day 194	July 13	Song of Songs 1:1–8:14
Day 195	July 14	Isaiah 1:1–6:13
Day 196	July 15	Isaiah 7:1–12:6
Day 197	July 16	Isaiah 13:1–18:7
Day 198	July 17	Isaiah 19:1–23:18
Day 199	July 18	Isaiah 24:1–27:13
Day 200	July 19	Isaiah 28:1–31:9
Day 201	July 20	Isaiah 32:1–35:10
Day 202	July 21	Isaiah 36:1–39:8
Day 203	July 22	Isaiah 40:1–48:22
Day 204	July 23	Isaiah 49:1–52:12
Day 205	July 24	Isaiah 52:13–55:13
Day 206	July 25	Isaiah 56:1–59:21
Day 207	July 26	Isaiah 60:1–66:24
Day 208	July 27	Jeremiah 1:1–6:30
Day 209	July 28	Jeremiah 7:1–10:25
Day 210	July 29	Jeremiah 11:1–15:21
Day 211	July 30	Jeremiah 16:1–20:18

Day 212	July 31	Jeremiah 21:1–24:10
Day 213	August 1	Jeremiah 25:1–29:32
Day 214	August 2	Jeremiah 30:1–33:26
Day 215	August 3	Jeremiah 34:1–38:28
Day 216	August 4	Jeremiah 39:1–45:5
Day 217	August 5	Jeremiah 46:1–52:34
Day 218	August 6	Lamentations 1:1–5:22
Day 219	August 7	Ezekiel 1:1–3:27
Day 220	August 8	Ezekiel 4:1–11:25
Day 221	August 9	Ezekiel 12:1–17:24
Day 222	August 10	Ezekiel 18:1–24:27
Day 223	August 11	Ezekiel 25:1–32:32
Day 224	August 12	Ezekiel 33:1–39:29
Day 225	August 13	Ezekiel 40:1–48:35
Day 226	August 14	Daniel 1:1–3:30
Day 227	August 15	Daniel 4:1–6:28
Day 228	August 16	Daniel 7:1–12:13
Day 229	August 17	Hosea 1:1–3:5
Day 230	August 18	Hosea 4:1–5:15
Day 231	August 19	Hosea 6:1–10:15

Day 232	August 20	Hosea 11:1–14:9
Day 233	August 21	Joel 1:1–2:27
Day 234	August 22	Joel 2:28–3:21
Day 235	August 23	Amos 1:1–2:16
Day 236	August 24	Amos 3:1–6:14
Day 237	August 25	Amos 7:1–9:15
Day 238	August 26	Obadiah
Day 239	August 27	Jonah 1:1–2:10
Day 240	August 28	Jonah 3:1–4:11
Day 241	August 29	Micah 1:1–2:13
Day 242	August 30	Micah 3:1–5:15
Day 243	August 31	Micah 6:1–7:20
Day 244	September 1	Nahum 1:1–3:19
Day 245	September 2	Habakkuk 1:1–3:19
Day 246	September 3	Zephaniah 1:1–3:20
Day 247	September 4	Haggai 1:1–2:23
Day 248	September 5	Zechariah 1:1–8:23
Day 249	September 6	Zechariah 9:1–14:21
Day 250	September 7	Malachi 1:1–4:6
Day 251	September 8	Matthew 1:1–4:25

Day 252	September 9	Matthew 5:1–48
Day 253	September 10	Matthew 6:1–34
Day 254	September 11	Matthew 7:1–29
Day 255	September 12	Matthew 8:1–10:42
Day 256	September 13	Matthew 11:1–13:52
Day 257	September 14	Matthew 13:53–15:39
Day 258	September 15	Matthew 16:1–18:35
Day 259	September 16	Matthew 19:1–20:34
Day 260	September 17	Matthew 21:1–23:39
Day 261	September 18	Matthew 24:1–25:46
Day 262	September 19	Matthew 26:1–28:20
Day 263	September 20	Mark 1:1–3:35
Day 264	September 21	Mark 4:1–7:23
Day 265	September 22	Mark 7:24–9:1
Day 266	September 23	Mark 9:2–10:52
Day 267	September 24	Mark 11:1–12:44
Day 268	September 25	Mark 13:1–37
Day 269	September 26	Mark 14:1–16:20
Day 270	September 27	Luke 1:1–4:13
Day 271	September 28	Luke 4:14–6:49

Day 272	September 29	Luke 7:1–9:50
Day 273	September 30	Luke 9:51–10:42
Day 274	October 1	Luke 11:1–54
Day 275	October 2	Luke 12:1–59
Day 276	October 3	Luke 13:1–14:35
Day 277	October 4	Luke 15:1–16:31
Day 278	October 5	Luke 17:1–19:27
Day 279	October 6	Luke 19:28–21:38
Day 280	October 7	Luke 22:1–71
Day 281	October 8	Luke 23:1–56
Day 282	October 9	Luke 24:1–53
Day 283	October 10	John 1:1–2:11
Day 284	October 11	John 2:12–3:36
Day 285	October 12	John 4:1–45
Day 286	October 13	John 4:46–6:71
Day 287	October 14	John 7:1–10:42
Day 288	October 15	John 11:1–12:50
Day 289	October 16	John 13:1–14:31
Day 290	October 17	John 15:1–17:26
Day 291	October 18	John 18:1–19:42

Day 292	October 19	John 20:1–21:25
Day 293	October 20	Acts 1:1–4:37
Day 294	October 21	Acts 5:1–7:60
Day 295	October 22	Acts 8:1–12:25
Day 296	October 23	Acts 13:1–15:35
Day 297	October 24	Acts 15:36–18:22
Day 298	October 25	Acts 18:23–21:16
Day 299	October 26	Acts 21:17–28:30
Day 300	October 27	Romans 1:1–3:20
Day 301	October 28	Romans 3:21–5:21
Day 302	October 29	Romans 6:1–8:39
Day 303	October 30	Romans 9:1–11:36
Day 304	October 31	Romans 12:1–16:27
Day 305	November 1	1 Corinthians 1:1–4:21
Day 306	November 2	1 Corinthians 5:1–6:20
Day 307	November 3	1 Corinthians 7:1–40
Day 308	November 4	1 Corinthians 8:1–11:1
Day 309	November 5	1 Corinthians 11:2–14:40
Day 310	November 6	1 Corinthians 15:1–16:24
Day 311	November 7	2 Corinthians 1:1–2:11

Day 312	November 8	2 Corinthians 2:12–7:16
Day 313	November 9	2 Corinthians 8:1–9:15
Day 314	November 10	2 Corinthians 10:1–13:14
Day 315	November 11	Galatians 1:1–2:21
Day 316	November 12	Galatians 3:1–4:31
Day 317	November 13	Galatians 5:1–6:18
Day 318	November 14	Ephesians 1:1–3:21
Day 319	November 15	Ephesians 4:1–6:24
Day 320	November 16	Philippians 1:1–30
Day 321	November 17	Philippians 2:1–30
Day 322	November 18	Philippians 3:1–4:1
Day 323	November 19	Philippians 4:2–23
Day 324	November 20	Colossians 1:1–2:23
Day 325	November 21	Colossians 3:1–4:18
Day 326	November 22	1 Thessalonians 1:1–3:13
Day 327	November 23	1 Thessalonians 4:1–5:28
Day 328	November 24	2 Thessalonians 1:1–2:17
Day 329	November 25	2 Thessalonians 3:1–18
Day 330	November 26	1 Timothy 1:1–20
Day 331	November 27	1 Timothy 2:1–3:16

Day 332	November 28	1 Timothy 4:1–6:21
Day 333	November 29	2 Timothy 1:1–2:26
Day 334	November 30	2 Timothy 3:1–4:22
Day 335	December 1	Titus 1:1–16
Day 336	December 2	Titus 2:1–15
Day 337	December 3	Titus 3:1–15
Day 338	December 4	Philemon
Day 339	December 5	Hebrews 1:1–2:18
Day 340	December 6	Hebrews 3:1–4:13
Day 341	December 7	Hebrews 4:14–7:28
Day 342	December 8	Hebrews 8:1–10:18
Day 343	December 9	Hebrews 10:19–13:25
Day 344	December 10	James 1:1–27
Day 345	December 11	James 2:1–3:12
Day 346	December 12	James 3:13–5:20
Day 347	December 13	1 Peter 1:1–2:10
Day 348	December 14	1 Peter 2:11–4:19
Day 349	December 15	1 Peter 5:1–14
Day 350	December 16	2 Peter 1:1–21
Day 351	December 17	2 Peter 2:1–22

Day 352	December 18	2 Peter 3:1–18
Day 353	December 19	1 John 1:1–2:27
Day 354	December 20	1 John 2:28–4:21
Day 355	December 21	1 John 5:1–21
Day 356	December 22	2 John–3 John 1:14
Day 357	December 23	Jude
Day 358	December 24	Revelation 1:1–3:22
Day 359	December 25	Revelation 4:1–5:14
Day 360	December 26	Revelation 6:1–8:5
Day 361	December 27	Revelation 8:6–11:19
Day 362	December 28	Revelation 12:1–14:20
Day 363	December 29	Revelation 15:1–16:21
Day 364	December 30	Revelation 17:1–20:15
Day 365	December 31	Revelation 21:1–22:21

Reading Plan ©1996 The Livingstone Corporation. Used by permission.

epiLoque

There's a lot of information in these pages, a lot of facts and numbers, a lot of details and stories. That's because the Bible is a lot of different stuff. It's not written like a novel with a beginning, middle, and end presented in a linear fashion. Instead, it is slices of life lifted from people who connected with God and experienced Him.

It's not enough to just know the details. It's about knowing God. The point of the Bible, the power of the Bible, is that God's Spirit speaks to us through it if we'll read and listen. Yes, even though most of it was written in a barbaric time of humanity. Yes, even though our understanding struggles with some of the concepts. Yes, even though we sometimes come to it with so many misconceptions that we don't give it a chance. Yes, even though it still includes some mysteries.

There is power in the Bible because God is in it. It is His outstretched hand. We can read it for the sake of information, but that's not why it was written. It was written for the sake of a connection between God and us. It was written so that we would know the lengths He has gone to for us to believe in Him and be His children. It was written so that we could know Him.

The best way to read any book is to open the book, then let the book open something in you. Open the Bible, and when you do, open your heart and let God speak to you.

It is relevant. To your life. Today.

Lists & Stuff

where to find it

Many editions of the Bible include a concordance in the back, similar to an index. Names, places, events, and words are listed there with their correlating scripture references. There are also larger, comprehensive concordances you can buy to accompany your Bible.

Included below is a short concordance of easily recognized people, events, and passages.

Abraham almost sacrifices Isaac . . . . Genesis 22:1–18

Adam and Eve: the first man and woman . . . . Genesis 2:1–3:24

Balaam and the talking donkey. . . . . .Numbers 22:21–35

Beatitudes: Jesus' Sermon on the Mount. . . . . Matthew 5:1–12

Cain kills Abel: the first murder . . . . Genesis 4

Creation . . . . Genesis 1:1–2:3

Daniel in the lions' den. . . . . .Daniel 6:1–23

Daniel's friends in the fiery furnace. . . . . .Daniel 3:1–30

David is anointed king . . . . .1 Samuel 16:7–13

Elijah faces Baal's prophets on Mt. Carmel . . . . 1 Kings 18:16–40

Elijah's chariot of fire . . . . 2 Kings 2:9–15

Esau, Isaac's son, sells his birthright . . . . Genesis 25:27–34

Faith chapter (aka the Hall of Faith). . . . . .Hebrews 11

First sin . . . . Genesis 3:1–24

John the Baptist is killed. . . . . Mark 6:14–29

John the Baptist's ministry . . . . Matthew 3:1–6

Jonah and the big fish. . . . . Jonah 1:1–2:10

Jordan River is parted by God . . . . Joshua 3:1–17

Joseph is taken to Egypt. . . . . Genesis 37:1–36

King David and Bathsheba . . . . 2 Samuel 11:1–27

King David and Goliath . . . . 1 Samuel 17:1–58

Lazarus, Jesus' friend, is raised from the dead. . . . . John 11:1–44

Lord's Prayer. . . . . Matthew 6:9–13

Lot's wife turns to salt. . . . . Genesis 19:15–26

Love chapter (a famous wedding reading) . . . . 1 Corinthians 13

Moses and the burning bush . . . . Exodus 3:1–22

Moses and the golden calf . . . . Exodus 32:1–35

Moses leads the Hebrews out of Egypt . . . . Exodus 12:31–14:31

Moses' protection as a baby . . . . Exodus 2:1–10

Naaman is healed of leprosy. . . . . 2 Kings 5:1–19

Nicodemus talks with Jesus . . . . John 3:1–21

Noah and the ark. . . . . Genesis 6:1–9:17

Noah and the flood . . . . Genesis 6:9–8:22

Passover in Egypt. . . . . Exodus 12:1–30

who's who?

Here's a list of well-known people from the Bible and where to find them.

Aaron: Moses' brother, the first high priest . . . . .Exodus 4

Abel: Adam and Eve's second son. . . . . .Genesis 4

Abraham: the father of the Jewish nation . . . . .Genesis 18

Adam: the first man God created . . . . .Genesis 2

Barnabas: Paul's early missionary companion . . . . Acts 13

Bathsheba: the woman with whom
King David had an affair. . . . . 2 Samuel 11

Boaz: the husband of Ruth . . . . .Ruth 2

Cain: Adam and Eve's first son . . . . .Genesis 4

Daniel: a young Israelite who became a leader
in Persia; also survived the lions. . . . . Daniel 1

David: a shepherd, a musician, and the
second king of Israel. . . . . 1 Samuel 17

Delilah: the woman who tricked
Samson into cutting his hair. . . . . Judges 16

Deborah: the only female leader (judge)
of the Hebrews whom we know of . . . . Judges 4

Disciples: the followers of Jesus—usually
refers to the twelve He was closest to: Simon Peter,
Andrew, James, John, Philip, Bartholomew, Thomas,
Matthew, James the son of Alpheus, Thaddeus,
Simon the Zealot, and Judas Iscariot. . . . . .Matthew 10

Elijah: a great prophet . . . . .1 Kings 17

Elisha: a great prophet who learned under Elijah . . . . .1 Kings 19

Esau: one of Isaac and Rebekah's twins, later named Edom . . .Genesis 25

Esther: the Jewish beauty who became queen of Persia. . . . . . . .Esther 2

Eve: the first woman God created. . . . . .Genesis 2

Gideon: a judge or leader of the Hebrews
who put a fleece before God. . . . . Judges 6

Hannah: Samuel's mother. . . . . 1 Samuel 1

Herod: the king who feared Jesus' birth
and so ordered all baby boys killed .Matthew 2

Isaac: Abraham's son. . . . . .Genesis 21–22

Jacob: one of Isaac and Rebekah's twins, later named Israel . . .Genesis 25

Jesus: the Son of God, Savior of the world . . . . .Luke 2

Jochebed: Moses' mother . . . . .Exodus 1–2

John the Baptist: Jesus' cousin who introduced
Jesus to the world. . . . . .Matthew 3

Jonathan: Saul's son and David's best friend . . . . 1 Samuel 18–20

Joseph: the favorite son of Jacob who established
leadership in Egypt. . . . . .Genesis 37

Joshua: the leader of the Hebrews after Moses . . . . Numbers 13–14

Judas Iscariot: the disciple who betrayed Christ . . . . .Matthew 26–27

Leah: Jacob's wife . . . . .Genesis 29

Levites: descendants of Levi whose tribe
was assigned to assist priests .... Numbers 1

Lot: Abraham's nephew who lived in
Sodom and Gomorrah ....Genesis 13, 19

Mary: the mother of Jesus.........................Matthew 1–2

Mary and Martha: friends of Jesus,
sisters of Lazarus ....Luke 10

Miriam: Moses' sister .... Exodus 2; Numbers 12

Mordecai: Esther's cousin who was like a father to her ....Esther 2

Moses: the leader of the Hebrews when they exited Egypt .....Exodus 2

Naomi: a Jewish woman who lost her husband
and sons in Moab and traveled back to Bethlehem
with her daughter-in-law ....Ruth 1

Noah: the only faithful man on the earth before the flood ...Genesis 5–6

Paul: the apostle who wrote many of the letters in the New Testament,
a persecutor of the church who converted to a missionary ..... Acts 8–9

Pilate: the governor who tried Jesus
but couldn't find Him guilty.........................Matthew 27

Priscilla and Aquila: friends of Paul the apostle .... Acts 18

Prophets: preachers in the Old and New Testaments
who called the people of God back to obedience
and sometimes spoke of the future.................. various books

Rahab: a prostitute in Jericho who helped
the Jewish spies and so saved her life and
the lives of her family members .... Joshua 2, 6

Shadrach, Meshach, and Abednego: friends
of Daniel taken captive in Persia. . . . . Daniel 1, 3

Silas: Paul's later missionary companion. Acts 15

Stephen: the first Christian martyr . . . . Acts 6–7

Rachel: Jacob's favorite wife . . . . .Genesis 29

Rebekah: Isaac's wife. . . . . .Genesis 24

Ruth: Naomi's daughter-in-law who
traveled with Naomi back to Bethlehem .Ruth 1

Samson: a judge whose long hair and Nazirite
code gave him superhuman strength . . . . Judges 13–14

Sarah: Abraham's wife. . . . . .Genesis 11, 17

Saul: the first king of Israel. . . . . 1 Samuel 9

Seth: Adam and Eve's third son. . . . . .Genesis 4

Solomon: the third and wisest king of Israel,
David and Bathsheba's son . . . . .1 Kings 1–2

Timothy: an apprentice of the apostle Paul. . . . . 1 Timothy 1

Zacchaeus: a short tax collector who saw Jesus
by climbing a tree. . . . . .Luke 19

women who made a difference

It's true that the Bible was written at a time when women were considered lower-class citizens than men. But that was a people thing, not a God thing. God used women in amazing ways. Here are some of the most well-known women of the Bible.

Abigail . . . . 1 Samuel 25:1–42; 2 Samuel 3:3

Anna . . . . Luke 2:36–38

Deborah . . . . Judges 4–5

Dorcas . . . . Acts 9:36–42

Elizabeth . . . . Luke 1:5–80

Esther . . . . the book of Esther

Eunice . . . . Acts 16:1–3; 2 Timothy 1:5

Eve . . . . Genesis 2–3; 2 Corinthians 11:3

Hannah . . . . 1 Samuel 1; 2:1–21

Jochebed . . . . Exodus 2:1–11; 6:20; Numbers 26:59

Lois . . . . 2 Timothy 1:5

Lydia . . . . Acts 16:12–15, 40

Martha . . . . Luke 10:38–41; John 11; 12:1–3

Mary Magdalene . . . . Matthew 27:56, 61; 28:1; John 19:25; 20:1–18

Mary, mother of Jesus . . . . Matthew 1; 2; 12:46; Luke 1; 2;
John 2:1–12; 19:25–27; Acts 1:14

parabLes OF JESUS

Jesus often taught by telling stories called parables. Parables are stories that may or may not have been true but always have a spiritual interpretation. Sometimes Jesus interpreted His parables for the people, and sometimes He left them to interpret them.

Jesus always used stories and illustrations like these when speaking to the crowds. In fact, he never spoke to them without using such parables. This fulfilled the prophecy that said, "I will speak to you in parables. I will explain mysteries hidden since the creation of the world"
(Matthew 13:34–35 NLT).

In his public teaching he taught only with parables, but afterward when he was alone with his disciples, he explained the meaning to them
(Mark 4:34 NLT).

"I have spoken of these matters in parables, but the time will come when this will not be necessary, and I will tell you plainly all about the Father"
(John 16:25 NLT).

The parables listed here are in the order in which they appear in the Gospels.

The Sower, the Seed, the Soils:
A story about seed sown on different types of soils. These soils reflect our own hearts and the way we accept God's truth.

Matthew 13:3–8; Mark 4:2–8; Luke 8:4–8

The Weeds and the Wheat:
An enemy of a farmer sows weeds into his wheat field. Alludes to the final judgment when God identifies those of true faith.

Matthew 13:24–30

The Mustard Seed:
Something so small as a seed can grow to be a large plant or tree. Faith works like this. A small amount goes a long way.

Matthew 13:31–32; Mark 4:30–32; Luke 13:18–19

The Yeast:
The kingdom of God is like yeast that, even in small amounts, changes the shape of a whole loaf of bread.

Matthew 13:33; Luke 13:20–21

The Treasure:
The kingdom of God is like a treasure.

Matthew 13:44

The Pearl:
The kingdom of God is like a precious pearl. It is more valuable than everything else.

Matthew 13:45–46

The Good and Bad Fish:
Alludes to the judgment when evil people are separated from good people.

Matthew 13:47–50

The Lost Sheep:
A shepherd's commitment to one sheep mirrors God's commitment to each of us.

Matthew 18:12–14; Luke 15:3–7

The Unforgiving Servant:
A man who has had a great debt canceled won't cancel a small debt owed to him. Deals with a lack of mercy.

Matthew 18:23–35

The Workers on Payday:
Explains the kingdom of heaven in terms of workers who are paid the same wage no matter when they signed on.

Matthew 20:1–16

The Two Sons:
One son says no, but then does as he is told. The other says yes, but never gets the job done.

Matthew 21:28–32

The Vineyard:
A man leaves some sharecroppers in charge of his vineyard. When they don't care for it, he finds others to take their place. Speaks to our accountability before God.

Matthew 21:33–44; Mark 12:1–9; Luke 20:9–16

The Marriage Feast:
Many are invited to a feast, but not many come. Speaks to our invitation into the kingdom of God.

Matthew 22:1–14

The Foolish Manager:
A manager ignores his superior's instructions and is caught red-handed. Speaks to our accountability at the final judgment.

Matthew 24:45–51; Luke 12:42–48

The Bridesmaids:
According to an old custom, the bridesmaids wait for the groom, but some are unprepared. Speaks to our final accountability before God.

Matthew 25:1–13

The Three Investors:
The boss goes away, leaving money to be invested. Only those who invest wisely are rewarded.

Matthew 25:14–30; Luke 19:11–27

The Wheat Harvest:
The kingdom of God is like a seed that by its own magic grows into a harvest.

Mark 4:26–29

The Watchful Servant:
A man leaves a servant in charge of his house but doesn't give the time of his return. That servant must always keep watch. Speaks to Christ's second coming.

Mark 13:34–37

The Canceled Loans:
Two loans are canceled. One is large; one is small. Which debtor will be the most grateful? Speaks to God's forgiveness.

Luke 7:40–43

The Good Samaritan:
A man who is undesirable himself is the true neighbor because he cares for someone.

Luke 10:30–37

The Request at Midnight:
Insight on prayer. A friend makes a request at an inconvenient time but gets what he wants because he keeps on asking.

Luke 11:5–10

The Rich Fool:
A rich man keeps storing more and getting more, but when he dies, he loses it all.

Luke 12:16–21

The Fruitless Fig Tree:
A tree that is supposed to produce fruit doesn't and is given one more year.

Luke 13:6–9

The Best Seat:
Don't pick the best seat at a feast, or you might be embarrassed. Pick the worst seat and let the host move you to the head table.

Luke 14:7–11

The Banquet Invitations:
A man invites many to his banquet, but when they don't come, he invites everyone he can find. Speaks to the kingdom of God.

Luke 14:15–24

The Lost Coin:
A woman's search for a lost coin mirrors God's commitment to people.

Luke 15:8–10

The Prodigal Son:
A son's journey away from family and home and his subsequent return mirror our journey through life and God's ever-welcoming arms.

Luke 15:11–32

The Shrewd Businessman:
A dishonest manager in danger of losing his job makes a few friends on his way down.

Luke 16:1–10

The Servant's Duty:
A servant shouldn't expect to be thanked for doing his duty.

Luke 17:7–10

The Unjust Judge:
Insight on prayer. A widow receives justice from an unjust judge because of her persistence.

Luke 18:1–8

The Prayers of the Pharisee and the Tax Collector:
The Pharisee prays out of his pride. The tax collector prays out of his humility. The tax collector is justified in God's eyes.

Luke 18:9–14

miracLes of jesus

This is a list of the miracles Jesus performed while He lived on earth as both God and man. They are in the order they appear in the Gospels. In the places where several Gospels record the same miracle, we've listed them together.

Herod was delighted at the opportunity to see Jesus, because he had heard about him and had been hoping for a long time to see him perform a miracle (Luke 23:8 NLT).

"But I have a greater witness than John—my teachings and my miracles. They have been assigned to me by the Father, and they testify that the Father has sent me" (John 5:36 NLT).

That was the main reason so many went out to meet him—because they had heard about this mighty miracle (John 12:18 NLT).

MIRACLES OF HEALING

Jesus heals a man with leprosy . . . . Matthew 8:1–4; Mark 1:40–42; Luke 5:12–13

Jesus heals a soldier's servant . . . . Matthew 8:5–13; Luke 7:1–10

Jesus heals Peter's mother-in-law . . . . . .Matthew 8:14–15; Mark 1:29–31; Luke 4:38–39

Jesus heals a paralyzed man. . . . . .Matthew 9:1–8; Mark 2:1–12; Luke 5:17–26

A woman is healed by touching Jesus' clothes . . . . .Matthew 9:20–22; Mark 5:25–34; Luke 8:43–48

Jesus heals a man's withered hand . . . . . . .Matthew 12:9–13; Mark 3:1–5; Luke 6:6–10

Jesus heals the blind . . . . Matthew 9:27–31; 20:29–34;
Mark 8:22–25, 10:46–52;
Luke 18:35–43; John 9:1–7

Jesus heals a man who cannot see or hear. . . . . Mark 7:31–37

Jesus heals a crippled woman. . . . . Luke 13:10–13

Jesus cures a sick man. . . . . .Luke 14:1–4

Jesus heals ten lepers. . . . . .Luke 17:11–19

Jesus reattaches a man's ear . . . . .Luke 22:49–51

Jesus heals an official's son without even meeting him. . . . .John 4:46–54

Jesus heals a man who had been an
invalid for thirty-eight years. . . . . .John 5:1–16

MIRACLES OF PROVISION

Jesus feeds over five thousand people . . . . .Matthew 14:15–21;
Mark 6:35–44; Luke 9:12–17; John 6:5–14

Jesus feeds over four thousand people. . . . . .Matthew 15:32–38;
Mark 8:1–9

The disciples make a miraculous catch of fish . . . . .Luke 5:1–7

Jesus turns water into wine . . . . .John 2:1–11

Jesus brings in another miraculous
catch of fish after His resurrection. . . . . .John 21:1–14

MIRACLES THAT INVOLVED RAISING SOME-ONE FROM THE DEAD

Jesus raises Jairus's daughter
from the dead. . . . . Matthew 9:18–26; Mark 5:22–24,
35–43; Luke 8:41–42, 49–56

A widow's son is raised from the dead . . . . .Luke 7:11–16

Lazarus is raised from the dead . . . . .John 11:1–45

MIRACLES THAT INVOLVED CASTING OUT DEMONS

Jesus casts demons out of a man
and sends them into pigs. . . . . Matthew 8:28–34; Mark 5:1–19;
Luke 8:26–39

Jesus casts out a demon and a mute man can speak. . . .Matthew 9:32–33;
12:22; Luke 11:14

Jesus casts a demon out of the
daughter of a foreigner. . . . . .Matthew 15:21–28; Mark 7:24–30

Jesus heals a boy possessed
by a demon . . . . .Matthew 17:14–18; Mark 9:14–26; Luke 9:37–42

Jesus casts out a demon at the synagogue. . .Mark 1:23–27; Luke 4:33–36

OTHER MIRACLES

Jesus stills the storm with His voice. . . . . .Matthew 8:23–27;
Mark 4:36–40; Luke 8:22–24

Jesus walks on top of rough waters . . .Matthew 14:22–33; Mark 6:45–52;
John 6:17–21

Jesus curses a fig tree . . . . . . Matthew 21:18–22; Mark 11:12–14, 20–22

Finding Topics That Interest You

There are a lot of resources these days that will help you find topics in the Bible. Many of recently published Bibles have lists in the back. There are also books in the bookstores that are full of these lists to accompany your Bible. We've included a list here just to get you started.

Abortion . . . . Psalm 139; Isaiah 49:1–5

Adultery. . . . . Exodus 20:14; Proverbs 6:28–32; Matthew 5:27–28; John 8:3–11

Anger. . . . . Psalm 145:8; Proverbs 29:11; Ephesians 4:25–32

Answered prayer . . . . Matthew 21:21–22; Philippians 4:6; Colossians 4:2; James 5:15

Bible . . . . 2 Timothy 2:15; Hebrews 4:12; 1 Peter 1:23–25

Church, Christ's body. . . . . .1 Corinthians 12, 14; Ephesians 1:18–23

Contentment. . . ., ... Proverbs 19:23; Philippians 4:11–12; 1 Timothy 6:6; Hebrews 13:5

Crucifixion . . . . Matthew 27; Mark 15; Luke 23; John 19

Death. . . . . .Psalm 116:15; John 11; 1 Corinthians 15

Dependence on God . . . . .Jeremiah 17:5–8; 2 Corinthians 12

Depression, despair, discouragement. . . . . . . .Psalm 42; 69; John 16:33

Drugs. . . . . Proverbs 23:29–35; Romans 13:11–14; 1 Corinthians 6:9–20; 1 John 3:7–10

Enemies. . . . . Exodus 23:4–5; Proverbs 16:7; 24:17; 25:21; 27:6

Faith in God. . . . . .Genesis 15:4–6; Matthew 8:5–10; Luke 8:43–48; Romans 5:1–8; Galatians 5:6

Family . . . . Proverbs 5:18–21; 1 Timothy 5:3–5; 2 Timothy 1:5–8

Forgiveness for others . . . . Matthew 18:21–35; Colossians 3:12–14

Forgiveness from God . . . . . Psalm 130:1–6; Ephesians 1:3–8; 1 John 1:9

Friendship . . . . Proverbs 17:17; 19:4; 22:24; 27:6; Ecclesiastes 4:10

Guidance from God . . . . Psalms 25:1–5; 139:1–10

Guilt . . . . Psalm 32:1–5; 1 John 3:18–20

Healing . . . . Psalm 103:2–5; Hosea 6:1–3; James 5:15–16

Heaven . . . . Luke 15:3–10; John 14:1–4; Philippians 3:18–20;
Hebrews 8:3–5; Revelation 21:10–27

Holy Spirit . . . . John 16:5–15; Acts 2:1–4; Romans 5:1–5;
1 Corinthians 6:18–20

Homosexuality . . . . Leviticus 18:22–29; Romans 1:18–27;
1 Corinthians 6:9–11

Hope . . . . Psalm 25:1–3; 147:7–11; Romans 5:1–5

Humility . . . . Proverbs 11:2; Philippians 2:1–9; James 4:6–10

Integrity . . . . Psalm 25:21; Proverbs 11:3; 1 Corinthians 15:33;
Titus 2:6–8

Jesus Christ . . . . Romans 3:21–26; Ephesians 1:3–14

Love of God . . . . Romans 5:1–8; Ephesians 2:4–10; 1 John 4:7–12

Marriage . . . . Genesis 2:18–24; Proverbs 6:27–35;
Matthew 19:3–6; Ephesians 5:21–33

Materialism . . . . Matthew 4:8–11; 19:21–30; Colossians 3:1–2

finding Help when you need it

WHEN YOU'RE. . .

Tired . . . . Psalm 23

Hurting. . . . . Hebrews 12

Tempted . . . . Daniel 1; James 1; 1 Corinthians 10

Needing some courage . . . . Joshua 1; Ephesians 6

Needing some good advice . . . . Proverbs

Depressed . . . . Psalm 42

Struggling with right and wrong . . . . Matthew 5–7; Colossians 2

Wondering who Jesus was. . . . . John 6–10

Trying to figure out the church . . . . 1 Corinthians 12

Feeling offended by someone . . . . 1 Corinthians 6

Finding it hard to believe . . . . Hebrews 11

Needing to forgive someone . . . . Philemon

Discouraged . . . . Romans 8

Afraid . . . . Psalm 27

Feeling like giving up . . . . 2 Timothy 2

Happy. . . . . Psalm 95

Wishing you hadn't said something. . . . . James 3

Struggling to do what's right . . . . Romans 7–8

Not sure you're worth anything. . . . . Genesis 1; Romans 4–5

Wanting to be closer to God . . . . John 3

Feeling guilty. . . . . 1 John 1–2; Psalm 51

Feeling lonely, left out . . . . Psalm 25

Trying to be more loving . . . . 1 Corinthians 13

Looking for God's will . . . . Philippians 2

Looking for guidance. . . . . Psalm 25

Wondering about abortion . . . . Psalm 139

Wondering if success will make you happy . . . . .Ecclesiastes

Wondering how to become a Christian . . . . .Romans 10

Famous Lists

There are several famous lists in the Bible. You've probably heard of most of them. For your quick reference, here they are plus a few you might not be so familiar with.

THE TEN COMMANDMENTS

1. *You shall have no other gods before me.*
2. *You shall not make for yourself an idol. . . .*
3. *You shall not misuse the name of the LORD your God. . . .*
4. *Remember the Sabbath day by keeping it holy. . . .*
5. *Honor your father and your mother, so that you may live long. . . .*
6. *You shall not murder.*
7. *You shall not commit adultery.*
8. *You shall not steal.*
9. *You shall not give false testimony against your neighbor.*
10. *You shall not covet your neighbor's house. You shall not covet your neighbor's wife, or. . .anything that belongs to your neighbor.*

(*Exodus 20:2–17 NIV*)

THE BEATITUDES
(FROM THE SERMON ON THE MOUNT GIVEN BY JESUS)

Blessed are the poor in spirit, for theirs is the kingdom of heaven.
Blessed are those who mourn, for they will be comforted.
Blessed are the meek, for they will inherit the earth.
Blessed are those who hunger and thirst for righteousness,
*   for they will be filled.*
Blessed are the merciful, for they will be shown mercy.
Blessed are the pure in heart, for they will see God.
Blessed are the peacemakers, for they will be called sons of God.
Blessed are those who are persecuted because of righteousness,
*   for theirs is the kingdom of heaven.*
Blessed are you when people insult you, persecute you and falsely say
*   all kinds of evil against you because of me. Rejoice and be glad,*
*   because great is your reward in heaven, for in the same way they per*
*   secuted the prophets who were before you.*

(*Matthew 5:3–12 NIV*)

THE ORDER OF CREATION

First Day: *God called the light "day," and the darkness he called "night." And there was evening, and there was morning—the first day (Genesis 1:5 NIV).*

Second Day: *So God made the expanse and separated the water under the expanse from the water above it. And it was so. God called the expanse "sky." And there was evening, and there was morning—the second day (Genesis 1:7–8 NIV).*

Third Day: *The land produced vegetation: plants bearing seed according to their kinds and trees bearing fruit with seed in it according to their kinds. And God saw that it was good. And there was evening, and there was morning—the third day (Genesis 1:12–13 NIV).*

Fourth Day: *God made two great lights—the greater light to govern the day and the lesser light to govern the night. He also made the stars. God set them in the expanse of the sky to give light on the earth, to govern the day and the night, and to separate light from darkness. And God saw that it was good. And there was evening, and there was morning—the fourth day (Genesis 1:16–19 NIV).*

Fifth Day: *So God created the great creatures of the sea and every living and moving thing with which the water teems, according to their kinds, and every winged bird according to its kind. And God saw that it was good. . . . And there was evening, and there was morning—the fifth day (Genesis 1:21–23 NIV).*

Sixth Day: *Then God said, "I give you every seed-bearing plant on the face of the whole earth and every tree that has fruit with seed in it. They will be yours for food. . . . God saw all that he had made, and it was very good. And there was evening, and there was morning—the sixth day (Genesis 1:29–31 NIV).*

Seventh Day: *By the seventh day God had finished the work he had been doing; so on the seventh day he rested from all his work. And God blessed the seventh day and made it holy, because on it he rested from all the work of creating that he had done (Genesis 2:2–3 NIV).*

THE FRUIT OF THE SPIRIT

But the fruit of the Spirit is

- *love*
- *joy*
- *peace*

- *patience*
- *kindness*
- *goodness*

- *faithfulness*
- *gentleness*
- *self-control*

Against such things there is no law (Galatians 5:22–23 NIV).

THE ARMOR OF GOD

Therefore put on the full armor of God, so that when the day of evil comes, you may be able to stand your ground, and after you have done everything, to stand.

Stand firm then, with the BELT OF TRUTH buckled around your waist, with the BREASTPLATE OF RIGHTEOUSNESS in place, and with your FEET FITTED WITH THE READINESS THAT COMES FROM THE GOSPEL OF PEACE.

In addition to all this, take up the SHIELD OF FAITH, with which you can extinguish all the flaming arrows of the evil one.

Take the HELMET OF SALVATION and the SWORD OF THE SPIRIT, which is the word of God.

And pray in the Spirit on all occasions with all kinds of prayers and requests. With this in mind, be alert and always keep on praying for all the saints.

(Ephesians 6:13–18 NIV)

THE DESCRIPTION OF LOVE

Love is patient,
 love is kind.
It does not envy,
 it does not boast,
 it is not proud.
It is not rude,
 it is not self-seeking,
 it is not easily angered,
 it keeps no record of wrongs.
Love does not delight in evil
 but rejoices with the truth.
It always protects,
 always trusts,
 always hopes,
 always perseveres.
Love never fails.
(1 Corinthians 13:4–8 NIV)

SEVEN THINGS GOD HATES

There are six things the LORD hates,
seven that are detestable to him:
> haughty eyes,
> a lying tongue,
> hands that shed innocent blood,
> a heart that devises wicked schemes,
> feet that are quick to rush into evil,
> a false witness who pours out lies
> and a man who stirs up dissension among brothers.

(Proverbs 6:16–19 NIV)

THE FAMOUS "FOR EVERY THING" LIST FROM ECCLESIASTES

There is a time for everything,
and a season for every activity under heaven:
> a time to be born and a time to die,
> a time to plant and a time to uproot,
> a time to kill and a time to heal,
> a time to tear down and a time to build,
> a time to weep and a time to laugh,
> a time to mourn and a time to dance,
> a time to scatter stones and a time to gather them,
> a time to embrace and a time to refrain,
> a time to search and a time to give up,
> a time to keep and a time to throw away,
> a time to tear and a time to mend,
> a time to be silent and a time to speak,
> a time to love and a time to hate,
> a time for war and a time for peace.

(Ecclesiastes 3:1–8 NIV)

unsung Bible Heroes

The culture described in the Bible was very different from our culture today. Still, the people of the Bible were much like us in their struggles and their successes. Even the greatest heroes we read about had frailties and moments of weakness. The biblical records don't even try to hide their idiosyncrasies from us.

But sometimes we have to look past the big-name, top-ten type of Bible heroes who worked from a platform much bigger than most of us ever see unless we buy a ticket. When we look past them, we start noticing that there were a lot of people who faithfully became a part of God's plan— some of them just for a moment. They were people who lived their lives like most of us do, behind the scenes, out of the spotlight. Their faithfulness and the fact that God used them can be an encouragement for us.

For instance, we often read, hear, and speak about the twelve disciples. Actually, Jesus had many disciples, but the Twelve were the ones closest to him. Luke 8:1–3 reveals some of the background of Jesus' ministry: "After this, Jesus traveled about from one town and village to another, proclaiming the good news of the kingdom of God. The Twelve were with him, and also some women who had been cured of evil spirits and diseases: Mary (called Magdalene) from whom seven demons had come out; Joanna the wife of Cuza, the manager of Herod's household; Susanna; and many others. These women were helping to support them out of their own means."

Wow! That is an amazing insight. In a culture that devalued women, were women involved in and even financially supporting Jesus' ministry. That tells you something about Jesus, but it also tells you something about us. We may not be one of the spotlighted few, like Peter or John, but we can be a Susanna or a Joanna.

We don't even know the names of some of the unsung heroes the Bible teaches us about. How about. . .

The servant girl of Naaman's wife:
Naaman was a leader who contracted leprosy, which, at that time, was career destroying and life changing. As the least powerful person in the whole scenario, this servant girl made a difference by directing Naaman to the prophet Elijah.

2 Kings 5:1–19

The widow who gave two mites:

What Sunday school child has not heard the story of the widow who stopped by the temple to give her offering? It was small, but it was all she had. She became an object lesson for Jesus in teaching His sometimes-stubborn disciples.

Mark 12:41–44; Luke 21:1–4

The Bible is full of people who lived their lives making good choices and being used by God. We might only know a sentence about them, but their fifteen (or fewer) minutes of the spotlight made it into God's best seller.

Abigail:

Her biggest mistake was marrying a jerk. But because she kept her wits about her, she eventually married King David (after she was widowed, of course).

1 Samuel 25:1–42

Anna:

When Jesus was taken to the temple as a baby, this widow recognized Him as the long-awaited Messiah.

Luke 2:36–38

Asaph:

You'll see Asaph's name scattered among the Psalms. He was the appointed praise and worship leader for the Jews. He wrote Psalm 50 and Psalms 73–83.

1 Chronicles 15:17; 16:5; 25:1; Nehemiah 12:46

Bezalel:

God actually subcontracted Bezalel to work on the tabernacle because of his excellent craftsmanship with metals and woods. How would you like to be referred by God?

Exodus 31:2; 35:30; 36:1; 37:1; 38:22

Epaphroditus:

A man sent by the Philippian church to help Paul, who risked his life in the process.

Philippians 2:25–30; 4:18

Gaius:

An all-around good guy who is noted for his hospitality, among other great qualities.

Acts 19:29; 20:4; Romans 16:23; 3 John 1

Hanani:

A prophet bold enough to stand up for truth and go to prison, just on principle.

2 Chronicles 16:7–10

Jairus:

A father who asked Jesus to heal his daughter and kept on believing even after he heard of her death.

Matthew 9:18–26; Mark 5:22–43

Miriam:

A little girl, a big sister, who got stuck babysitting and ended up saving her brother's life and thus her nation from slavery. She later became a worship leader for the whole nation of Jews.

Exodus 15:20–21

Simon of Cyrene:

He carried Jesus' cross for Him up the hill.

Matthew 27:32; Mark 15:21; Luke 23:26

Tabitha:

A woman who built a reputation for always helping the poor.

Acts 9:36

Zerubbabel:

After the Jews had been exiled in Babylon, this man led the first group back home and began to restore their temple and their homes.

Ezra 3:8; 4:3–4; Nehemiah 12:47; Haggai 2:2; Zechariah 4:6

Did you know this was from the Bible?

People all around us are quoting from the Bible and don't even know it. Even now, more than two thousand years (and counting) later, there are still biblical phrases numerous used in popular language.

Am I my brother's keeper? . . . . Genesis 4:9

Apple of his eye . . . . Psalm 17:8

Blind leading the blind. . . . . Luke 6:39

By the skin of my teeth. . . . . Job 19:20

Doubting Thomas. . . . . John 20:27

Drop in a bucket . . . . Isaiah 40:15

Eat, drink, and be merry . . . . Luke 12:19

Entertaining angels unaware. . . . . Hebrews 13:2

Eye for an eye. . . . . Leviticus 24:19–20

Fall from grace . . . . Galatians 5:4

Fat of the land . . . . Genesis 45:18

Feet of clay. . . . . Daniel 2:33–34

Fire and brimstone. . . . . Genesis 19:24 KJV

Fly in the ointment. . . . . Ecclesiastes 10:1 KJV

Handwriting on the wall. . . . . Daniel 5:5

Having someone's head on a platter . . . . Matthew 14:8

Holier than thou. . . . . Isaiah 65:5 KJV

Spirit is willing, but flesh is weak . . . . Matthew 26:41 KJV

Still small voice . . . . 1 Kings 19:12–13 KJV

Straight and narrow . . . . Matthew 7:13–14 KJV

Sweating blood. . . . . Luke 22:44

The Lord gives, and the Lord takes away . . . . Job 1:21

Thorn in my flesh. . . . . 2 Corinthians 12:7

Wits' end . . . . Psalm 107:27

Wolf in sheep's clothing . . . . Matthew 7:15

names of god

God is called a lot of different things in the Bible. In fact, in the original languages of the Bible, there were many names to describe the variety of ways that God meets His children. Here are some of them.

Ancient of Days . . . . Daniel 7:9

Almighty . . . . Genesis 17:1

Compassionate and gracious God. Exodus 34:6

Eternal God . . . . .Deuteronomy 33:27

Eternal King. . . . . Jeremiah 10:10

Everlasting God . . . . .Isaiah 40:28

Father. . . . . .Deuteronomy 1:30

Father of the heavenly lights. . . . . .James 1:17

Father of our Lord Jesus Christ. . . . . Romans 15:6

Fortress . . . . 2 Samuel 22:2

Great and awesome God. .Deuteronomy 7:21

Great King . . . . .Psalm 48:2

God of heaven and earth . . . . Genesis 24:3

God of Abraham, Isaac, and Israel . . . . 1 Kings 18:36

God of Israel. . . . . .Psalm 68:35

God of our fathers . . . . .Ezra 7:27

God of truth. . . . . .Psalm 31:5

Lord of lords................................Deuteronomy 10:17

Lord of the Sabbath ....James 5:4 KJV

Lord our God................................Deuteronomy 1:6

Maker of all things .... Proverbs 22:2

Maker of heaven and earth........................Psalm 115:15

Merciful God ....Deuteronomy 4:31

Mighty One of Israel...............................Isaiah 1:24

Most High ....Deuteronomy 32:8

Our strength................................. Exodus 15:2

Ruler .... 1 Timothy 6:15

Shield...................................... Genesis 15:1

Sovereign Lord...............................Deuteronomy 9:26

Spring of living water........................... Jeremiah 17:13

Strong tower.....................................Psalm 61:3

names of christ

Names in the ancient world meant a lot more than names do today. Several times in the Bible God changed people's names to mark a huge turn in their lives (Abram to Abraham, Jacob to Israel, Sarai to Sarah).

Advocate . . . . 1 John 2:1 KJV

Almighty . . . . Revelation 1:8

Alpha and Omega. . . . . Revelation 1:8; 22:13

Arm of the Lord . . . . Isaiah 51:9; 53:1

Author and perfecter of Faith. . . . . Hebrews 12:2

Beginning of the creation of God. . . . . Revelation 3:14 KJV

Beloved Son . . . . Matthew 12:18

Blessed and only Sovereign . . . . 1 Timothy 6:15 NRSV

Bread of Life . . . . John 6:35, 48

Chief Shepherd. . . . . 1 Peter 5:4

Chosen One . . . . Isaiah 42:1

Christ of God . . . . Luke 9:20

Consolation of Israel. . . . . Luke 2:25

Cornerstone . . . . Psalm 118:22 NKJV

Creator . . . . John 1:3

Deliverer . . . . Romans 11:26

Door . . . . John 10:7 KJV

Everlasting Father.................................... Isaiah 9:6

First and Last .... Revelation 22:13

Firstborn....................................... Revelation 1:5

Glory of the Lord .... Isaiah 40:5

God..................................... Isaiah 40:3; John 20:28

Good Shepherd..................................... John 10:11

Great High Priest .... Hebrews 4:14

Head of the church.............................. Ephesians 1:22

Heir of all things................................. Hebrews 1:2

Holy and Righteous One .... Acts 3:14

Holy One of God .... Mark 1:24

Holy Servant....................................... Acts 4:27

I Am .... John 8:58

Image of God .... 2 Corinthians 4:4

Immanuel .... Isaiah 7:14

Jesus .... Matthew 1:21

Jesus of Nazareth .... Luke 24:19

Judge of Israel.............................. Micah 5:1 KJV

King.. Zechariah 9:9

King Eternal .... 1 Timothy 1:17

fulfilled prophecies

Since the Bible ultimately has one author's inspiration (God's), there is a congruence between the promises and the prophecies of the Old Testament and the big news of the New Testament: Jesus Christ, God in the flesh. Here are some specific prophecies of the Old Testament that were fulfilled by the life of Jesus, the Messiah.

You'll notice that several of these prophecies come from several psalms. You might even hear these psalms called the "messianic" psalms because they so strongly foretold Jesus' coming. If you're interested, check them out.

The Messiah Will Not Die Permanently

For you will not leave my soul among the dead or allow your godly one to rot in the grave (Psalm 16:10 NLT).

For God had promised to raise him from the dead, never again to die. This is stated in the Scripture that says, "I will give you the sacred blessings I promised to David." Another psalm explains more fully, saying, "You will not allow your Holy One to rot in the grave" (Acts 13:34–35 NLT).

He Will Be Abandoned by God

My God, my God! Why have you forsaken me? Why do you remain so distant? Why do you ignore my cries for help? Every day I call to you, my God, but you do not answer. Every night you hear my voice, but I find no relief (Psalm 22:1–2 NLT).

At about three o' clock, Jesus called out with a loud voice, "Eli, Eli, lema sabachthani?" which means, "My God, my God, why have you forsaken me?" (Matthew 27:46 NLT).

The Messiah Will Be Rejected by People

But I am a worm and not a man. I am scorned and despised by all! (Psalm 22:6 NLT).

Then they spit in Jesus' face and hit him with their fists. And some slapped him (Matthew 26:67 NLT).

He was despised and rejected—
a man of sorrows, acquainted with
bitterest grief. We turned our backs
on him and looked the other way
when he went by. He was despised,
and we did not care (Isaiah 53:3 NLT).

But although the world was made
through him, the world didn't
recognize him when he came. Even
in his own land and among his own
people, he was not accepted.
(John 1:10–11 NLT).

He Will Trust God from Birth

Yet you brought me safely from my
mother's womb and led me to trust you
when I was a nursing infant. I was thrust
upon you at my birth. You have been my
the moment I was born
(Psalm 22:9–10 NLT).

The child grew up healthy and
strong. He was filled with wisdom beyond his years, and God placed his
special favor upon him God from
(Luke 2:40 NLT).

His Hands and Feet Will Be Pierced

My enemies surround me like
a pack of dogs; an evil gang closes
in on me. They have pierced my
hands and feet (Psalm 22:16 NLT).

[Thomas] replied, "I won't believe
it unless I see the nail wounds in his
hands, put my fingers into them, and
place my hand into the wound in
his side" (John 20:25 NLT).

Then [Jesus] said to Thomas,
"Put your finger here and see my
hands. Put your hand into the
wound in my side. Don't be faith-
less any longer. Believe!"

"My Lord and my God!" Thomas
exclaimed (John 20:27–28 NLT).

The Soldiers Will Divide His Garments

They divide my clothes among
themselves and throw dice for
my garments (Psalm 22:18 NLT).

After they had nailed him to the cross,
the soldiers gambled for his clothes
by throwing dice (Matthew 27:35 NLT).

His Bones Will Not Be Broken

For the LORD protects them from
harm—not one of their bones
will be broken! (Psalm 34:20 NLT).

But when they came to Jesus, they
saw that he was dead already, so they
didn't break his legs (John 19:33 NLT).

He Will Be Betrayed by a Friend

Even my best friend, the one I trusted completely, the one who shared my food, has turned against me (Psalm 41:9 NLT).

But even as he said this, a mob approached, led by Judas, one of his twelve disciples. Judas walked over to Jesus and greeted him with a kiss (Luke 22:47 NLT).

He Will Be Rejected by His Family

Even my own brothers pretend they don't know me; they treat me like a stranger (Psalm 69:8 NLT).

When his family heard what was happening, they tried to take him home with them. "He's out of his mind," they said (Mark 3:21 NLT).

He Will Given Vinegar to Drink

But instead, they give me poison for food; they offer me sour wine to satisfy my thirst (Psalm 69:21 NLT).

One of them ran and filled a sponge with sour wine, holding it up to him on a stick so he could drink (Matthew 27:48 NLT).

He Will Teach in Parables

For I will speak to you in a parable. I will teach you hidden lessons from our past. (Psalm 78:2 NLT)

Jesus always used stories and illustrations like these when speaking to the crowds. In fact, he never spoke to them without using such parables. This fulfilled the prophecy that said, "I will speak to you in parables. I will explain mysteries hidden since the creation of the world" (Matthew 13:34–35 NLT).

He Will Be Born to a Virgin

"All right then, the Lord himself will choose the sign. Look! The virgin will conceive a child! She will give birth to a son and will call him Immanuel—'God is with us" (Isaiah 7:14 NLT).

All of this happened to fulfill the Lord's message through his prophet: "Look! The virgin will conceive a child! She will give birth to a son, and he will be called Immanuel (meaning, God is with us)" (Matthew 1:22–23 NLT).

The Spirit of God Will Be on Him

And the Spirit of the LORD will rest on him—the Spirit of wisdom and understanding, the Spirit of counsel and might, the Spirit of knowledge and the fear of the LORD (Isaiah 11:2 NLT).

Then John said, "I saw the Holy Spirit descending like a dove from heaven and resting upon him" (John 1:32 NLT).

God Will Send One to Prepare the Way for Him

Listen! I hear the voice of someone shouting, "Make a highway for the LORD through the wilderness. Make a straight, smooth road through the desert for our God" (Isaiah 40:3 NLT).

John replied in the words of Isaiah: "I am a voice shouting in the wilderness, 'Prepare a straight pathway for the Lord's coming!'" (John 1:23 NLT).

"Look! I am sending my messenger, and he will prepare the way before me. Then the Lord you are seeking will suddenly come to his Temple. The messenger of the covenant, whom you look for so eagerly, is surely coming," says the LORD Almighty (Malachi 3:1 NLT).

When John's disciples had gone, Jesus began talking about him to the crowds. "Who is this man in the wilderness that you went out to see? . . .Were you looking for a prophet? Yes, and he is more than a prophet. John is the man to whom the Scriptures refer when they say, 'Look, I am sending my messenger before you, and he will prepare your way before you" (Matthew 11:7–10 NLT).

He Will Stand Silent Before His Accusers

He was oppressed and treated harshly, yet he never said a word. He was led as a lamb to the slaughter. And as a sheep is silent before the shearers, he did not open his mouth (Isaiah 53:7 NLT).

"Don't you hear their many charges against you?" Pilate demanded. But Jesus said nothing, much to the governor's great surprise (Matthew 27:13–14 NLT).

He Will Be Sinless

He had done no wrong, and he never deceived anyone. But he was buried like a criminal; he was put in a rich man's grave (Isaiah 53:9 NLT).

For God made Christ, who never sinned, to be the offering for our sin, so that we could be made right with God through Christ (2 Corinthians 5:21 NLT).

He Will Be Born in Bethlehem

But you, O Bethlehem Ephrathah, are only a small village in Judah. Yet a ruler of Israel will come from you, one whose origins are from the distant past (Micah 5:2 NLT).

And because Joseph was a descendant of King David, he had to go to Bethlehem in Judea, David's ancient home. He traveled there from the village of Nazareth in Galilee. He took with him Mary, his fiancée, who was obviously pregnant by this time (Luke 2:4–5 NLT).

He Will Ride into Jerusalem on a Donkey

Rejoice greatly, O people of Zion! Shout in triumph, O people of Jerusalem! Look, your king is coming to you. He is righteous and victorious, yet he is humble, riding on a donkey—even on a donkey's colt (Zechariah 9:9 NLT).

As Jesus and the disciples approached Jerusalem, they came to the town of Bethphage on the Mount of Olives. Jesus sent two of them on ahead. "Go into the village over there," he said, "and you will see a donkey tied there, with its colt beside it. Untie them and bring them here. If anyone asks what you are doing, just say, 'The Lord needs them,' and he will immediately send them" (Matthew 21:1–3 NLT).

His Followers Will Be Scattered for a Time

"Awake, O sword, against my shepherd, the man who is my partner, says the LORD Almighty. Strike down the shepherd, and the sheep will be scattered, and I will turn against the lambs" (Zechariah 13:7 NLT).

Then Jesus said to the crowd, "Am I some dangerous criminal, that you have come armed with swords and clubs to arrest me? . . . But this is all happening to fulfill the words of the prophets as recorded in the Scriptures." At that point, all the disciples deserted him and fled (Matthew 26:55–56 NLT).

A Harmony of the Gospels

As you know, the Gospels are the first four books in the New Testament. They tell about Jesus' life from four different perspectives. They don't all list the same events or list them in the same order.

You know us humans: We love to organize things so they are as easy to understand as possible. So here's a "harmony" of the Gospels. It's a table that puts together all of the stories, sermons, and events in the Gospels in a logical order. (Each harmony you see may be in a little different order.)

	MATTHEW	MARK	LUKE	JOHN
How can God become human?				1:1–18
Jesus' genealogy	1:1–17		3:23–38	
Jesus' coming is announced to Zechariah, Mary, and Elizabeth			1:5–56	
John the Baptist is born			1:57–80	
Jesus' birth is announced to Joseph	1:18–25			
Jesus is born			2:1–20	
Baby Jesus goes to the temple for the first time			2:21–40	
The wise men come	2:1–12			

	MATTHEW	MARK	LUKE	JOHN
Jesus' family escapes to Egypt	2:13–23			
Jesus grows up			2:41–52	
The work of John the Baptist	3:1–12	1:2–8	3:1–20	1:19–28
Jesus is baptized	3:13–17	1:9–11	3:21–22	1:29–34
Jesus is tempted	4:1–11	1:12–13	4:1–13	
The first disciples	4:18–22	1:16–20	5:1–11	1:35–51
Jesus performs His first miracle: making wine			2:1–11	
Jesus takes a stand in the temple				2:12–25
Jesus and Nicodemus				3:1–21
John the Baptist teaches about Jesus				3:22–36
Jesus and the Samaritan woman				4:1–42
Jesus teaches in Galilee	4:12	1:14–15	4:14–15	4:43–45
Jesus heals a royal official's son				4:46–54
Jesus teaches in Capernaum	4:13–17		4:31	

	MATTHEW	MARK	LUKE	JOHN
Jesus begins a ministry of healing and teaching	4:23–25 8:1–4, 14–17 9:1–8	1:21–2:12	4:31 4:33–44 5:12–26	
Jesus eats at Matthew's house	9:9–13	2:13–17	5:27–32	
Jesus talks about fasting and introduces a new way of thinking	9:14–17	2:18–22	5:33–39	
Jesus heals on the Sabbath (This creates a conflict)	12:1–21	2:23–3:12	6:1–11	5:1–47
The twelve disciples are confirmed	10:2–4	3:13–19	6:12–16	
The Beatitudes ("Blessed are the. . .")	5:1–16		6:17–26	
Jesus discusses the law	5:17–48		6:27–36	
Jesus discusses giving and prayer	6:1–8; 6:14–7:12		6:37–42	
Jesus teaches about getting to heaven	7:13–29		6:43–49	
A Roman centurion shows faith	8:5–13		7:1–10	

	MATTHEW	MARK	LUKE	JOHN
Jesus raises a widow's son is raised from the dead			7:11–17	
Jesus responds to the doubts of John the Baptist	11:1–30		7:18–35	
Religious leaders express their doubts whether Jesus' power comes from God	12:22–45	3:20–30		
Jesus redefines His true family	12:46–50	3:31–35	8:19–21	
Jesus teaches a series of kingdom parables including the parable of the sower	13:1–52	4:1–34	8:4–18	
Jesus miraculously stills a storm	8:23–27	4:35–41	8:22–25	
Jesus casts demons out and sends them into pigs	8:28–34	5:1–20	8:26–39	
Jesus heals people of disease and death	9:18–34	5:21–43	8:40–56	
Jesus is rejected in His hometown: Nazareth	13:53–58	6:1–6	4:16–30	

	MATTHEW	MARK	LUKE	JOHN
Jesus commissions the ministry of the twelve disciples	9:35–10:42	6:7–13	9:1–6	
John the Baptist is beheaded	14:1–12	6:14–29	9:7–9	
Jesus feeds over five thousand people by multiplying bread and fish	14:13–21	6:30–44	9:10–17	6:1–15
Jesus walks on water to the disciples' boat	14:22–36	6:45–56		6:16–21
Jesus says He is the bread of life, but the people do not understand				6:22–71
Jesus explains true purity (being clean inside) rather than just ceremonial purity (being clean outside)	15:1–20	7:1–23		
Jesus casts out a demon	15:21–28	7:24–30		
Jesus miraculously feeds over four thousand people by multiplying fish and bread	15:29–39	8:1–10		

	MATTHEW	MARK	LUKE	JOHN
Religious leaders ask for a sign and tension grows between their teaching and Jesus' teaching	16:1–12	8:11–21		
Jesus heals a blind man		8:22–26		9:1–41
Peter confesses that Jesus is the Messiah God promised	16:13–20	8:27–30	9:18–20	
Jesus begins to prepare the disciples for His death and predicts His death for the first time	16:21–28	8:31–9:1	9:21–27	
Jesus is transfigured on the mountain, His body takes on a more heavenly form, and He talks to Elijah and Moses, who had been dead for years	17:1–13	9:2–13	9:28–36	
Jesus casts out a demon	17:14–21	9:14–29	9:37–43	
Jesus continues to prepare His disciples and predicts His death a second time	17:22–23	9:30–32	9:44–45	

	MATTHEW	MARK	LUKE	JOHN
Peter finds a coin in the fish's mouth and usesit to pay a temple tax	17:24–27			
Jesus warns against temptation	18:1–35	9:33–50	9:46–50	
Jesus addresses the cost of being a disciple	8:18–22; 19:1–2			9:59–62
Jesus teaches with authority at the temple and the controversy surrounding Him becomes heated				7:10–53
Jesus forgives a woman caught in adultery				8:1–11
Jesus speaks openly about Himself as deity and is almost stoned				8:12–59
Jesus explains Himself as the Good Shepherd				10:1–21
Jesus commissions seventy-two other disciples			10:1–24	
Jesus tells the story of the Good Samaritan			10:25–37	

	MATTHEW	MARK	LUKE	JOHN
Jesus visits Mary and Martha in their home			10:38–42	
Jesus teaches about prayer	6:9–13		11:1–13	
Jesus confronts the religious leaders			11:14–54	
Jesus teaches with some very sobering parables			12:1–13:21	
Religious leaders threaten to stone Jesus				10:22–42
Jesus spends time healing and teaching			13:22–14:35	
Jesus tells parables about a lost coin, a lost sheep, and a lost son			15:1–32	
Jesus teaches His disciples within hearing distance of the Pharisees			16:1–17:10	
Jesus raises Lazarus, His friend, from the dead				11:1–44

	MATTHEW	MARK	LUKE	JOHN
Jesus heals ten lepers, but only one says "thanks"			17:11–19	
Jesus talks about the unexpected coming of the kingdom			17:20–37	
Jesus tells two parables about prayer			18:1–14	
Jesus teaches about marriage	19:3–12	10:2–12		
Jesus welcomes, honors, and blesses little children	9:13–15	10:13–16	18:15–17	
Jesus talks with the rich young man	19:16–20:16	10:17–31	18:18–30	
Jesus teaches about having a servant's heart	20:17–28	10:32–45		
Jesus heals the blind	20:29–34	10:46–52	18:35–43	
Zacchaeus follows Jesus in faith			19:1–10	

	MATTHEW	MARK	LUKE	JOHN
The parable of the servants who invested the king's money differently			19:11–27	
Religious leaders begin to plan Jesus' assassination				11:45–57; 12:9–11
Jesus takes His famous ride into Jerusalem to a cheering crowd	21:1–11, 14–17	11:1–11	19:28–44	12:12–19
Jesus curses a fig tree and it quickly dies	21:18–19	11:12–14		
Jesus takes a stand in the temple again	21:12–13	11:15–19	19:45–48	
Jesus clarifies His mission even more boldly				12:20–50
Jesus speaks to the power of prayer	21:20–22	11:20–26		
Jesus stumps the religious leaders	21:23–27	11:27–33	20:1–8	

	MATTHEW	MARK	LUKE	JOHN
Jesus tells more parables about the kingdom of God	21:28–22:14	12:1–12	20:9–19	
Jesus fields significant questions from the religious leaders	22:15–40	12:13–34	20:20–40	
Jesus stumps the religious leaders again and tension mounts	22:41–46	12:35–37	20:41–44	
Jesus openly warns people about the religious leaders	23:1–39	12:38–40	20:45–47	
A widow gives all she has and Jesus teaches from her example		12:41–44	21:1–4	
Jesus talks with His disciples more about being ready for the events to come	24:1–25:46	13:1–37	21:5–38	

	MATTHEW	MARK	LUKE	JOHN
Religious leaders agree on the strategy for Jesus' arrest	26:1–5	14:1–2	22:1–2	
A woman anoints Jesus with expensive perfume	26:6–13	14:3–9	7:36–8:3	12:1–8
Judas closes the deal to betray Jesus	26:14–16	14:10–11	22:3–6	
Jesus and the disciples prepare for the Passover meal (an important Jewish celebration)	26:17–19	14:12–16	22:7–13	
Jesus humbles His disciples by taking the role of a servant and washing the disciples' feet (a custom of the day in light of the unpaved roads)				13:1–20
Jesus hints at Judas's plans to betray Him	26:20–25	14:17–21	22:14–16 21–30	13:21–30

	MATTHEW	MARK	LUKE	JOHN
Jesus and His disciples celebrate the Passover by sharing a meal that we now call "the Last Supper"	26:26–28	14:22–24	22:17–20	
Before they leave their last meal together, Jesus talks with His disciples about the future	26:29–30	14:25–26		13:31 14:31–
Jesus foretells Peter's denial (which Peter, of course, denies)	26:31–35	14:27–31	22:31–38	
Jesus describes our relationship with God in terms of a grapevine and teaches about the Holy Spirit				15:1 16:33

	MATTHEW	MARK	LUKE	JOHN
Jesus agonizes and prays for Himself, His disciples, the believers of His day, and us before He faces His betrayal	26:36–46	14:32–42	22:39–46	17:1–18:1
Jesus is betrayed by Judas and arrested by the soldiers	26:47–56	14:43–52	22:47–53	18:2–11
Jesus stands a religious trial before Caiaphas	26:57, 59–68; 27:1	14:53 55–65;	22:54, 63–71	18:12–14, 19–24
Sure enough, Peter denies knowing Jesus	26:58, 69–75	14:54, 66–72	22:54–62	18:15–18, 25–27
Judas kills himself after betraying Jesus for thirty coins	27:3–10			*see also* *Acts 1:18–19*

	MATTHEW	MARK	LUKE	JOHN
Jesus stands a political trial before Pilate and Herod	27:2, 11–31	15:1–20	23:1–25	18:28-19:16
Jesus is executed by hanging on a cross	27:31–56	5:20–41	23:26–49	19:16–37
Jesus is buried in a borrowed grave	27:57–66	15:42–47	23:50–56	19:38–42
Jesus returns to life and appears to women who loved Him	28:1–15	16:1–11	24:1–12	20:1–18
Jesus appears to two believers on the road to Emmaus		16:12–13	24:13–35	
Jesus enters a room through locked doors to be with the disciples		16:14	24:36–43	20:19–23
Jesus confronts Thomas's doubts (This is where the term "doubting Thomas" comes from)				20:24–31

	MATTHEW	MARK	LUKE	JOHN
Jesus cooks breakfast on the beach for the disciples				21:1–25
Jesus gives what we now call "the Great Commission" before returning to a heavenly existence	28:16–20	16:15–18		
Jesus appears to the disciples one last time			24:44–49	*see also Acts 1:3–8*
Jesus returns to heaven		16:19–20	24:50–53	*see also Acts 1:9–12*

web sites you might want to try

You know how the Internet goes. Things change all the time, so we can't guarantee these will be helpful to you, but they sure are worth checking out.

Bible.com

Bible.org

Biblenotes.net

Biblequizzes.com

Biblestudytools.net

Biblegateway.com

Bible.christiansunite.com

Bible-history.com

Christianitytoday.com

Netministries.org

Newlivingtranslation.com

StudyLight.org

Theoneyear.com

sources

A lot of great books and study helps are out there. Here are a few referred to in the making of this book.

1001 Things You Always Wanted to Know about the Bible, Thomas Nelson, 1999

The Ancient World of the Bible, Viking Press, 1994

Applying the Bible, Zondervan, 1990

Bible Almanac, Publications International, Ltd., 1997

Bible Clues for the Clueless, Promise Press, 1999

The Bible: An Owner's Manual, Paulist Press, 1983

Bruce and Stan's Guide to the Bible, Harvest House, 1998

Discovering the Bible, Eerdmans, 1986

How to Apply the Bible, Baker, 1999

Illustrated Dictionary of Bible Life and Times, Reader's Digest Association, 1997

The Illustrated Guide to the Bible, Oxford University Press, 1995

Life Application Bible, Tyndale, 1988

The New International Dictionary of the Bible, Zondervan, 1987

Manners and Customs in the Bible, Hendrickson, 1991

Pictorial Introduction to the Bible, Hendrickson, 1982

Strong's Exhaustive Concordance, Abingdon Press, 1981

Unger's Bible Dictionary, Moody Press, 1967

Vine's Expository Dictionary, Revell, 1981

notes

notes

notes

notes

notes

notes

notes

Other popular Bible reference books
from Barbour Publishing

The Illustrated Guide to Bible Customs and Curiosities
6" x 9" / Paperback / 256 pages / $9.97
ISBN 978-1-59310-703-1

If you've ever wondered why Bible people did such strange things, *The Illustrated Guide to Bible Customs and Curiosities* will answer your questions.

Who's Who and Where's Where in the Bible
6" x 9" / Paperback / 400 pages / $14.97
ISBN 978-1-59310-111-4

Here's a Bible dictionary that's actually fun to read! Dig deeply into the stories of five hundred people and places that make the Bible such a fascinating book.

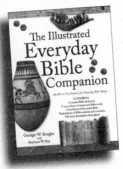

The Illustrated Everyday Bible Companion—An All-in-One Resource for Bible Study
7" x 9½" / paperback / 704 Pages / $24.97
ISBN 978-1-59310-905-9

Open the door to better Bible study with The *Illustrated Everyday Bible Companion*! You'll find a dictionary, concordance, handbook, and more—plus more than 200 full-color illustrations.

Available wherever Christian books are sold.